Able Learners
in the Middle Level School:
Identifying Talent and Maximizing Potential

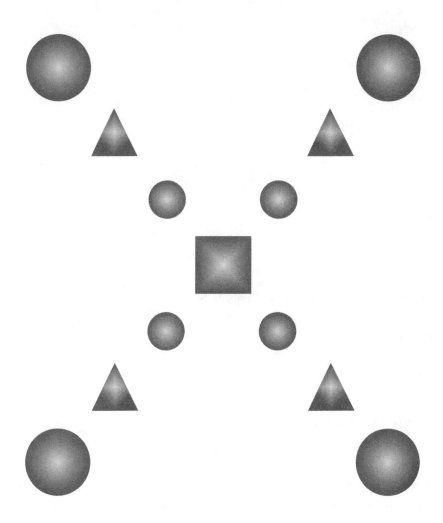

Ronald D. Williamson
University of North Carolina at Greensboro

J. Howard Johnston
University of South Florida

Editors

To our families: Marsha, Lucinda, Kevin, Christoper, Sarah, Kristin.
Special people with special gifts.

Timothy J. Dyer, Executive Director

Thomas F. Koerner, Deputy Executive Director

John A. Lammel, Associate Executive Director, Director of High School
Services and the National Alliance of High Schools

Susan Galletti, Associate Executive Director, Director of Middle Level
Services and the National Alliance of Middle Level Schools

Robert Mahaffey, Director of Communications

Patricia George, Associate Director of National School Alliances, Editor

Jan Umphrey, Assistant Editor

Eugenia Cooper Potter, Technical Editor

ISBN: 0-88210-325-3

ABLE LEARNERS IN THE MIDDLE LEVEL SCHOOL:
Identifying Talent and Maximizing Potential

TABLE OF CONTENTS

Introduction

One of the characteristics of middle level education that distinguishes it most clearly from other reform initiatives is the emphasis on challenging many of the assumptions about what is right and appropriate in the education of early adolescents. Middle level educators pride themselves on their attentiveness to these unique learners and the accompanying efforts to modify curricular and instructional practice.

While middle level education is at the forefront of these reform efforts, its critics have raised serious and significant questions about whether the needs of the most able and talented middle level students are being met.

This book is designed to engage principals and teachers, researchers and professors, parents and community members in a conversation about this issue. The authors raise significant questions, present a variety of perspectives, and offer an abundance of suggestions for ways in which middle level schools can strengthen service to their most talented students.

The impetus for this volume came from a Symposium on Gifted and Talented Students and the Middle Level School sponsored by the National Association of Secondary School Principals and attended by teachers, principals, professors, and representatives of several educational advocacy organizations. It reflects the Association's commitment to examine the most pressing issues facing the nation's middle level schools and to offer practitioners, principals, and teachers information to better inform their practice.

We believe this book raises provocative questions and we encourage you to engage your faculty in thoughtful and reflective discussions about its implications.

Timothy Dyer
Executive Director
National Association of
Secondary School Principals

Susan Galletti
Associate Executive Director,
Director of Middle Level Services

About the Authors

Gwendolyn Cooke is director of urban services at the National Association of Secondary School Principals. A former middle school principal, she has done extensive research and writing about gifted education in the middle grades.

Cassandra Countryman is principal of Muirlands Middle School, LaJolla, Calif. She worked with the Edna McConnell Clark Foundation on middle school reform directed at improved student achievement.

Susan E. Galletti is associate executive director of the National Association of Secondary School Principals. A former middle level principal, she provides leadership to NASSP's Office of Middle Level Services.

Laurel K. Johnson is instructional consultant and resource teacher in the Dexter (Mich.) Public Schools with responsibility for assisting teachers with curriculum development and delivery strategies for meeting the diverse needs of students. She was academic enrichment coordinator and gifted/talented coordinator in Michigan and New Hampshire.

J. Howard Johnston is professor of secondary education at the University of South Florida. His interests include school restructuring-particularly meeting the needs of diverse populations.

Lucinda L. Johnston is director of the Center for High Achieving Schools in Tampa, Fla. A former assistant principal and middle grades teacher, she specializes in applications of technology to improve student achievement.

Peggy S. Mayer is a humanities and mathematics teacher at Lake Stevens Middle School in Everett, Wash. She specializes in integrated curriculum, use of computers for instruction, and portfolio assessment.

Jay McIntire is coordinator of the National Training Program for Gifted Education at the Council for Exceptional Children, Reston, Va.

Karen H. Nathan is a doctoral student at the University of South Florida with an interest in the inclusion of students with various exceptionalities in regular classrooms.

John H. Powell is a clinical psychologist in private practice at the Family Center of Temple Terrace, Fla.

Hilda Rosselli is associate professor of special education at the University of South Florida. She is currently the interim director of the Suncoast Area Teacher Training Program, and her interests are in gifted and talented education.

Janine Shahinian is president of the Advocates for Able Learner Education in Ann Arbor, Mich. The parent of a middle school child, she is an advocate for improved educational services to gifted and talented middle grades students.

Carol Tomlinson is assistant professor at the University of Virginia. A former middle school educator, she specializes in curricular and instructional strategies for meeting the needs of gifted students in the middle grades.

Jaclynn C. Tracy is associate professor of educational leadership at Eastern Michigan University, specializing in community education, school/community relations, and adult education.

Ronald D. Williamson is assistant professor of educational leadership and cultural foundations at the University of North Carolina at Greens-boro with an interest in the school principalship, leadership development, and the principal's impact on school culture and student achievement.

Preface

Leaders of the nation's middle level schools are confronted by increasing demands to provide high quality academic programs for students—programs characterized by greater rigor and challenge for all students but particularly the most talented. Parents, teachers, and community leaders have united to demand more from the school's curricular and instructional programs.

Several factors contribute to the demands, including the perception, right or wrong, that the middle level school with its focus on responding to the developmental needs of students has resulted in reduced academic standards. This perception is compounded by the fact that middle level schools are often in the forefront of educational change, particularly the modification of traditional grouping practices. Furthermore, it is at the middle level that parents and students are often confronted by the competitive nature of selection for high school courses and subsequent college admission.

No single factor drives this discussion. However, together, they create a milieu in which teachers and principals are increasingly asked to examine their programs and ensure that all students, particularly the most talented, are well served.

In response to these concerns, the Office of Middle Level Services at the National Association of Secondary School Principals (NASSP) convened a colloquium to examine several critical questions:

- What is the role of the middle level school in the education of able learners?
- What is a definition of able learners at the middle level?
- How do middle level schools best serve identified able learners?

Eleven participants met in October 1995 to examine these issues. Representatives from NASSP's Middle Level Council, the NASSP Board of Directors, middle level principals, researchers on the education of the gifted, and leaders from the National Middle School Association and the Council for Exceptional Children joined in the discussion.

The colloquium provoked intense debate, for rarely have middle level advocates joined with advocates for the gifted to discuss, debate, and seek agreement on strategies for more effectively serving able learners. Diverse and at times quite contradictory points of view were shared. Occasionally, participants disagreed. The focus, however, remained on seeking ways in which the middle level school, with its long-standing commitment to meeting the needs of all students, could work collaboratively with advocates for gifted education to more effectively address the needs of able students.

A foundation for the discussion was agreement on what is meant by the term "able learner." As a result of the discussion, colloquium members developed a working definition of able learners:

A student who, by virtue of experience or aptitude, has the ability to identify, attempt to solve, or solve problems and/or demonstrate creativity in a field of endeavor that is beyond the learning needs of their age peers.

This definition led to discussion about the role of the middle level school. Colloquium members agreed to the following mission statement:

Within the mission of the middle level schools we have a responsibility to find, understand, and meet the specific learning needs of students with exceptional gifts and/or talents.

Together, the working definition and the mission statement chart a new course for the middle level school. They commit the school to a more assertive stance on behalf of student learners—obligating the school to find and meet the needs of capable students. In so doing, the middle level school affirms its long-standing emphasis on developmental responsiveness and meeting the needs of each and every student.

This book had its origins at the 1995 colloquium. During those discussions it became clear there was a need for researchers and practitioners to share their perspectives about serving able learners. The colloquium, while building sound linkages among advocacy groups, clarified the varying points of view held by advocates for both middle level education and gifted education. While there are many similarities, there is no uniform set of beliefs held by all middle level educators or all gifted educators.

Three purposes guided the preparation of this work. First, it permits advocates for both middle level education and able learner education, in a single volume, to express their thinking about how best to serve this segment of the student population. It also provides an opportunity for the reader to analyze and reconcile the varied points of view. We believe there is no one model for serving able learners. Each middle level school must engage faculty and parents in discussion and debate, in analysis of options, and in design of appropriate programs. Finally, this book provides an outlet to hear from a variety of perspectives-school-based, university-based, advocacy groups-and from voices often unheard in this debate—parents and students.

This book was designed to provide a voice for these varying perspectives. It was carefully constructed to include those most affected by school practice-students, teachers, principals, parents, community members-as well as researchers and advocacy groups.

The different perspectives present in this volume reflect the dynamic nature of this debate. Each of the chapters raises significant questions about how middle level schools meet the needs of their most capable students. They offer specific strategies proven effective in other settings. They do not, however, provide a road map for how to address the needs of able learners in all middle level schools, for no single approach will work at all sites.

Pay close attention to the voices of students, parents, teachers, and others present in this work. They raise difficult questions. They challenge some of our accepted norms. They demand that we examine some of our most cherished practices.

This book does not provide easy answers. It does, however, provide an opportunity for the reader to gain greater awareness of the issues and concerns that surround education of able learners in the middle grades.

What Is an Able Learner?

Perhaps the most contentious issue in this debate is defining the population to be served. Throughout this book the authors use the definition developed by the 1995 colloquium and stated on p.v. Other terms will also be used, terms such as gifted and talented, high achieving, high performing, accelerated, and academically talented. In each case they are synonomous with able learner.

The debate should center on services to students rather than terms and definitions. Therefore, we believe that able learners include students who have demonstrated success. They also include those students who possess the potential—fulfilled and unfulfilled, recognized and unrecognized. We are unconcerned with policy definitions or matching diagnostic criteria. The primary focus of this work is discussing the issues that affect identification and service to this specific group of students.

Assumptions About Able Learner Education

Three assumptions guided the development of this book—professional stances implicit in each of the chapters. First, we believe that the practices advocated for able learners are equally effective for all learners. The converse may not be true. Thus, the curricular and instructional strategies suggested throughout this volume are worthy of consideration for all students.

The second assumption guiding our work is that every middle level school has a responsibility to find, nurture, and cultivate talent and potential. Such a stance challenges accepted practice in many schools. It requires that middle level educators adopt a more aggressive stance in seeking talented students, and providing for their specific educational needs. It embraces an approach that uses multiple indicators of talent and provides varied service models.

Finally, implicit throughout this book is the need to ensure equity in serving able learners. There is no evidence that talent is based on ethnicity, language, socioeconomic status, or any other learning disability or handicap. Therefore, middle level schools must aggressively seek and identify talented students from all groups for inclusion in their programs for able learners.

Ronald Williamson
J. Howard Johnston

CHAPTER 1

Able Learners and the Middle Level School

Ronald D. Williamson and J. Howard Johnston

Today's school leaders face a multitude of problems, but none felt with more passion and discomfort than the perceived decline in academic challenge and rigor, particularly for the nation's most able and talented. Nowhere is this passion felt with more urgency than at the middle level—when schools more actively distinguish the abilities and talents of students and when students and parents come face-to-face with the impending need to make choices about high school coursework and potential college enrollment.

Justified or not, the trend during the past 30 years to reform schooling for early adolescents has become linked with the perceived decline in academic rigor and standards.

In 1968, William Alexander et al. suggested modifications in the education of early adolescents that were built on the premise that schools should respond to the developmental needs of students. Alexander and colleagues described the importance of this characteristic: "A truly effective school program . . . must be based on knowledge about the learner who is to be served by the school" (p. 23).

The movement to reform middle level education was energized by Alexander's work and subsequent publications spoke passionately about the characteristics of the early adolescent learner and the most appropriate teaching and learning strategies (Alexander and George, 1981). As a result, a finite set of characteristics of the middle level school emerged. Such schools, it was suggested, included grades 6-8, were organized into interdisciplinary teams of teachers, initiated teacher-based advisory programs, abandoned interscholastic sports in favor of intramurals, began exploratory courses, and implemented heterogeneous grouping. Writers and professional associations described essential characteristics of middle level schools (Georgiady, Riegle, and Romano, 1973; National Middle School Association, 1981; Johnston et al., 1985).

During the 1970s, some schools began to examine their programs, and increasing numbers adopted a 6-8 grade organization and some of the recommended program characteristics (Brough, 1995).

In the 1980s the Carnegie Council on Adolescent Development established the Task Force on Education of Young Adolescents to examine the education of early adolescents. *Turning Points: Preparing American Youth for the 21st Century* (1989), written by the Task Force, recommended eight areas that would improve the education of early adolescent students. Among the recommendations were:

- Creating learning communities within each school—places where students would develop close and trusting relationships with teachers and other students

- Teaching a core curriculum with high standards for critical thinking, ethical and moral decision making, and development of healthy lifestyles

- Ensuring the success of every child, regardless of prior achievement level

- Engaging teachers and administrators in decision making about their schools
- Establishing vital and engaging links among schools, students' families, and the local communities.

Identifying the Needs of Middle School Students

To be responsive to the characteristics and needs of early adolescent learners, educators began developing general profiles of those students. In many schools, these profiles became "emblems" of middle grades learners. For example, one midwestern state issued a position paper that characterized middle level students as "awkward and uncoordinated" and "less concerned for academics than social issues." While these statements may be true for some or even many middle level students, it is woefully inappropriate to use them to characterize all early adolescents.

As a result of such profiles and an emphasis on making school a supportive and caring environment, in the minds of the public and educators at other levels, middle schools became disassociated from student achievement. The resultant dichotomy—that middle schools are either caring and supportive places or they focus on academics and student achievement—does a tremendous disservice to middle school students, implying there is no link between the two—that caring and support must be sacrificed to address legitimate achievement needs.

Middle school advocates repeatedly describe their schools as "developmentally responsive"— a laudable goal. Unfortunately, references to developmental responsiveness are viewed by parents and others as code words for lowering standards, subverting rigor, and ignoring academics.

Different Views of the Function and Purpose of Middle Schools

As a result of this dichotomy, parents and faculty members raise serious questions about the purpose and function of the middle level school. Is it self-esteem or academics? Rigor and challenge or fun and games? Those schools advocating support, sensitivity, and a focus on self-esteem are linked to promoting lower standards.

Lost in the debate are the 10 to 14-year-olds whom both groups profess to serve. Student profiles and other identifiers that seek to categorize and subscribe certain characteristics to all middle level learners oversimplify the enormous and rich diversity in this dynamic group. Such an oversimplification is a cruel disservice to this deserving population of young people.

At the center of this debate are high achieving middle level students. Those students and their parents are rightly concerned about the "one size fits all" approach to teaching and learning. Service to these students has all too often come to represent this dichotomy about the function and purpose of the middle level school.

There are no simple solutions. In many middle level schools, able learners are neglected— heterogeneous grouping results in teaching to the middle, and high achievers are left to fend for themselves. In other schools, able learners are perceived to receive a disproportionate share of the schools' resources.

Serving Able Students

Defining an able student presents a dilemma for the middle level school. Is the term "able" a code word for "gifted?" Does it imply that all students are able or that all high potential students are high achievers? Does it expand the group of students to be served?

A publication from the ERIC Clearinghouse on Handicapped and Gifted Children at the Council for Exceptional Children (1990) provides some guidance. It suggests a definition from the U. S. Commissioner of Education that describes high achievers as "children who require differentiated educational programs and/or services beyond those normally provided by the regular school program in order to realize their contribution to self and society" (p. 1).

In October 1995, the National Association of Secondary School Principals convened a colloquium to examine the education of gifted students in the middle level school. Attended by teachers, principals, professors, and researchers, the colloquium developed a working definition of able learners: a student who, by virtue of experience or aptitude, has the ability to identify, attempt to solve, or solve problems and/or demonstrate creativity in a field of endeavor that is beyond the learning needs of their age peers.

This definition was complemented by the development of a mission statement outlining the commitment of middle level schools to the education of able learners: Within the mission of the middle level schools we have a responsibility to find, understand, and meet the specific learning needs of students with exceptional gifts and/or talents.

Together, the proposed mission statement and the definition of high achievement recommit middle level schools to serving all students, including the most talented. They affirm the importance of finding, nurturing, and meeting the needs of talented students.

What, then, is the role of the middle level school? How does the school ensure it meets this high standard? Several components emerge as critical to such a venture: identification, supportive programs and services, and curricular and instructional practices.

Characteristics of Able Students

Identifying the able student is a daunting task because no single measure can be used. In a discussion of this issue, Parke (1992) found that three factors were cited most often by classroom teachers in identifying able students:

First, [able] students tend to get their work done quickly and may seek further assignments or direction. Second, they ask probing questions that tend to differ from their classmates in depth of understanding and frequency. Finally, they have interests in areas that are unusual or more like the interests of older students (p. 1).

One midwestern district struggled to find a way to serve talented students in its middle schools. Programs were in such disarray that a parent advocacy group was formed to lobby the board of education and school administrators. From these efforts, a committee of parents and staff was formed to examine the gifted program and recommend modifications. As a result of the deliberations, the district acknowledged and designed a program around several beliefs: that talented students exist in all populations, parents should be active partners in the identification process, there is no single measure of talent, and there should be multiple entry points for receipt of services.

Parents were invited to nominate their children for participation in the program. Parent and teacher observations were given as much weight in identification as were standardized test data or academic achievement. This process legitimized the role of parents as contributors to their children's program. The number of students referred to the program did not change substantially; however, parents and others developed greater ownership of the identification process.

Services

A school is obligated to serve *all* of its students, including its most talented. At the middle level, the challenge is acute because the middle school philosophy espouses responsiveness, yet in practice often adheres to a one-size-fits-all delivery model based on projections of "developmental needs" onto individual students. Serious questions about the middle level model's impact on gifted students have surfaced (Tomlinson, 1992) and beliefs about how middle level students learn are challenged.

For example, Tomlinson cites a commonly held belief that "most middle school youngsters are concrete learners" and suggests that accepting such a profile of the middle level learner leads teachers to provide students with limited opportunities for complex and challenging work.

Instructional Practices

Curriculum modification, teacher preparation, and grouping were identified as issues requiring the greatest attention in an investigation of attitudes of middle school and gifted educators conducted by the Gifted Studies Program at the University of North Carolina at Chapel Hill (Coleman and Gallagher, 1992). Both groups agreed that the standard middle school curriculum is often not sufficiently challenging for gifted students. They also agreed that middle level teachers need enhanced staff development to help them meet the needs of capable students. The study revealed that teachers were ready and willing to differentiate curriculum and instruction for talented youngsters, but lack the resources—time, materials, and staff development—to accomplish the task.

There was disagreement about whether gifted students should be educated in a heterogeneous or homogeneous setting. Nevertheless, both groups agreed that grouping issues must be addressed. Several strategies emerge that can facilitate the process and enhance the delivery of sound instructional programs for the most able learners.

Engage in Thoughtful Analysis and Planning

Middle level leaders must assess, refine, and strengthen their school programs so able learners are well served. Essential to this effort is involving those most affected by such a program—parents, teachers, and students.

An abundance of guidelines exist for planning school programs (Toepfer, 1989; Williamson and Johnston, 1991; Raebeck, 1992). Each places a premium on thoughtful deliberation and consideration of alternatives. Several essential planning ideas emerge:

- Agree on a clear statement of purposes for programs for able learners. Value the conversations and discussions that lead to a shared vision (Toepfer, 1989; Williamson and Johnston, 1991).

- Discuss and develop grouping practices that are appropriate for middle level learners and meet the needs of able learners (Toepfer, 1989; Tomlinson, 1992).

- Design and use multiple measures of student talent. Reliance on a single measure is likely to result in many talented students not being identified (Toepfer, 1989; Johnston and Markle, 1991).

- Engage parents and others as active partners in conversations about the school's program for high achievers. Provide specific information about program and course options, identification processes, and ongoing evaluation practices (Toepfer, 1989; Williamson and Johnston, 1991).

- Ensure that procedures are in place that allow students to enter, exit, and re-enter curricular programs based on their interests and abilities. Provide multiple opportunities for able learners to receive services (Toepfer, 1989; Tomlinson, 1992).

- Plan and implement a process for ongoing monitoring of services to able learners. Identify measures of program success, routinely collect data, and provide opportunity for conversations with parents, faculty members, and students about program success (Williamson and Johnston, 1991).

Thoughtful and comprehensive planning is essential to the success of programs for high achievers. Engaging constituents in the process builds support, encourages risk taking, and reduces misunderstanding and distrust.

Challenge the Norms

Middle level leaders must be prepared to question the accepted norms of middle level programs. Over time, program innovations and recommendations invariably become the standard by which program success is measured. Such is the case with the middle level school. For example, one model for evaluating middle level programs suggests that a middle school is effective if it has inter-disciplinary teams and uses heterogeneous grouping. Such models provide a simplistic view of the success of schools. They imply that the mere presence of an organizational feature ensures effectiveness.

Growing unrest with established norms for middle level schools (Tomlinson, 1992; Williamson and Johnston, 1996) reflects concern that the middle level movement, initiated as a response to established doctrine and practice, has matured into an orthodox and inflexible approach to early adolescent education.

Middle level leaders must be willing to question the established norms, to engage their communities in thoughtful and reflective discussion about the success of their programs, and to abandon those practices that no longer meet the needs of students.

The experience of one Ohio middle school illustrates the point. Three years ago the school converted to a 6–8 structure, implementing teams and abandoning ability grouping, although there was some resistance among parents. Following a recent board of education election, questions arose about the program's impact on able learners. The principal, aware that the new program had not met all its stated outcomes, established a study group of parents and teachers to examine the issue. She urged the group to review all aspects, including teaming and grouping, in search of solutions. As a result of these deliberations, the debate focused on *how* grouping could be used to enhance student learning rather than *whether* grouping should or should not be used. This approach provided options, including use of grouping where appropriate.

Welcome Advocates as Friends

It is easy to discount the motives of those who ask difficult questions or suggest that schools are less effective than they can be. Many school administrators recognize that ignoring dissent and serious questions is often counterproductive. Ignoring concerns usually hands dissenters another issue—unresponsive school leadership.

An alternative approach is to treat dissent and disagreement as rational. When administrators legitimize differing points of view and welcome difficult questions they turn dissent into an advantage.

Often dissent is based on personal perceptions of what is currently taking place. While the perceptions may not always be accurate, they still reflect serious and legitimate concerns. Understanding that issues raised by advocacy groups must be addressed in some fashion, many school leaders structure opportunities for discussion and dialogue.

A school in Oregon was contemplating changes in its grouping practices. As word of the proposed changes spread throughout the community, parents called the principal, wrote letters to the board of education, and met with the superintendent, all before any deliberations or plan was developed. Responding to this concern, the principal convened a study committee of parents, teachers, and students to examine the issue. He ensured that the committee had representatives from all key constituent groups—parents of high achievers, parents of low achievers, teachers, students, senior citizens. He also ensured that a leader of the most vocal parent group was a member of the panel.

The committee members struggled with their task. They read, held community forums, attended workshops, conducted surveys, and deliberated for hours. Their recommendations resulted from this structured interaction of those most affected by the decision. While no one group achieved all their objectives in the final plan, each acknowledged that they had been heard, had an opportunity to influence the plan, and learned much from those with differing points of view.

One key to the success of any reform effort is acceptance by constituent groups. Structuring opportunities to learn from these "known dissenters" often results in clearer thinking, stronger and more strongly endorsed recommendations, and greater ownership and acceptance of any new initiative.

Address Rigor and Challenge for All Students

Underlying concern about the achievement of able students is the perception that the standard curriculum is not rigorous or challenging. While these perceptions may or may not be accurate, they must be addressed.

Suggest a lack of "rigor" and "challenge" in schools and members of most audiences will nod in agreement. Engage those members in a conversation to define those terms, and you meet an unsettling quiet. Most of us know rigor and challenge when we see it, yet we find it difficult to define.

In recent conversations with middle level teachers, principals, and parents, a set of characteristics or attributes of rigor and challenge emerged:

- Students feel challenged to stretch beyond their perceived level of competence.
- Complex problems that lend themselves to more than one answer are addressed.
- Students feel empowered to accomplish something difficult but important.
- The activity is purposeful, with a clear goal and the presence of support.
- There is some degree of anxiety about the task.

These characteristics, while not finite, serve as useful guideposts for examining current middle level programs. Rigor and challenge are issues for all students, not just the most able. As part of a comprehensive assessment of their middle level program, principals should engage faculty members and parents in discussions about rigor and how to ensure its presence in all aspects of the program, not just those serving able learners.

Identify and Implement Program Models

How do teachers and principals meet the needs of able learners? This question is central to any effort to provide high quality programs for able learners.

Three ways able learners differ from their classmates are the pace at which they learn, the depth of their understanding, and their interests (Maker, 1982). To address the curricular and instructional needs of high achievers "it is necessary to address and accommodate these defining characteristics" (Parke, 1992).

Although an abundance of approaches for serving high achievers is available, an examination of three general approaches (Johnston et al., 1992)—grouping and tracking, enrichment, and cooperative learning-provides some guidance. Each strategy is shown to have both strengths and weaknesses, but the research, often ambiguous about specific approaches, supports the combined use of all approaches.

A report from the ERIC Clearinghouse on Disabilities and Gifted Education (Winebrenner and Berger, 1994) offers several strategies for providing curriculum alternatives, including curriculum compacting and contracts.

Curriculum compacting is an approach in which "students who demonstrate previous mastery spend less time with the regular curriculum and more time with extension and enrichment opportunities" (Winebrenner and Berger, 1994, p. 1). This approach permits teachers to present alternative activities to able learners, activities that "provide for challenge, promote cognitive growth, and are based on student interests" (p. 2).

A contract is a "written agreement between teacher and student, that outlines what students will learn, how they will learn it, in what period of time, and how they will be evaluated" (Winebrenner and Berger, 1994, p. 1). Contracts engage able students in decisions about their own learning. Students identify their own interests, assume responsibility for constructing the learning process, and participate in assessing and measuring their success.

Another strategy is acceleration—an option that raises intense debate because some people equate acceleration with grade skipping and believe it has a negative social and emotional impact on able learners. Grade skipping is but one form of acceleration. Analysis of the literature on acceleration (Southern and Jones, 1991; Rogers and Kimpston, 1992) identified as many as 17 different models, including placement in a non-graded or multigrade classroom, grade telescoping (three grades in two years), or curriculum compacting. The negative social and emotional consequences of acceleration did not surface in the literature.

Summarizing the efforts at implementing sound programs for high achievers Johnston and colleagues (1992) remark:

> It is clear that [these] programs will continue to be provided, will be criticized and will be altered to meet changing social, political, and instructional demands. The question, then, is not whether to offer programs for special student needs, but how to do so (p. 56).

Provide Staff Development

Key to reforming any school program is building the capacity among those who must implement the reforms. Staff development is vital and was identified by teachers and principals as one of the most pressing issues related to the education of talented students (Coleman and Gallagher, 1992).

In the prologue to *Changing School Culture Through Staff Development* (Joyce, 1990) the importance of staff development is noted:

> The future culture of school will be fashioned largely by how staff development systems evolve. How good schools will be as educational institutions—how humane and vital they will be as places to work-will be functions of the energy and quality of the investment in their personnel (p. xv).

Modifying curricular practice to more effectively meet the needs of able learners requires substantial investment in school personnel. "Successful change involves learning how to do something new," says Fullan (1990) in describing the importance of staff development. Implementation of any new program, practice, or innovation is essentially a learning practice. It requires the support—training and skill development—to ensure that the personnel charged with implementation do so confidently.

Barriers to the effective implementation of program innovations have also been identified (Pink, 1989). They include:

- Too little time for teachers to plan for and learn new skills and practices

- Lack of sustained support from the office

- Underfunding

- Managing projects from the central office or school office rather than developing leadership capacity among teachers
- Inadequate awareness of the limitations of teacher and administrator knowledge about implementation
- Competing demands
- Failure to adjust for differences among school sites.

The benefits of quality staff development programs are manifold. Fullan (1990) concludes that "staff development, implementation of innovation, and student outcomes are closely interrelated" (p. 7). He states that there are other benefits from staff development besides improved teacher practice and student achievement, including a residual effect of increasing collegiality and collaboration among teachers, which has a positive impact on the culture of the school and therefore increases the likelihood that teachers will be willing to participate in further innovations.

Ensuring that teachers have the confidence and capability to effectively serve able learners must be a priority. Effective school leaders understand the need, plan thoughtfully to provide staff development, and support the implementation of innovative practice.

Conclusion

Probably the most contentious issue in the middle grades is how to provide for the education of able learners. Everyone has an opinion, each strongly held and passionately conveyed. Advocates for varied program options quickly polarize and assume staunchly held positions. Such zeal and passion is important. It can generate enthusiasm for reform and energize implementation.

The school leader plays a pivotal role as forceful advocate for the achievement of all students, including the high achieving. To advance this agenda, the leader must be willing to work collaboratively with constituent groups to examine current practice and promote needed reforms.

High achieving schools, where all students succeed, embrace conversations about achievement, about rigor and challenge, about raising standards, and about serving students more appropriately. They understand the importance of achievement and unabashedly promote it as their school's primary goal.

The challenge is great. The potential exhilarating. The options limited only by our imaginations. Solutions to this challenge will come only from vision and creative innovation, not from adherence to orthodoxy.

References

Alexander, W. M., and George P. *The Exemplary Middle School*. New York: Holt, Rinehart and Winston, 1981.

Alexander, W.; Williams, E.; Compton, M., Hines, V.; Prescott, D.; and Kealy, R. *The Emergent Middle School*. New York: Holt, Rinehart, and Winston, 1968.

Brough, J. "Middle Level Education: An Historical Perspective." In *Educating Young Adolescents*, edited by M. J. Wavering. New York: Garland Publishing, 1995.

Carnegie Council on Adolescent Development. *Turning Points: Preparing American Youth for the 21st Century*. Washington, D.C.: CCAD, 1989.

Coleman, M. R., and Gallagher, J. *Middle School Survey Report: Impact on Gifted Students*. Chapel Hill: Gifted Education Policy Studies Program, 1992.

Doda, N.; George, P.; and McEwin, K. "Ten Current Truths About Effective Schools." *Middle School Journal* 3(1987): 3-5.

The Council for Exceptional Children. "Giftedness and the Gifted: What's It All About?" Reston, Va.: CEC. ERIC Digest #E476.

Fullan, M. T*he New Meaning of Educational Change*. New York: Teachers College Press, 1990.

Georgiady, N.; Riegle, J.; and Romano, L. "What Are the Characteristics of the Middle School?" *In The Middle School: Selected Readings on an Emerging School Program*. New York: Nelson-Hall, 1973.

Johnston, J. H., and Markle, G. C. "Gifted and Talented Education Part 1: Definition, Identification, and Rationale." *Middle School Journal* 2(1991): 52-55.

Johnston, J. H.; Arth, A.; Lounsbury, J.; and Toepfer, C. *An Agenda for Excellence at the Middle Level*. Reston, Va.: National Association for Secondary School Principals, 1985.

Johnston, J. H.; Markle, G. C.; Arth, A.; Roh, L.; Tonack, D.; and Trawinski, P. "Gifted and Talented Education Part II: Programs, Curricula, and Outcomes." *Middle School Journal* 4(1992): 53-57.

Joyce, B. "Prologue." *In Changing School Culture Through Staff Development*, edited by B. Joyce. Alexandria, Va.: Association for Supervision and Curriculum Development, 1990, pp. xv-xviii.

Maker, J. *Curriculum Development for the Gifted*. Rockville, Md.: Aspen Systems Corporation, 1982.

National Middle School Association. *This We Believe*. Columbus, Ohio: NMSA, 1982.

Parke, B. *Challenging Gifted Students in the Regular Classroom*. Reston, Va.: ERIC Clearinghouse on Disabilities and Gifted Children, 1992.

Pink, W. "Effective Development for Urban School Improvement." Paper presented at the annual meeting of the American Educational Research Association, San Francisco, Calif., 1989.

Raebeck, B. *Transforming Middle Schools*. Lancaster, Pa.: Technomic, 1992.

Rogers, K. B., and Kimpston, R. D. "Acceleration: What We Do vs. What We Know." *Educational Leadership* 2(1992): 58-61.

Southern, W. T., and Jones, E. D. "Academic Acceleration: Background and Issues." In T*he Academic Acceleration of Gifted Children,* edited by W. T. Southern and E. D. Jones. New York: Teacher's College Press, 1991.

Toepfer, C. F. "Planning Gifted/Talented Middle Level School Programs: Issues and Guidelines." *Schools in the Middle,* May 1989.

Tomlinson, C. A. "Gifted Education and the Middle School Movement: Two Voices on Teaching the Academically Talented." *Journal for the Education of the Gifted* 3(1992): 206-38.

Williamson, R., and Johnston, J. H. *Planning for Success: Successful Implementation of Middle Level Reorganization.* Reston, Va.: National Association of Secondary School Principals, 1991.

Williamson, R., and Johnston, J. H. *Through the Looking Glass: The Future of Middle Level Education.* Reston, Va.: National Association of Secondary School Principals, 1996.

Williamson, R.; Johnston, J. H.; and Kanthak, L. "The Achievement Agenda for Middle Level Schools." *Schools in the Middle* 2(1995): 6-8.

Winebrenner, S., and Berger, S. *Providing Curriculum Alternatives to Motivate Gifted Students.* Reston, Va.: ERIC Clearinghouse on Disabilities and Gifted Children, 1994.

CHAPTER 2

Selection and Identification of Students of Promise: In Favor of Fluidness

Hilda C. Rosselli, University of South Florida

S chools or districts seeking to meet the needs of high achieving students usually design a selection process. Regardless of the philosophical intentions, the most probable process will include a set of guidelines or procedures that suffer the same problems faced by education for the gifted in general: complaints of elitism, violation of educational equity, and misuse and abuses of tests. Therefore it is wise to examine these issues and discuss alternative pathways that may be more applicable. Throughout this chapter the term "high ability/talent" will be used to refer to students who either demonstrate high ability or talent or who are believed to have high potential for the same. We are including within this term the following: accelerated, promising, gifted, academically talented, able, and talented.

Addressing the Philosophical Issues

Although both the Marland Report (Marland, 1972) and the more recent *National Excellence: Developing America's Talent* (U.S. Department of Education, 1993) attempted to broaden the definition of giftedness to include such areas as creativity, leadership, and artistic talent, reviews of current practices indicate that a more limited and monolithic view still prevails. IQ is still the most commonly used and accepted criterion for the identification of giftedness (Birch, 1984; Shore et al., 1991).

Interestingly, one of the misconceptions underlying this practice has been an assumption that high academic achievement begets adult giftedness. Yet, what seems to be more accurate is that the predictors of academic success are conversely related to achievement in the world outside formal education (Richert, 1997). Thus, if one is looking to influence the probability that students will become creative and productive thinkers in their respective fields, quite a different set of characteristics/behaviors should be sought and developed, e.g., passion, intrinsic motivation, and creativity (Treffinger, 1989; Richert, 1997).

Issue of Elitism

For more than a quarter of a century, educators have been warned against practices that may encourage students to perceive themselves as entitled to status and privileges denied others. "...[I]f they look down upon less able students and feel that society owes them recognition...then such classes are socially undesirable" (Goldberg, Passow, and Lorge, 1958). The current debates on grouping by ability also encompass morally infused issues related to equity, access, and privilege that demand attention in today's educational system.

As Richert (1997) points out, the responses to these debates range from those who could defend grouping practices if reserved only for the "highly gifted" to those who would support a more egalitarian view, providing "enrichment for all." Unfortunately, the global nature of the latter approach would most likely ignore the individual nature of the student whom the approach was originally intended to benefit.

The Dichotomy of Labeling

Using labels to identify students for special services/programs is one of the unfortunate by-products resulting from most identification and selection processes. Proponents argue that the practice is vital to the delivery of services to students. Labeling can facilitate passage of legislation, create categories for funding services and programs, and provide a cohesive element to volunteer organizations (Hobbs, 1975).

Yet, labeling also creates many ethical dilemmas for educators. Borland (1996) asks:

Is it possible that by implicitly or explicitly positing two categories of children—gifted children and whatever we choose to call the rest—we are thereby actually creating those categories, grossly simplifying reality, and acting on the basis of an abstract categorization that has no objective reality but does have the potential to influence the course of children's lives?

In essence, labeling becomes a social construct with the defining qualities, cut-offs, and procedures determined by values, beliefs, and cultural contexts (Sapon-Shevin, 1996). Some believe, however, that any undesirable social consequences resulting from labeling emerge not from the philosophy that guides these actions, but from the climate in which the provisions are made and the self-concepts that the students are helped to develop—both of which are elements that can be observed and subsequently monitored in all educational settings. Goldberg, Passow, and Lorge (1958) contend that "...where poor attitudes result from special grouping, the parent and the teacher are likely to be at fault."

Still others caution that when we view labels such as "gifted" or "high-achieving" as an absolute concept, practitioners may begin to view students as either "having it" or "not having it" (Renzulli, 1981; Borland, 1996) or viewing some students as being gifted in every area and others in none (Cox, Daniel, and Boston, 1985). Therefore, as soon as a system is developed to identify students as having promise, by its very nature it also identifies students as not having promise. As a result, if students do not meet the selection criteria, parents, teachers, and students themselves may lower their academic and personal expectations. This may appear to be a necessary offshoot of any selection system, but the overall loss to self-esteem and change in perceptions is unfathomable (Sapon-Shevin, 1996; Treffinger and Feldhusen, 1996).

Systematic Approaches

The dichotomous effect of labeling is worsened by the nature of institutions to concretize and codify procedures for every new idea. While this behavior can help create more continuity in practice, it can also strangle the sometimes more fluid systems that, when allowed to exist informally, can more adequately address the original need.

Another unfortunate outcome of labeling may be the inferred transfer of responsibility for the gifted student's education to the staff assigned to that particular program, releasing others who may still work with the student from providing appropriate levels of challenge and support (Sapon-Shevin, 1996). This split of responsibility has already been witnessed in special education programs and may, in part, have fueled interest and support for the Regular Education Initiative and the subsequent inclusion movement.

Educational Equity

Salkind (1988) believes two types of equity should be considered when examining services for high ability students:

- Horizontal equity involves the equal treatment of individuals who have similar needs.

- Vertical equity, on other hand, exists "when children who have different needs are treated differently; that is, the unequal treatment of unequals."

Still another type of educational equity is violated when considering access to services. Many programs for the gifted have ignored the assertion that giftedness emerges as a result of the interaction between innate abilities and learning or experience and have sought to "select" rather than "nurture" ability. As a result, the processes typically used to identify and select students for gifted programs have encountered waves of societal disapproval for poor and culturally diverse students (Patton, Prillaman, and Van Tassel-Baska, 1990; Borland, 1994; Frasier and Passow, 1994).

In response to the under-representation of minorities in gifted programs, many school districts have modified their identification procedures to include multiple sources of information (Borland, 1994; Frasier and Passow, 1994; Richert, 1997). Yet, not only have these more pluralistic approaches sometimes suffered from statistically invalid practices such as equal weighting or inappropriately designed matrices, but many have placed a weighted emphasis on subjective measures that are *still* more aligned with the majority population—in this case, white middle class students.

Finding a Programmatic Fit

Many methods of identification have weak linkages between the student's characteristics and the services to be delivered. For example, programs for the gifted sometimes use a creativity test as part of their district identification procedures and then place the identified students in academically accelerated programs. Sole use of an IQ test to select a student for accelerated learning opportunities is also inappropriate. A high IQ does not directly predict success in advanced academics. More applicable might be the use of an out-of-level test that indicates student potential for achieving on a level more advanced than their age peers (Benbow, 1994). Even programs that have successfully increased the number of under-represented students identified as high achieving have often failed to use the additional data obtained to plan and provide appropriate individualized services (Bernal, 1979).

The potential for matching the results of an identification system with the services provided to high achieving students has perhaps best been realized by approaches that provide options, choices, and revolving participation approaches.

Defining Promise in High Achieving Students

Traditional Views: The Academically Gifted

Traditionally, high achieving students have included those usually labeled as academically gifted, based most often on results of a combination of aptitude and/or achievement measures. Terman (1925) solidified the view that these academically gifted students were well-rounded, healthy, socially adept, and generally well adjusted. A differing view was offered by Hollingsworth (1926), whose studies of highly gifted students indicated that the more gifted the child, the greater the risk for social maladjustment.

As mentioned earlier, the most common practices for identifying students of promise have centered primarily around the use of intelligence tests, achievement tests, or some combination of these (Coleman and Gallagher, 1992). Much has been written about the limitations and weaknesses of IQ measures, including the resulting narrow interpretation of the identification process (Birch, 1984); the generalized results that ignore varying differences between verbal and performance abilities (Keating, 1976); the reality of cultural, economic, or racial biases (Frasier and Passow, 1994); and the over-reliance on mathematical and linguistic forms of intelligence (Gardner, 1983). The use of standardized achievement tests has drawn similar criticisms, yet, the practice is favored when specific goals for a program can be linked to appropriate test instruments, such as in the case of an accelerated math program.

Although the objective nature of both intelligence tests and achievement tests is seen as a strength along with their purported link to success in some kinds of learning, students with high ability that "top" out on easy achievement tests in particular may have their abilities underestimated. Although some believe that IQ tests provide a more favorable consideration of underachievers than do achievement tests, the expense of administering individual IQ tests can seriously threaten equitable access to programs and services. Until all students are automatically assessed using individual measures of intelligence, this problem perpetrates unfair practices.

Nontraditional Views

Perhaps as a result of dissatisfaction with gifted programs or as a natural evolution of practice over time, a variety of non-traditional views of ability that affected the identification and selection of students of promise have surfaced, some from gifted education and some from general education.

A renaissance has revived the concepts of talent and the talent development. Long recognized as important, the belief in multiple ways of being smart was mirrored in the original Marland definition of giftedness (Marland, 1972), the Multiple Talents Model (Taylor, 1968; Schlichter, 1986); and even Guilford's Structure of the Intellect (1956). The latest wave appears to have been fueled by Gardner's theory of multiple intelligences (1983) and OERI's report, *National Excellence: Developing America's Talent* (1993) in which "the term 'gifted' connotes a mature power rather than a developing ability."

Conceptions of Talent

Treffinger and Feldhusen (1996) define talent as "potential for the development of competence or expertise across a broad range of human endeavors in which there are opportunities for meaningful and valuable expressions and productivity" (p. 183). They recommend abandoning the concept of "gifted" and focusing on ways to identify and develop talent in all youth. On the other hand, Richert (1997) cautions that the use of the word "talent" may create another elitist hierarchy in which "gifted" refers to general intellectual ability, while "talent" refers to other gifted abilities, which may have other connotations now that the under-representation of minority students in gifted programs is finally receiving the attention it deserves.

Nontraditional Identification Methods

Emphasis on Students' Needs.

The field of special education, long known for its categorical approach to education, has recently begun to re-examine the traditional process of labeling students for purposes of providing services. The questions now being asked are, "Does a categorical program best meet all students' needs?"

and "In what ways can this student's needs best be met, regardless of the label?" Both of these questions realign the initial intent of special education programs by focusing on the student first.

Several states, including Florida, are dramatically changing the way special programs are funded by matching severity of needs with intensity of services for each student individually. Although still in the embryonic stages of implementation, this shift in focus from a clearly-identified student population to an identification of students' instructional needs holds potential for schools that wish to provide appropriate levels of challenge for high ability students. Several models have already emerged that emphasize programmatic flexibility and greater attention to student needs (Renzulli and Reis, 1985; Feldhusen, 1992; Feldhusen and Kolloff, 1986; Treffinger, 1986).

Schoolwide Programs

Based on 15 years of development that include research on the Enrichment Triad Model (Renzulli, 1977), the Revolving Door Identification Model (Renzulli, 1981), and Curriculum Compacting (Renzulli, Smith, and Reis, 1982), the Schoolwide Enrichment Model (Renzulli and Reis, 1985; Renzulli, 1994) offers a way to weave together the instructional methods and curricular practices originating in programs for high ability learners within the context of school improvement. The model Renzulli proposes is not intended to "replace the schools' focus on traditional academic achievement, but it does emphasize the development of a broader spectrum of the multiple potentials of young people" (p.10). In essence, the issue of identification and selection shifts in Renzulli's model to emphasize abilities, interests, and styles of all students. Evidence for a student's portfolio can include standardized test scores, grades, evidence of interests, teacher ratings, performance evaluations based on student products, and instruments that examine environmental, instructional, learning, thinking, and expression style preferences.

Schools and districts that embrace such a pluralistic view of abilities and move toward the nurturing and developing of students' talents can ask a different set of questions than those traditionally used by gifted programs. Instead of simply asking if they are "gifted" or not, Treffinger and Sortore (1992) suggest questions such as:

- What strengths or talents do we see in this student?
- What is happening now in the student's program?
- What modifications (if any) are necessary or desirable?
- What data give us a full picture of this student?
- What additional data are needed?
- What particular interests and accomplishments tell us about this student's learning needs?
- How does information about the student's ability, interests, and motivation guide us in instructional planning?

Non-Graded Programs

Still another organizational approach that bypasses the need for formal selection and identification processes involves a non-graded approach or flexible grading structure. The continuum for such a practice can stretch from within-class individualized pacing to the elimination of grade-level classes. One such example has existed for more than 20 years at Thomas Jefferson Junior High School in Merritt Island, Fla., where materials and teaching methods are chosen for their suitability for a specific group of students at a precise moment in time without regard to grade placement.

Readiness Testing

Some middle school educators use models such as the Cognitive Levels Matching (CLM) to recognize the need of matching instruction with student cognitive readiness. Epstein (1981) describes the CLM as giving teachers the skills to identify and diagnose student cognitive levels; organize learning activities that match student readiness to learn information; help students consolidate and mature previously initiated thinking skills; and introduce new and higher level thinking skills as students demonstrate their readiness.

Such tests as the Arlin Test of Formal Reasoning are recommended to help teachers identify students' cognitive levels. In addition, general consideration should be given to differentiation of the curriculum experiences based on differences in interests, motivation, and goals; differences in intellectual responsiveness and attitudes related to social maturity; and differences in personal adjustment.

Special Populations of Gifted Students

Although not originally acknowledged by early research in the field of gifted education, there is now a growing belief in the heterogeneous nature of students who are identified as gifted or high ability. Betts and Neihart (1988) have recognized at least six categories of gifted students including those who are underground, autonomous, challenging, double-labeled, and those who are dropouts. The research literature and federally funded Javits projects have helped spotlight the diversity and special needs found in gifted populations such as girls, students from cultural diverse background, underachieving students, students from economically disadvantaged backgrounds, highly gifted students, students with limited English proficiency, "twice exceptional" students who also have disabilities, and even creative students.

The same issues/questions that are now being raised in gifted education must be examined in light of the selection and identification of students of promise. Richert, Alvino, and McDonnel (1982) recommend that "if any identification process results in more than a 5 to 10 percent under representation of any of these sub populations," measures should be taken to overcome the apparent bias.

What About the Others? Gifted But Not Achieving

Even in the 1960s, proponents of gifted education understood and advocated for students whose abilities might be hidden by under-achievement, lack of motivation, or other variables that might inhibit achievement. The term "underachieving gifted" or UAG was coined to describe this facet of the population; although more than a dozen definitions appear in the literature, the most common method of identification is still a comparison of achievement test scores with intelligence test scores (Dowdell and Colangelo, 1982). Undetected learning disabilities, family relations, low self-esteem, socialization, and emotional disturbances have all been cited as potential conditions leading to gifted underachievement.

Although the literature clearly supports the need for early intervention (Whitmore, 1980; Dowdell and Colangelo, 1982; Rimm, 1986), efforts must continue to recognize the signs of under-achievement; policies should not exclude students from selection for high-end learning experiences merely on the basis of past performance.

Best Practices To Guide the Process

1. Identification systems should not only parallel the type of services we intend to provide, but also provide valuable information/data that are subsequently used for planning instruction and documenting student progress.

2. Procedures should allow students to enter, exit, and re-enter additional options offered to maximize their abilities as their profiles of interests and abilities change during adolescence.

3. High ability students represent a range of students whose special characteristics must be considered when developing procedures of identification and selection.

4. No single criterion is viable for use as identification and selection procedure; rather, a combination is recommended that invites input from teachers, families, and students themselves in combination with other more standardized processes.

5. Schoolwide talent searches hold much promise for finding and addressing the broad area of needs that students have for challenging educational experiences. The services or experiences offered sometimes can serve as the best identifiers possible as they tap student motivation and interest in ways that more formalized searches may miss.

6. Students seen as underachieving may very well benefit from exposure to or participation in activities deemed challenging. We must avoid a false assumption that only students who are currently achieving should be eligible for enrichment, acceleration, or individualized instruction.

7. Over-reliance on standardized measures of identification and selection ignore the value of more subjective measures.

8. Whenever possible, a fluid approach that allows students choice, control over their participation, and flexibility without labeling is preferable.

REFERENCES

Benbow, C. P. "Mathematical Talent: Its Nature and Consequences." In *Talent Development: Proceedings from the 1993 Henry B. and Jocelyn Wallace National Research Symposium on Talent Development,* edited by N. Colangelo, S. Assouline, and D. Ambroson. Dayton, Ohio: Ohio Psychology Press, 1994.

Bernal, E. M. Jr. "The Education of the Culturally Different Gifted." In *The Gifted and the Talented: Their Education and Development. Seventy-Eighth Yearbook of the National Association for the Study of Education: Part 1.* Chicago, Ill.: University of Chicago Press, 1979.

Betts, G., and Neihart, M. "Profiles of the Gifted and Talented." *Gifted Child Quarterly* 32(1988): 248-53.

Birch, J. W. "Is Any Identification Procedure Necessary?" *Gifted Child Quarterly* 28(1984): 157-61.

Borland, J.H. "Gifted Education and the Threat of Irrelevance." *Journal for the Education of the Gifted* 2(1996): 129-47.

————. "Identifying and Educating Young Economically Disadvantaged Urban Children: The Lessons of Project Synergy." In *Talent Development: Proceedings from the 1993 Henry B. and Jocelyn Wallace National Research Symposium on Talent Development,* edited by N. Colangelo, S. Assouline, and D. Ambroson. Dayton, Ohio: Ohio Psychology Press, 1994.

Callahan, C. M. "A Critical Self-Study of Gifted Education: Healthy Practice, Necessary Evil, or Sedition?" *Journal for the Education of the Gifted* 2(1996): 148-63.

Coleman, M. R., and Gallagher, J. J. *Report on State Policies Related to Identification of Gifted Students.* Chapel Hill, N.C: Gifted Education Policy Studies Program, University of North Carolina-Chapel Hill, 1992.

Cox, J.; Daniel, N.; and Boston, B. O. *Educating Able Learners: Programs and Promising Practices.* Austin, Tex.: University of Texas Press, 1985.

Dowdell, C. B., and Colangelo, N. "Underachieving Gifted Students: Review and Implications." *Gifted Child Quarterly* 35(1982): 99-105.

Epstein, H. "Learning How to Learn: Matching Instructional Levels." *The Principal* 5(1981): 25-30.

Feldhusen, J. F. *Talent Identification and Development in Education: TIDE.* Sarasota, Fla.: Center for Creative Learning, 1992.

Feldhusen, J. F., and Kollof, P. B. "The Purdue Three Stage Enrichment Model for Gifted Education at the Elementary Level." In *Systems and Models for Developing Programs for the Gifted and Talented,* edited by J. S. Renzulli and S. M. Reis. Mansfield Center, Conn.: Creative Learning Press, 1986.

Feldhusen, J. F.; Asher, J. W.; Hoover, S. M. "Problems in the Identification of Giftedness, Talent, or Ability." *Gifted Child Quarterly* 28(1984): 149-151.

Frasier, M. M., and Passow, A. H. *Toward a New Paradigm for Identifying Talent Potential.* Research Monograph 94111. Storrs, Conn.: The National Research Center on the Gifted and Talented, 1994.

Gardner, H. *Frames of Mind: The Theory of Multiple Intelligences.* New York: Basic Books, 1983.

Goldberg, M.; Passow, H.; and Lorge, I. "Issues in the Social Education of the Academically Talented." *The Social Education of the Academically Talented.* Washington, D.C.: National Council for the Social Studies, 1958.

Guilford, J. P. "Structure of Intellect." *Psychological Bulletin* 53(1956): 267-93.

Hobbs, N. *The Futures of Children: Categories, Labels and Their Consequences.* San Francisco, Calif.: Jossey-Bass, 1975.

Hollingsworth, L. *Gifted Children: Their Nature and Nurture.* New York: Macmillan, 1926.

Keating, D. P. "Discovering Quantitative Precocity." In *Intellectual Talent: Research and Development,* edited by D. P. Keating. Baltimore, Md.: Johns Hopkins University Press, 1976.

Marland, S. P., Jr. *Education of the Gifted and Talented.* Report to the Congress of the United States by the U.S. Commissioner of Education. Washington, D.C.: U.S. Department of Health, Education, and Welfare, 1972.

Patton, J. M.; Prillaman, D.; VanTassel-Baska, J. "The Nature and Extent of Programs for the Disadvantaged/Gifted in the United States and Territories." *Gifted Child Quarterly* 34(1990): 94-96.

Renzulli, J. S. *The Enrichment Triad Model.* Mansfield, Conn.: Creative Learning Press, 1977.

———. *The Revolving Door Identification Model.* Mansfield, Conn.: Creative Learning Press, 1981.

———. *Schools for Talent Development: A Practical Plan for Total School Improvement.* Mansfield, Conn.: Creative Learning Press, 1994.

Renzulli, J. S., and Reis, S. M. *The Schoolwide Enrichment Model: A Comprehensive Plan for Educational Excellence.* Mansfield, Conn.: Creative Learning Press, 1985.

Renzulli, J. S.; Smith L.H.; and Reis, S. M. "Curriculum Compacting: An Essential Strategy for Working with Gifted Students." *The Elementary School Journal* 82(1982): 185-194.

Richert, E. S. "Excellence with Equity in Identification and Programming." In *Handbook of Gifted Education,* edited by N. Colangelo and G. Davis. Boston, Mass.: Allyn and Bacon, 1997.

Richert, E. S.; Alvino, J.; and McDonnel, R. *The National Report on Identification: Assessment and Recommendation for Comprehensive Identification of Gifted and Talented Youth.* Sewell, N.J.: Educational Improvement Center-South, 1982.

Rimm, S. B. *Underachievement Syndrome: Causes and Cures.* Watertown, Wis.: Apple, 1986.

Salkind, N. "Equity and Excellence: The Case for Mandating Services for the Gifted Child." University of Kansas, 1988.

Sapon-Shevin, M. "Beyond Gifted Education: Building a Shared Agenda for School Reform." *Journal for the Education of the Gifted* 2(1996): 194-214.

Schlichter, C. L. "Talents Unlimited: An Inservice Education Model for Teaching Thinking Skills." *Gifted Child Quarterly* 30(1986): 119-23.

Shore, B. M.; Cornell, D. G.; Robinson, A.; and Ward, V. S. *Recommended Practices in Gifted Education.* New York: Teachers College Press, 1991.

Taylor, C. W. "Be Talent Developers as well as Knowledge Dispensers." *Today's Education,* December 1968.

Terman, L. M. *The Mental and Physical Traits of a Thousand Gifted Children.* Stanford, Calif.: Stanford University Press, 1925.

Slavin, R. E. "Are Cooperative Learning and 'Untracking' Harmful to the Gifted? *Educational Leadership* 6(1991): 68-71.

Treffinger, D. J. *Blending Gifted Education With the Total School Program.* East Aurora, N.Y.: DOK, 1986.

————. "From Potential to Productivity: Designing the Journey to 2000." *GCT*, March-April 1989.

Treffinger, D. J., and Feldhusen, J. F. "Talent Recognition and Development: Successor to Gifted Education." *Journal for the Education of the Gifted* 2(1996): 181-93.

Treffinger, D. J., and Sortore, M. R. "Volume 1: Programming for Giftedness—A Contemporary View." Sarasota, Fla.: Center for Creative Learning, 1992.

U.S. Department of Education. *National Excellence: A Case for Developing America's Talent.* Washington, D.C.: USDE, 1993.

Whitmore, J. R. *Giftedness, Conflict, and Underachievement.* Boston, Mass.: Allyn & Bacon, 1980.

CHAPTER 3

Curriculum and Instruction for Gifted Learners in the Middle Grades: What Would It Take?

Carol Tomlinson, University of Virginia

On some level, schooling is about finding and developing talent in students who pass through the schoolhouse doors. Never an easy charge, the task becomes even more complex at the middle level when early adolescents must chart the variable landscape bridging the relative certainties of what they were as children and the alluring uncertainties of what they might be as young adults. For highly able early adolescents, the rigors of the journey are marked with competing calls to achieve and to belong. Developing classroom environments in which curriculum and instruction are contributors to a good transition and to positive outcomes for advanced or gifted learners is a challenge little examined in the literature of middle school and important in the lives of these learners whom middle schools will serve—poorly or well.

Who Are Gifted Middle Schoolers?

An insightful educator noted in a speech to colleagues that he believed there was no such thing as a homogeneous class unless he was in a room by himself. He continued, "...and even then, I'm not so sure." His comment is apt on a number of levels and certainly might be applied to middle school learners, to gifted learners, and to middle school learners who are gifted.

Early adolescents are childlike and adult-like, mature and immature, sensitive and unaware, seekers of independence and clingers to dependence, concrete and ideological, interested and detached. Sometimes all these characteristics are evident within a single individual and within a brief span of time. Adolescents are in a state of transition from a more predictable, prescribed, limited, and familiar place in the world to one less familiar, more unpredictable, more self-directed, and fuzzier in its boundaries. They are travelers—joining forces to protect against any threat to the adventure and simultaneously longing for times and places left behind. They are growing in every possible way—and there is both pain and exultation in the changes. Some early adolescents make the journey sooner, some later; some with relatively few impediments, some encountering bandits behind outcropping rocks every step of the way. Middle schoolers are not a homogeneous group, yet they are bound by common threads and themes.

Likewise, gifted learners are a mixed lot. They may be compliant or rebellious, divergent or convergent thinkers, talented in one area or many. They may come from opportunity-rich homes, or homes that fail to raise windows on the world. The strengths of gifted students may be in domains easily embraced by schools, such as math or writing. Their talents may be in areas less readily served in school, such as spatial or spiritual ones. They may embrace school, or deplore it, may be joyful learners or grade addicts.

Despite their differences, however, they also share some common traits. At least in their talent areas, they are likely to process ideas more rapidly and at greater depth than many agemates.

They tend to make more connections among ideas, probe more deeply for meaning, persist longer, and challenge adults with a bit more pluck than many agemates. Perhaps because of their large fund of information, depth of understanding, and connection-making, they may be more sensitive to what goes on around them in the world. For some of the same reasons, they may laugh at somewhat different things than agemates—and may see the world at a slightly odd angle when compared with peers who are less advanced cognitively.

So, what about early adolescents who are very advanced as learners, whom we sometimes call "gifted"? If they share common traits of both early adolescence and giftedness, what is their journey like?

For these learners, the middle years are a pivotal time for accepting or rejecting their potential as part of their identity, and for developing attitudes, habits, understandings, and skills likely to lead toward expert-level performance and production (Bloom, 1985; Csikszentmihalyi, Rathunde, and Whalen, 1993). If they are to come into their own, early adolescents who are advanced learners must affirm their exceptional ability and develop self-efficacy by extending it. And they must do this at a time when being different from peers feels risky. They must become self-critical thinkers and skilled evaluators of their own work, for soon they may pass their teachers in one or more domains of knowledge. And they must develop these skills at a time when self-criticism threatens to gobble them up. They need to become intrinsically motivated to achieve personal excellence, at a time when they are already well-schooled to aim for grades typically computed and awarded based on yardsticks better suited to less advanced peers.

All these and other benchmarks they must accomplish at a time when they are developmentally propelled to question adult endeavors (such as schooling) in favor of a peer group (whose members often find it less compromising than do advanced learners to eschew things educational).

In other words, gifted early adolescents face the same developmental challenges and uncertainties as other early adolescents, but with a slightly different spin and a set of unique complications.

What's Difficult About Defining Curriculum for Gifted Middle Level Learners?

Defining appropriate curriculum and instruction for middle level learners whose ability is advanced well beyond that of many agemates poses two particular challenges. One has to do with the variety of gifted middle schoolers; the other has to do with the absence of consensus regarding what constitutes appropriate middle school curriculum in general.

High Ability Comes in Many Packages

Because the middle years are a time of transition, adolescents chart their passages on varied timetables and with varied routes. Thinking back to hundreds of high ability middle level students with whom I worked, I am struck by the diversity of their transitions from childhood to adolescence.

Some of them were as socially and emotionally precocious as they were academically advanced. At 13, Gregg read and understood Stephen Hawking's *A Brief History of Time*. He also coached elementary students in a highly successful Odyssey of the Mind team. At 12, Teresa studied algebra I, algebra II, geometry, and trigonometry in a single summer, with mastery and deep understanding. In her leisure activities, she felt far more at home with high school seniors and college students as friends than with agemates.

On the other hand, some of the high ability middle schoolers had very adult minds, but social and emotional development that was more typical of agemates, or even a bit behind. Erika's store of knowledge about world cultures and anthropology would have served her well among college majors in the field, but she giggled over elementary school jokes and enjoyed the company of younger children in her neighborhood. Ray interpreted the works of Edgar Allan Poe in a way that left his academic peers in awe, but had limited capacity to make it through a day with basic classroom supplies and materials in tow.

Some of the middle schoolers were convergently bright, but feared divergent risk. Debra would sob in the face of an open-ended assignment, yet relished the chance to tackle immensely complex, but highly prescribed material. Others were divergently or creatively brilliant, and consistently stymied by basic requirements for academic conformity. John, for example, thrived on the opportunity to develop new approaches to mathematical problem solving and innovative ways of expressing understandings. He found it so loathsome to keep a notebook or to follow a particular writing format that his grades seldom reflected his brilliance.

A notable number of middle level students who peopled my past were bright—and lost. Jason consistently did battle with an inner urge to learn and excel and a peer group that told him if he made good grades, he was "acting white." Samantha first lied about her good grades to win the good graces of peers with lesser achievement, then gave up the good grades because she got clear messages from a variety of sources that boys aren't looking for brains.

Like many other middle schoolers, Robbie was a highly abstract thinker in one subject and stunningly concrete in others. He developed computer programs that surpassed the ability of school district and university computer specialists to mentor. In the same year, he wrote that the theme of "The Gift of the Magi," a story about sacrificial giving as a measure of love, is "Don't give Christmas gifts."

Ariana had immense talent in one area—mathematics. Geoff was an omnibus talent—a poet, an electrician, a historian, a scientist, a computer expert, a dancer.

Joe's talents were in the school-friendly subjects of math, language, and science. Robin's talents were lonelier ones—an inner compass, self-awareness, sensitivity to the needs of others, an eye for justice, gifts of the soul.

David and Rhett were very learning disabled, and very gifted. Their ideas were laser sharp. Their capacity to give written form to the ideas, however, was leaden. By middle school, few teachers even saw them as gifted. David and Rhett had learned to doubt their abilities, too.

Common among these advanced middle level learners, to be sure, was a keenness of mind, a depth of insight, a stunning ability to make unique and appropriate connections among seemingly disparate elements. Common among them also is their variance. While the first commonality provides some guidance about the sorts of learning experiences likely to foster talent development in these young learners, the second "commonality" provides ample caution that there is no curricular, instructional, or programmatic formula that will serve all these high potential early adolescents well.

Ambiguity Regarding Appropriate Middle School Curricula in General

In the past 25 years, a range of individuals associated with middle level education have proposed varied curricular frameworks for middle schools, including:

- A curriculum centered on consolidating previously learned skills (Strahan, 1985)
- Curriculum by themes relevant to early adolescents rather than by disciplines (Beane, 1990)

- Interdisciplinary curricula (Lounsbury, 1992)

- Integrated instruction (Stevenson and Carr, 1993).

Nonetheless, there has been no widely espoused or broadly accepted framework for what constitutes appropriate curriculum for middle level learners (Beane, 1990; Tomlinson, 1992; Stevenson and Carr, 1993). In fact, it can be argued that the least well-defined element of middle level education is curriculum (Tomlinson, 1992).

Typically, curriculum for gifted learners would be conceived, at least in part, in comparison to curriculum prescribed for learners who are more academically "typical" at a given developmental stage. The absence of consensus regarding what constitutes appropriate curriculum in general at the middle level results in the lack of a point of comparison for describing curriculum for middle level learners who are more advanced academically than the standard curriculum is designed to serve.

In other words, curriculum for exceptional learners (including those who are gifted) is often said to be "differentiated" or modified from the norm in ways that make it more appropriate for the needs of those exceptional learners. Because middle school curriculum has yet to be clearly defined, the question of differentiation for gifted middle schoolers becomes: "Different from what?"

Developing Promise: A Framework for Thinking About Curriculum for Advanced Middle Level Learners

Despite the variance among high ability early adolescents and the lack of clarity related to middle level curriculum, a number of principles can safely guide development of curriculum for middle level learners who are academically advanced. In concert with one another, these principles are key to developing the potential with which gifted early adolescents enter the middle school doors. They are the principles that would guide talent development in any area for young adolescents—athletic, musical, mathematical, and so on:

1. Curriculum for advanced learners at the middle level would help these students develop deep roots in the areas of their ability or talent.

2. Appropriate curriculum for advanced learners at the middle level would guide these students in developing passion for one or more facets of learning.

3. Curriculum for advanced learners at the middle level would ensure that these students learn to embrace challenge.

4. Appropriate curriculum for advanced learners at the middle level would establish the journey of these students on a path toward expertise.

A sensitive teacher will understand the variability in early adolescents who are advanced learners, and will give emphasis to various principles as a student's development and needs warrant.

Developing Deep Roots

No author ever became great without the basic skills of writing well in hand. No person ever became a great mathematician without knowing how to compute and problem solve. Great discoveries in science begin with an understanding of the rudiments of science. Thus, for all students, including those who are gifted, future promise in a given arena begins with a more humble foundation in the essential understandings and skills of that field. "Basics" such as literacy and numeracy indeed *are* basic. So is developing facility with essential concepts and principles of the discipline, high level thinking, and production.

Curriculum for early adolescents should ensure that they develop deep roots in their talent areas by:

- **Using with accuracy and ease the essential skills of the discipline or area in which they have advanced talent** (For example: use of varied maps or almanacs as information sources in geography, approaches to problem solving in mathematics, clarity and power of expression in writing, and so on).

- **Understanding and appropriately using the vital concepts and principles that govern the discipline(s) of their talent** (For example: the concepts of scarcity and conflict in history, the concepts of change and energy in science, the principle in literature that our personal stories help us make sense of life, the principle in history that all of history is an ebb and flow of stability and change).

- **Developing an understanding of various types of thinking that typify a given discipline or area, selecting appropriately from among the various types of thinking to solve problems, and assessing the effectiveness of their thinking in solving problems.**

- **Developing and applying the standards that typify production in a given discipline** (For example: methods and standards of research in history, developing and presenting findings from an experiment in science, drawing to scale and creating three-dimensional representations in mathematics).

A young adolescent becomes deeply rooted in an area of study when he or she develops frameworks or structures that make a subject more than a collection of disparate facts, more than a series of isolated skills. Rather, the subject becomes a way of inquiring about the world—a method of operating. As talented young athletes learn the basic terms and skills of basketball, the rules of the game, ways of responding under pressure on the court, and what constitutes an effective player as well as an effective game, so talented young scientists, musicians, mathematicians, writers, and so forth must become rooted in their subjects or areas so that they really "know the game" in a way that invites their skilled participation.

Developing Passion

Early adolescence is a time ripe for passion. Middle level learners are developing a multi-dimensional view of the world with both its possibilities and its injustices. They are beginning to understand that they are on the brink of the moment the world will be theirs. They care about many things. The middle years offer the perfect opportunity for teachers to seize upon the learner's passion and turn it into a passion for learning. In fact, we know that young adolescents who develop a passion for learning in some area (whether it is an in-school or out-of-school area) are far more likely to emerge from adolescence whole and healthy than are peers who fail to develop such a passion (Csikszentmihalyi, Rathunde, and Whalen, 1993).

Few young adolescents find a drill and practice approach to the basic skills and facts of a subject to be a gateway to passion. Certainly that approach is stultifying for an advanced middle level learner who has long since found those facts and skills redundant and flat. Even a more amplified "deep roots" approach to middle level curriculum—one that emphasizes the concepts, principles, thinking patterns, and production requirements of a discipline-can seem uninspired to an 11-year-old with a taste for adventure.

Thus, curriculum for academically advanced early adolescents must begin with deep roots, but cannot stop there. The curriculum must capture the sense of possibility nascent in the learner.

There is no recipe for developing passion in a young learner. In fact, it is a highly individual proposition. What "hooks" the imagination of one middle schooler may bore another. Nonetheless, there are some general prompts for evoking passion in advanced middle school learners. Given that the curriculum would be grounded in the key concepts, principles, and skills of the subject or discipline, passion may be encouraged through:

- **High relevance.** Important strands of study should be able to be tied directly to the world of the middle schooler. If misunderstanding among cultures leads to conflict in history, it is no less the case in the world of the 12-year-old. An insightful middle level physical science teacher taught his students that all of physical science is a study of observers, events, and relationships. He began the study by having the students discuss what they had observed their first day in school, what events were likely to be important to them this year, and which relationships in their lives helped define them. All year, physical science remained close to their own experiences.

- **The romance of the real.** A middle level teacher helped her learners explore the concepts of "old" and "new" by visiting a neonatal unit in a local hospital, interviewing participants at a senior citizens' center, and interacting with a scientist who does carbon dating. Abstract ideas became real and intriguing because the people and settings were real and intriguing.

- **Student choice.** It is generally possible to provide structure in student assignments that ensure mastery and application of key concepts, principles, and skills while still encouraging students to apply those essential elements to areas of their own interest. Students in a middle level social studies class were encouraged to relate essential understandings about causes and effects of the Civil War to science during that period, music of the era, lives of early adolescents who experienced the impact of the war, literature of the day, politics in the decade ahead, and so on. They were also helped to select a preferred mode of expressing their research findings-including producing a documentary, participating in an interdisciplinary symposium, writing historical fiction, and so on. The balance of teacher-developed structure and student-developed choices can breathe amazing life into what might otherwise have been dry bones.

- **An action orientation.** A group of advanced young writers surveyed agemates to determine key issues in their lives. They then studied the effectiveness and ineffectiveness of their community in understanding and addressing those issues. They made recommendations to a whole raft of agencies (including their school) about addressing the needs of adolescents in their community. Government, writing, and research became immensely more important to these students because they became actively involved in the issues.

- **Digging holes, making tunnels, building bridges.** Student interest is a first step toward passion. Adolescents have much to explore. When a middle level learner shows interest in a topic, prompting that student to study a facet of it in greater depth, study the whole topic in breadth, or make connections between a topic of interest and other topics, this can be important in the evolution from curiosity to interest to passion. When students "dig holes," they study one facet of a larger topic in great depth (for example, pursuing an in-depth study of black holes when the class has been investigating space). When students "make tunnels," they study a larger topic in breadth (for example, looking at the history of space travel, colonizing space, ethics and space colonization, medicine and space, the economics of space exploration, and so on, as an extended study of pioneers in space). When students "build bridges," they link a key concept from one topic or discipline to others (for example, using space as a concept and investigating similarities and differences in how space is dealt with in a study of "outer space" vs. architecture, psychology, art, oceanography, and so on). The hole, tunnel, bridge approach encourages testing and expanding frameworks of meaning of a discipline, exploring thinking, and applying essential skills in a context that is of interest to the learner.

Embracing Challenge

Humans learn best in a state of moderate challenge (Caine and Caine, 1994)—that is, when they are pushed a bit beyond their comfort zones into risk, and when they are then supported in succeeding at that level. A talented young gymnast would never reach her potential in the sport, for example, if a coach were not insisting that she attempt and then master increasingly complex moves in her routines. Similarly, advanced middle level learners will never reach their potential in their talent areas unless they are being coached to attempt and then master increasingly difficult and risky content, processes, and products in their areas of strength.

While it is true for all learners that growth and self-efficacy come from undertaking and succeeding at endeavors that the learners felt were beyond their grasp, advanced learners seldom have this opportunity in school. They "do what comes naturally" on an assignment, and because it looks more astute than their agemates' results, we tell them it is excellent. Not surprisingly, these students become addicted to the trappings of "excellence" such as grades and adult favor. Also not surprisingly, when they are faced with a challenge designed for them (rather than one designed for the whole), they balk. It is uncomfortable to have reward, status, and identity threatened.

Katherine Patterson, a noted writer for young adolescents, keeps a sign above the typewriter where she writes her highly acclaimed novels. It says, "Before the gates of excellence, the high gods have placed sweat" (Patterson, 1981, p. 3). She is likely correct. Advanced learners will probably not achieve excellence without accepting and ultimately embracing genuine challenge. Further, in the middle years when developing a sense of self-efficacy is of prime importance, highly able learners cannot achieve this benchmark without a clear sense that their talents have been put to a high test, and that, in the end, despite some failures along the way, they have prevailed.

Thus, curriculum for advanced or gifted middle level learners must not only lead to deep roots in students' talent area(s) and evoke passion for one or more facets of learning, but it must also cause these learners to experience, accept, and ultimately embrace challenge as important, dignifying, and exhilarating. So what are the characteristics of curriculum and instruction that push advanced middle schoolers beyond their comfort zones in knowledge, understanding, insight, cognition, metacognition, basic skills, and production? Among them are these elements:

- **Curricular, supplementary, and research materials are advanced.** That is, they contain vocabulary and levels of information, and call on a level of reasoning from a middle level reader that would be too difficult for most of the advanced learner's agemates.

- **Pace of study, exploration, and production are alternately brisker than would be appropriate for most agemates in general study, and slower than would be of interest to most agemates in order to allow for depth or range of study.** (What we call "acceleration" is probably the natural pace for an advanced learner. It only appears accelerated when we define it in terms of the whole group.)

- **Content (what students learn), processes (how students make sense of what they learn), and products (how students demonstrate and extend what they have learned) for advanced learners should be at a high "degree of difficulty."** In some sports such as diving and gymnastics, certain moves are said to have a higher "degree of difficulty" than others. That is, they take more skill, involve more risk, and represent a more advanced proficiency in the sport than do other moves assigned a lower "degree of difficulty." For advanced middle level learners, that means that the three curricular elements (content, process, product) will need to be more abstract, complex, multi-faceted, and open-ended than would be appropriate for most agemates. Content, process, and products should also require greater transformation of ideas and skills, mental leaps, ability to deal with problem ambiguity, and independence than would be appropriate for most agemates.

Middle schools have often eschewed high challenge as damaging for early adolescents (e.g., Epstein and Toepfer, 1978; Hester and Hester, 1988; Toepfer, 1990; National Middle School Association, 1992). In reality, early adolescence is a time of becoming, a time of realizing oneself. For academically advanced students in this age group, it is highly likely that realization of self and potential can only occur when curricula have deep roots, are passion-provoking, and are presented at a high level of challenge.

Movement Toward Expertise

Curriculum and instruction for gifted or academically advanced middle level learners must also move these young adolescents down a path toward expertise in their talent area(s). We are accustomed to gifted young athletes, actors, or musicians working assiduously in early adolescence to develop the attitudes, skills, and practices of adult professionals in their fields. Similarly, early adolescents with advanced talent in one or more academic domains will likely benefit from learning experiences and learning environments that help them develop the sorts of attitudes, skills, and practices that typify experts in their fields.

Among elements of curriculum and instruction likely to facilitate movement toward expertise (in addition to establishing deep roots in the subject area, developing passion for some facet of learning, and accepting and embracing challenge) are the following:

- **Honing the skills of independent learning and production.** By early adolescence, if not before, highly able learners sometimes think beyond their teachers. It is important for middle level learners to become increasingly comfortable in identifying problems or issues to be tackled in their interest areas, determining methods for addressing the problems, setting short and long-term goals toward task completion, establishing timelines for accomplishing goals, knowing how to assess progress and when to revise plans, knowing how to get meaningful in-process feedback, coming to see glitches as important sources of information, persisting in the face of difficulty, and so on.

  Virtually all expert-level professionals demonstrate these sorts of learned skills of independence. As early adolescents are looking for increased independence in their lives in general, ensuring that they also develop comfort with skills of independence in their talent area(s) is affirming in the short term, and essential for long-term movement toward expertise.

- **Working like a professional in the field.** Curriculum for advanced middle level learners should provide them with consistent opportunities to identify, address, and work to solve problems that are authentic to the discipline in question—using the procedures, processes, guidelines, tools, and criteria of experts in the field. Mathematicians do not go to work and do problems from a book on a blackboard. They use mathematics as a means of solving problems that exist in the world and/or as a language to communicate understandings about the world. Historians do not go to work to answer questions at the end of text chapters. Rather, they gather and interpret information to help us more fully understand the people, places, and events in our world. Scientists do not typically execute pre-crafted experiments with highly predictable outcomes. Instead, they employ heuristics of questioning, observing, weighing information, and posing possible solutions to an immense range of problems and uncertainties around them. Writers doggedly write, and so on.

  Students do not move toward expertise by reading about and completing worksheets on archaeology or sculpting nearly so effectively as by working like an archaeologist or sculptor or botanist or poet. Early adolescence is a prime time for developing a sense of adult roles, and middle level students with advanced potential in one or more areas are ripe for coming to understand what it is like to be an expert in those domains.

- **Developing real products that are shared with meaningful audiences.** A highly able young computer graphic artist develops an animation about the environment for her science class. Upon completion, she shows it to her classmates, and her teacher grades it. Another student with similar talents works closely with a local environmental agency to develop a graphic animation that will be used as part of a television ad campaign to build public support for a particular environmental initiative. During part of the process, the student works with a scientist who helps her better understand the environmental issue and the audience for the campaign. She also consults with professional animators who point out strengths in the animation sequence and make suggestions for revisions. There is no comparison in the amount of movement toward expertise likely to take place in the two scenarios. Becoming producers of knowledge and/or solutions to real problems and receiving both formative and summative feedback from experts in the field provides the sort of stretch rarely encountered in the classroom alone.

- **Assessment according to rubrics or "guidelines for success" that point toward expertise.** In school, students are often given guidelines for success for a task or project that have accuracy and completeness as a ceiling of expectations. Advanced middle level learners should work with guidelines and rubrics that move them from accuracy as a baseline of performance to levels of insight and elegance of thought and production (e.g. Wiggins, 1996). Coming to understand the difference between something crafted adequately and something crafted in a surprising and sophisticated way is an important step toward expertise.

Learning Environment as an Element of Curriculum and Instruction

In *The Mozart Season* (Wolff, 1991), Allegra, a talented young violinist, is offered by her music teacher the option of participating in a demanding musical competition. The music teacher elects to wait until the softball season is over before discussing the competition with Allegra, because he knows she needs that season in her life as well. During the summer of the Mozart season, Allegra gives much of every day to practice. She struggles to move from skillful performance to inspired performance by trying to experience the music as its composer did. In the process, she learns to value a man she encounters who is "different," senses the tragedy that has shaped the life of a beloved family friend and mentor, plays with an adult orchestra during summer concerts in the park, and misses her best friend who is away for the summer. Her teacher models, cajoles, encourages, stands back, asks essential questions but refrains from providing answers, and helps her tolerate risk. Allegra does not "win" the competition, but she comes to see music as a metaphor that pulls together all the emotions and discoveries of the summer. In doing so, she plays with the soul of a composer. Ultimately, she knows she is a different and stronger person—and a better musician. As the book ends, she is lying in her bed, cat curled up beside her, and smiles as she hears a song on the radio dedicated to her by a boy who played in the competition with her.

It's fiction, of course, but in order to help talented young learners establish deep roots, develop passion for learning, accept and embrace challenge, and move toward expertise, the fictional learning environment created by the teacher in the novel must be a reality in the classroom. Learning environments that promote talent development in academically advanced middle level learners:

- **Balance joy and rigor.** In the environment there must be invitation and expectation for hard work and struggle, counterbalanced with a sense of joy in learning, celebration of personal growth, invigoration at a challenge accepted, and a sense of satisfaction in having strived and prevailed.

- **Support risk with scaffolding that promotes success.** Many very bright middle level learners have moved through elementary school earning "A's" with little effort. Those grades become a part of their identity. They often believe people expect the "A's" of them, and might value them less without the grades. A classroom that points the way to deep roots, challenge, and expertise raises the ceilings of expectations. Students often feel threatened because their success no longer seems inevitable. A wise teacher understands that discomfort and simultaneously raises the standards while helping the young learner reach the new heights. Encouragement, clear criteria for success, in-process feedback with time to revise assignments before they are due, support in learning to tackle more demanding assignments, and a sense of partnership between teacher and student can make all the difference between a classroom that is challenging and one that is threatening.

- **Balance the pull of early adolescence with the pull of advanced accomplishment.** Students like Allegra need both the softball season and the Mozart season. An effective teacher for these students understands their need to giggle and their need to excel—their need to achieve and their need to belong—their need to be children and their need to make forays into adulthood. Such a teacher helps a talented young person encounter complexity and still enjoy the pleasures that should accompany the middle years. Such a teacher ensures that highly able learners do not have to sacrifice acceptance of their ability in order to have a peer group, and do not have to sacrifice a peer group in order to affirm their talent.

Curriculum for Advanced Middle Level Learners: Curriculum Good for One and All?

Just as gifted or academically advanced middle level learners are both like and unlike their age-mates in traits and learning profiles, so it is that curriculum and instruction for these learners should be both similar to and different from that of their agemates. Some elements of effective curriculum and instruction for advanced middle level learners would benefit most students of that age. For example, most middle level learners would benefit from curriculum that is concept-based and principle-driven, teaches essential skills in context, promotes high level thinking, balances student choice with teacher structure, is relevant, is action-oriented, links the classroom with a broader world, promotes exploration, ensures challenge, and so on.

What makes appropriate curriculum and instruction for academically advanced middle level learners distinct from that which benefits their agemates is the degree of abstractness, complexity, open-endedness, independence, problem ambiguity, multi-facetedness, and mental leap necessary to stretch and propel these learners—and the variance in pace of learning that is appropriately challenging for these learners in comparison with many agemates.

Thus, it is not the case that a "good" middle level curriculum would be good for all learners—unless that curriculum has built into it consistently varied avenues to content, process, and product, so all learners are continually engaged with materials, activities, and products that stretch them a bit beyond their individual comfort zones. For advanced middle level learners, that requires a depth and breadth of core study and exploratory study likely to be overwhelming to many middle level learners, consistent engagement with materials likely to be too complex and abstract for many middle level learners, tasks and products with specifications at too high a degree of difficulty to be appropriate for many middle level learners, escalation toward expertise likely to be too demanding for many middle level students, and an environment that supports the paradoxes of talent development at a level perhaps unnecessary for many middle level learners.

How Are We Doing with Curriculum and Instruction for Academically Advanced Middle Level Learners?

Many middle level schools have historically rejected grouping by ability or readiness (Klingele, 1979; George, 1988; National Middle School Association, 1992; Carnegie Council on Young Adolescents, 1995), and have moved away from special programs or services for gifted or academically advanced learners (O'Connell-Ross, 1993). In many instances, then, curriculum and instruction delivered in the regular classroom becomes the sole academic fare for these learners.

In regular classrooms, middle level teachers often feel uncomfortable with differentiating instruction for academically diverse learners, including those who are advanced well beyond grade level expectations (Tomlinson, 1995). A recent national survey of beliefs and practices of middle level teachers regarding curriculum and instruction for academically diverse learners (Moon, Tomlinson, and Callahan, in press) suggests there is much to be done before establishing deep roots, developing passion for learning, accepting and embracing challenge, and moving toward expertise become the norm in middle level classes.

In the survey:

- 76 percent of teachers believe middle level learners are concrete thinkers
- 78 percent believe middle level learners are more social than academic
- 92 percent believe middle level learners work best with routine
- 65 percent believe middle level learners are easily discouraged
- 21 percent believe middle level learners think at high levels.

And despite years of contradictory admonitions (Hutson, 1985; Carnegie Council on Adolescent Development, 1989; Stevenson, 1992; Arnold 1993) 47 percent still believe middle level learners are in a brain plateau period and are thus not capable of complex thinking and should be protected from taxing learning experiences.

Further, few of the teachers reported consistent use of any instructional strategy that invites modification of curriculum and instruction for advanced learners. Fifty percent of teachers suggested that middle level teachers do not modify instruction for academically diverse learners (including those who are advanced) because they see no reason to do so.

These indicators coupled with a general lack of clarity on what constitutes appropriate curriculum for the middle level in general bode poorly for environments that commend and support high levels of talent development in highly able early adolescents at a pivotal developmental phase in their lives. At 12, Kathleen wrote a poem that clearly expresses the challenge to middle level educators of developing talent in academically advanced students.

Push me!

See how far I go!

Work me 'til I drop,

Then pick me up.

Open a door,

Then make me run to it before it closes.

Teach me so that I might learn,

But then show me the tunnel of experience

And let me walk through it alone.

Then, near the end,
When I look back
And see another in the tunnel
With you watching,
I shall smile.

References

Arnold, J. "A Curriculum to Empower Young Adolescents." *Midpoints* 1(1993): 1-11.

Beane, J. *A Middle School Curriculum: From Rhetoric to Reality*. Columbus, Ohio: National Middle School Association, 1990.

Bloom, B. *Developing Talent in Young People*. New York: Ballentine, 1985.

Caine, R., and Caine, G. *Making Connections: Teaching and the Human Brain*. Menlo Park, Calif.: Addison-Wesley, 1994.

Carnegie Council on Adolescent Development. *Turning Points: Preparing American Youth for the 21st Century*. Washington, D.C.: Carnegie Corporation, 1989.

Carnegie Council on Young Adolescents. *Great Transitions: Preparing Adolescents for a New Century*. New York: Carnegie Corporation, 1995.

Csikszentmihalyi, M.; Rathunde, K.; and Whalen, S. *Talented Teenagers: The Roots and Success of Failure*. New York: Cambridge University Press, 1993.

Epstein, H., and Toepfer, C. "A Neuroscience Basis for Reorganizing Middle Grades Education." *Educational Leadership* 35(1978): 656-60.

George, P. "Tracking and Ability Grouping." *Middle School Journal* 1(1988): 21-28.

Hester, J., and Hester, P. "Brain Research and the Middle School Curriculum." *Middle School Journal* 1(1988): 4-7.

Hutson, B. "Brain Growth Spurts: What's Left by the Middle School Years?" *Middle School Journal* 2(1985): 8-10.

Klingele, W. *Teaching in Middle Schools*. Boston, Mass.: Allyn & Bacon, 1979.

Lounsbury, J., ed. *Connecting the Curriculum Through Interdisciplinary Instruction*. Columbus, Ohio: National Middle School Association, 1992.

Moon, T.; Tomlinson, C.; and Callahan, C. *Academic Diversity in the Middle School: Results of a National Survey of Middle School Administrators and Teachers*. Storrs, Conn.: National Research Center on the Gifted and Talented, (in press).

National Middle School Association. *This We Believe*. Columbus, Ohio: NMSA, 1992.

O'Connell-Ross, P. *National Excellence: A Case for Developing America's Talent*. Washington, D.C.: U.S. Office of Education, 1993.

Patterson, K. *The Gates of Excellence: On Reading and Writing Books for Children*. New York: Elsevier/Nelson Books, 1981.

Stevenson, C. *Teaching Ten to Fourteen Year Olds*. New York: Longman, 1992.

Stevenson, C., and Carr, J. *Integrated Studies in the Middle Grades: Dancing Through Walls*. New York: Teachers College Press, 1993.

Strahan, D. "Brain Growth Spurts and Middle Grades Curriculum: Readiness Remains the Issue." *Middle School Journal* 2(1985): 11-13.

Toepfer, C. "Implementing *Turning Points:* Major Issues To Be Faced." *Middle School Journal* 5(1990): 18-21.

Tomlinson, C. "Deciding To Differentiate Instruction in Middle School: One School's Journey." *Gifted Child Quarterly* 39(1995): 77-87.

———. "Gifted Education and the Middle School Movement: Two Voices in Teaching the Academically Talented." *Journal for the Education of the Gifted* 15(1992):206-38.

Wiggins, G. "Anchoring Assessment with Exemplars: Why Students and Teachers Need Models." *Gifted Child Quarterly* 40(1996): 66-69.

Wolff, V. *The Mozart Season*. New York: Henry Holt, 1991.

CHAPTER 4

Utilizing the Community To Support Able Learners

Jaclynn C. Tracy, Eastern Michigan University

Laurel K. Johnson, Dexter Public Schools

The middle school years are often pivotal in the lives of high achieving students. This is a time when many high achievers begin to focus their strengths, talents, and sustained interests by identifying with a particular area of study and tenaciously pursuing knowledge and skill. Other high achieving students, often those with multiple talents and abilities, seem to drift through these years, never settling down, unable to focus their strengths or identify strong areas of interests. Still others become stressed trying to excel in many areas, unable to focus and identify their passion.

Consider John, the mathematical wizard of his elementary classroom, renowned for his mastery of popular computer games. John enters middle school after a summer of self-study in BASIC programming using his uncle's old college text. John's goal in life is to create new and exciting computer games and to sell them to the highest bidder. John is both persistent and precocious in his learning. He has focused his mathematical ability on the field of computers and he is anxious to learn as much as possible.

Similar stories can be told about Jennifer, the voracious reader who has fallen in love with Celtic literature; about Tanisha, the budding scientist who has become absorbed in saving endangered species; or about Aaron, the talented artist who has become fascinated with painting people's faces. All these children were high achievers in elementary school; all have entered middle school ready to focus their interest and their energies to develop an area of expertise. What responsibility do middle level educators have in the development of these talents? How can middle level educators, with their limited resources and expertise, support these individual students?

Consider also Mary, whose talents and abilities are superior, who has entered middle school as a voracious reader, an accomplished dancer, a budding violinist, and an excellent student in mathematics who shows promise as a leader because she is popular and well-liked. Mary is beginning to show signs of stress as she attempts to excel in all these areas and to keep up with the vigorous practice and concentration required to remain proficient in several ways. What can middle level educators do to support Mary?

Another multi-talented, high potential student is Andrew. Andrew has always excelled at school without much effort, and middle school continues to be easy for him. Andrew's parents are concerned because they feel their son is not being challenged and that he is not developing a work ethic. Andrew's teachers are concerned because he shows no interest in class, is putting forth minimal effort, and becoming a class clown. How can middle level educators help focus Andrew's abilities and refocus his energies?

Or, what about Sandi? Sandi has always done well in school. Her grades have been excellent and her test scores indicate superior ability. Sandi has developed a new interest in middle school—boys—and has decided that excelling academically inhibits her social standing. Her grades are slipping, as is her confidence in her abilities. How can the school guide Sandi, redirecting her energies and re-inspiring her to develop her potential?

Typical middle level schools do not have the resources to assist a student with an individual interest, nor the expertise or time to guide the talented student toward a more focused pursuit of interest and talent. Focusing and developing talent during these critical years is the responsibility of the middle level educators, but alone they are limited in what they can do.

Finding solutions to the educational needs such as those of John, Jennier, Tanisha, Aaron, Mary, and Andrew is not a simple task, but one that can be accomplished when approached in creative and innovative ways. The philosophy reflected in *It Takes a Village and Other Lessons Children Teach Us* (Clinton, 1996) can be one answer to meeting the needs of high achieving students. Extending middle level classrooms into the community and opening doors to the community provides opportunities for a myriad of creative possibilities to emerge that support and enrich the developing talents of young adolescents.

Witham (1991) suggests that activities for high achieving students include projects and independent studies that are interdisciplinary in nature, designed to ensure an appropriate fit of complexity and pacing for individual students. Experiential learning theory suggests that when students are actively engaged in learning, and that learning is meaningful and challenging, students are empowered and successful. Community resources can be utilized to develop projects and independent study activities that engage students as they develop areas of strong interest and ability.

Volunteerism

How do middle level educators begin to gather community resources needed to expand its talent development efforts? There are several ways such resources can be tapped. Asche (1989), in materials prepared for the National Association of Partners in Education, recommends that teachers and administrators consider the use of volunteers. Specific roles for volunteers that may support talent development include:

- *Intergenerational Programs*—Seniors helping students write oral histories, introducing them to the "lost" arts, creating and building community history and pride

- *Tutoring Programs*—Community volunteers tutoring students in a field of endeavor that is beyond the learning needs of their age peers

- *School/Community Partnerships*—Formalized support for talent development programs by community agencies or businesses

- *Corporate Released Time Programs*—Local company employees released from work at corporate expense working with students on individual projects in areas of student interest

- *Career Exploration/Employability Skills/Shadowing Programs*—Short-term, off-campus, specialized assistance to students in occupational areas of interest

- *Mentor Programs*—Long-term, off-campus, specialized assistance to students in academic and occupational areas of interest

- *Supplementary Programs*—Formalized supplementary programs integrated with the school curriculum to expand learning opportunities

- *After-School Student Contact*—Support enrichment services after the regular school day

- *Recognition Activities*—Organization of recognition events for community members and high achieving students involved in curriculum extensions

- *Decision-Making Groups*—Service on various school-based input committees and school representation on community-based councils.

Coordinating expanded volunteer services and matching volunteer resources with student talents and needs can come from parent teacher organizations, from parent talent development advocacy groups, from part-time paid staff, or from school/community partnerships. Leadership is critical to program success. It provides direction for the development of policies and procedures to guide and manage volunteer programs.

Formal assessment of volunteer resources and student needs is often a useful starting point. The goal is to match volunteer resources with student abilities, interests, and needs in a sustained effort that stimulates and develops the talent of bright young adolescents.

Training and orientation programs enhance the potential for successful community volunteer-based talent development programs. Ongoing coordination, supervision, and assessment contribute to the growth and success of the program. Finally, appropriate recognition for the contribution of volunteers is essential.

Active, vibrant school volunteer programs provide middle level educators with extensive resources and increased options for the individualization necessary to help high achieving students develop their talents. Such efforts could help John pursue his interest in computers, help Aaron increase his skill in portrait painting, and help Sandi identify and explore areas of strong interest.

Use of volunteers is one way to support high achieving students. Deeper, richer commitments are also available. They build on volunteer programs and establish vibrant school/community partnerships.

School/Community Partnerships

The past decade has given rise to the notion that schools working with their communities can address serious issues and concerns of youth, including the needs of high achieving students. Volunteerism in schools and classrooms is one avenue. Another form of support is school/community partnerships. "Partnerships are formal, voluntary relationships between the schools and their communities for the purpose of educational improvement. Partners match available resources with identified needs to meet mutually agreed upon goals and objectives. All partners benefit" (Partnerships for Education Task Force, 1989). These benefits include:

- Improved community support for education—personally, financially, and legislatively
- Additional instructional resources—materials, equipment, and personnel
- A curriculum enhanced by experiential learning, expanded content, and real-world exposure
- Greater motivation to stay in school and graduate
- Better career information—greater awareness of and access to job opportunities and placement
- Expanded use of school facilities and resources by the entire community (Partnerships for Education Task Force, 1989; Oakes and Thomas, 1991).

The scope of school/community partnerships varies, depending on the level of the organization at which the commitment is made, the resources available to the partners, the perceived need in the community, the degree of personal and organizational commitment, and the demographic make-up and political milieu of the community (Schmitt and Tracy, 1996). Thus, partnerships take many different forms.

Two partnership arrangements that support and promote student achievement are service learning and mentorship programs. These programs benefit all students, but have particular benefits for high achieving students. They serve as excellent pathways to enhance the regular school curriculum and individualize student learning and talent development.

Service Learning

The National Service Act of 1993 defines service learning as a method:

- Under which students learn and develop through active participation in thoughtfully organized service experiences that meet actual community needs and that are coordinated in collaboration with the school and community

- That is integrated into the students' academic curriculum or provides structured time for students to think, talk, or write about what the student did and saw during the actual service activity

- That provides students with opportunities to use newly acquired skills and knowledge in real-life situations in their own communities

- That enhances what is taught in school by extending student learning beyond the classroom and into the community and helps to foster the development of a sense of caring for others.

Kinsley and McPherson (1995) quote Sawyer: "Service learning is a powerful educational experience where interest collides with information, values are formed, and action emerges. The learning part has two dimensions: an inner dimension (i.e., learning about yourself, your motivation, and your values); and an outer dimension (i.e., learning about the world, its ways, and the underlying cause of the problems that service work addresses)" (p. 5). Twenty years of teaching community service in the classroom, accompanied by a review of research in the field, led Conrad and Hedin (1989) to identify the following benefits from well-designed community service programs:

Personal Growth and Development

- Self-esteem
- Personal efficacy (sense of worth and competence)
- Ego and moral development
- Exploration of new roles, identities, and interests
- Willingness to take risks, accept new challenges
- Revised and reinforced values and beliefs
- Taking responsibility for, accepting consequences of own actions

Intellectual Development and Academic Learning

- Academic skills (expressing ideas, reading, calculating)
- Higher-level thinking skills (open-mindedness, problem solving, critical thinking)
- Content and skills directly related to service experiences
- Skills in learning from experience (to observe, ask questions, apply knowledge)
- Motivation to learn and retention of knowledge

- Insight, judgment, understanding—the nuances that can't be explained in a book or lecture but often the most important things of all to know

Social growth and development

- Social responsibility, concern for the welfare of others
- Political efficacy
- Civic participation
- Knowledge and exploration of service-related careers
- Understanding and appreciation of, and ability to relate to, people from a wider range of backgrounds and life situations (Kinsley and McPherson, 1995).

Let's examine service learning experiences for some of the students described earlier. For Tanisha, such an experience would help her develop her scientific research interests and would appeal to her altruistic environmental concerns. Imagine Tanisha joining the local Sierra Club and becoming involved in their efforts to reverse the declining population of the sandhill crane. By joining people with similar interests, Tanisha benefits intellectually, personally, and socially. By matching Tanisha's interests and abilities to community resources, her talents would be expanded and her energies joined with others sharing similar concerns.

Andrew is another high achieving student who would benefit from a service learning experience. Through his social studies class, Andrew became interested in an upcoming local election and connected with a candidate of his choice. Imagine the engagement when Andrew is invited to become part of the campaign team. Andrew has the opportunity to use his computer and writing skills to create campaign brochures, to participate in both telephone and door-to-door promotion, and to be present and involved in the local election night festivities. By matching Andrew's interests and abilities to community resources, his talents are focused productively and his energies and work ethic constructively developed.

Mentorships

Closely related to service learning but quite different in terms of programmatic and student outcomes, are mentoring programs. They provide another use for community volunteers to enhance student learning and talent development (Glasgow, 1996). Such programs often accomplish the following:

- Mentored activities supplement, enhance, and validate existing curricular activities. Once implemented, they can become an integral part of the everyday curriculum.
- Many times, students gain a sense of relevance and context for the schoolwork within the mentored project.
- Mentored project activities are open ended in nature and students have the ability, with the collaboration of their mentors, to explore and create their own project pathways and explore their personal interests.
- Abstract ideas about many occupations become concrete for those experiencing a taste of what they view as a potential career.
- Many mentored projects require responsibilities that aid students in role and behavior transitions.
- Longer-term relationships with mentors offer greater immersion and more meaningful experiences than do job shadowing, career day, or guest speakers.

- Mentors become community advocates for education and the school.

- Relationships with businesses, industry, and public agencies can provide resources that the school cannot.

- The mentor program model is open ended, which allows many people, businesses, industries, and public agencies to contribute in mutually designed programs within their own comfort zone.

- The community, much as in sports programs, becomes an active, not a passive, participant in your academic program.

A mentorship would be an excellent way to meet John's focused talent development needs. John's computer interests would be a good match for Mr. Schneider's expertise in computer generated animation. Both Mr. Schneider and John would benefit from this mentoring relationship. John would learn another interesting application of computers and Mr. Schneider would be making a contribution to the growth and development of young talent.

Connecting Sandi, a potentially at-risk student, with a mentor is one way to change this direction. The owner/realtor of the most successful realty company in the region, Jamie Raines, would be a good mentor for Sandi. Observing Jamie's leadership and management of more than 250 highly competent professionals creates a new vision of personal success for Sandi. Inspired by the identification of a potential career, Sandi is able to restore her confidence and regain her academic standing.

Youth Program Opportunities

Community resources are also delivered to high achieving students via extended day/year programs. Many school districts, community education departments, local recreation councils, and area libraries and museums offer programs and services that supplement the regular school curriculum. These programs and services provide additional venues for stimulation and enrichment and are most often offered after school, on weekends, and during the summer months. Minzey and LeTarte (1994) state that capitalizing on the availability of varied local opportunities "provides students with an opportunity to pursue their own goals and to expand their abilities in areas of their own choice, as dictated by their personal interests. This includes providing an opportunity to try out new courses and new techniques, and to have the opportunity to fail without feeling like a failure" (p. 136).

Participation in youth program opportunities would offer both Aaron and Jennifer a chance to learn and grow in their area of interest. When Aaron attends Camp Brighton for two weeks during the summer, he receives one-on-one instruction from the resident artist who is impressed with Aaron's ability to capture emotion in portraits. Aaron's works are showcased in a local art exhibit.

Jennifer's interest in Celtic literature is discovered by her English teacher who shares this with the university librarian. Jennifer is invited to participate in a literature discussion group that meets monthly at the university. Again, by matching student needs with community resources, student talents develop.

Involvement in Decision Making

Advocates for high achieving students are needed to serve in decision-making capacities throughout the schools and community, including representation on Chambers of Commerce boards, school improvement teams, parent resource councils, booster clubs, advisory councils, school boards, site-based management teams, interagency collaboratives, curriculum councils, talent development advocacy groups, and local task forces. Through their input and advocacy for the programs and services serving youth (i.e., volunteer programs, school/community partnerships, service learning, mentorship programs, and expanded youth programming) adults can influence their peers in a variety of ways garnering greater understanding for these programs, extending financial contributions, and expanding human resource support.

Parents of high achieving students should also be encouraged to join in the advocacy efforts. Their need for personal and family support can be addressed as families make connections with people of similar interests and concerns. Mary's parents might benefit from the wisdom and experiences of parents of other high achieving students. This would help them guide Mary as she makes choices about her future vocation.

Conclusions

Although it is the responsibility of the middle level educators to focus and develop the talents of high achieving students, these educators have neither the resources nor the expertise to accomplish this task on their own. By utilizing school volunteers, creating school/community partnerships, engaging students in service learning opportunities and mentorships, accessing youth program opportunities, and involving parents and community members in decision-making processes the middle level school opens its doors to a myriad of creative possibilities that both support and enrich the developing talents of young adolescents.

High achieving students like John, Jennifer, Tanisha, Aaron, Mary, Andrew, and Sandi can be well-served by these approaches. Individual opportunities for learning and growth that are engaging, meaningful, and challenging can be found in the community at large. Talents are developed when these opportunities are matched with student interests and abilities. Creating partnerships to this end is a difficult, yet rewarding and productive way for people to join together sharing resources and expertise.

Partnership is something more than the words "parent involvement" or "community involvement" convey. True partnership indicates a *sustained relationship involving mutual expectations, responsibilities, and benefits*. It evolves from the recognition that the potential of children is enhanced when educators and educative institutions work together. As the village comes together to serve its children, the potential to affect the achievement of all students is strengthened.

References

Asche, J. *Handbook for Principals and Teachers: A Collaborative Approach for the Effective Involvement of Community and Business Volunteers at the School Site.* Alexandria, Va.: The National Association of Partners in Education, Inc., 1989.

Clinton, H. R. *It Takes a Village and Other Lessons Children Teach Us.* New York: Simon & Schuster, 1996.

Conrad, D., and Hedin, D. *High School Community Service: A Review of Research and Programs.* Washington, D.C.: National Center on Effective Secondary Schools, U.S. Department of Education, Office of Educational Research and Improvement; and Madison, Wisconsin Center for Education Research, School of Education, University of Wisconsin-Madison, December 1989.

Glasgow, N. E. *Taking the Classroom into the Community: A Guidebook.* Thousand Oaks, Calif.: Corwin Press, 1996.

Kerr, B. A. *Smart Girls Two: A New Psychology of Girls, Women and Giftedness.* Dayton, Ohio: Ohio Psychology Press, 1994.

Kinsley, C. W., and McPherson, K., eds. *Enriching the Curriculum Through Service Learning.* Alexandria, Va.: Association for Supervision and Curriculum Development, 1995.

Minzey, J. D., and LeTarte, C. E. *Reforming Public Schools Through Community Education.* Dubuque, Iowa: Kendall/Hunt, 1994.

Oakes, J., and Thomas, D. "A Sound Investment." *Thrust for Educational Leadership* 5(1991): 12-14.

Partnerships for Education Task Force. *Michigan Partnership for Education.* Lansing, Mich.: Michigan Department of Education, 1989.

Schmitt, D., and Tracy, J. *Gaining Support for Your School: Strategies for Community Involvement.* Thousand Oaks, Calif.: Corwin Press, 1996.

Thompson, S. "The Community as Classroom." *Educational Leadership* 8(1995): 17-20.

Witham, J. "Full-Time Solutions to Part-Time Problems." *The Gifted Child Today* 6(1991): 10-12.

CHAPTER 5

Technology for Able Learners: Promoting Engagement and Learning

Lucinda L. Johnston, The Center for High Achieving Schools, Tampa Florida

Emily loves technology! When she was four years old her favorite toy was a Mickey Mouse calculator with a large smiling face and 14 buttons to press. She would spend hours pushing buttons and watching the figures on the screen change. As time passed, she discovered that the figures were numbers and that they changed in specific, predictable ways when she pressed certain buttons. By the time she reached her fifth birthday she had discovered arithmetic and could add, subtract, multiply, and divide with the best of us.

Emily grew up in a highly technical world. Her parents use technology to make every aspect of their lives less complicated and more efficient. They do their banking electronically, use microwave ovens to cook, and correspond using e-mail, voice mail, and pagers. Emily chooses from 180 channels when watching TV and amuses herself playing video games and computer simulations that are more sophisticated than some of the technology employed by NASA to put earthlings on the moon.

Emily is truly a Nintendo Kid: technically literate, intellectually curious, able and racing into the 21st century with hopeful anticipation of the exciting innovations in store for humankind. She, along with the rest of her generation, holds the key to the future of this planet. They will use their earnest curiosity and available technology to solve the problems of poverty, conflict, pollution, racism, intolerance, and injustice. They are filled with the kind of optimistic curiosity it will take to learn from the past and solve the problems that have been so intractable for the current adult generation.

Now imagine what happens to this unbridled enthusiasm for learning and discovery when Emily walks into her seventh grade classroom. Five days a week Emily rediscovers that her school, like most others, has not kept pace with the technical advances in our society. Although she spends part of her day in "special" classes for able learners, her day-to-day instruction is very similar to that of her parents 25 years ago or her grandparents 25 years before that. Emily, like most students today, spends most of her time in classrooms listening to teachers give information, reading textbooks, and completing assignments that require memory and recall. In the school, little has changed since the technology race began in the early 1950s.

If we are to meet the needs of our most able learners, schools must confront the challenge of catching up with the rest of our highly technical society. We must change our view of teaching and learning in the same ways we have had to change the way we view banking, shopping, communicating, and other areas of our lives (Johnston and Johnston, 1996). To do so we need to understand the role of technology in instruction and work toward integrating it into the daily lives of all our students, especially our most able and talented.

Computers, video, multi-media, telecommunications, and other forms of information technology give students and teachers the power to transform ordinary classrooms into dynamic learning communities in which students engage in productive knowledge production and information utilization tasks. More than any other student population, able learners can use technology to enhance the way they access, analyze, process, and communicate information.

Access to technology, along with appropriate guidance and encouragement, can help maximize the remarkable potential of able learners at the same time it enables teachers to differentiate instruction for this special population. In addition, able learners who are encouraged to explore the possibilities of available technology in a school can become the fearless navigators we need to lead us into the information age with the rest of society. But where do we begin?

Planning for the use of technology in a program for able learners begins with careful consideration of the ways technology can affect learning. There are four practical applications for technology in academic settings that form an organizer for integrating technology into the school program: technology exists as a separate subject, a surrogate teacher, an instructional tool, and a catalyst for transforming the learning process for both teacher and students (Johnston and Johnston, 1996).

Technology as an Academic Subject

If our most able learners are to be pioneers in the 21st century, they require a thorough understanding of the technology available to them. Because of the increasing technological sophistication of students coming to the middle level school—particularly able and talented learners—computer literacy instruction must be more than a half-semester enrichment segment focused mainly on software and keyboarding. Indeed, the very concept of "computer literacy" must change as the overall technological competency of our nation's children grows.

The content for a computer literacy course is taken from our society itself. Computers have a history. They have affected our society and empowered people to be more effective and efficient learners. Guided exploration through the most important aspects of technology's impact on society is essential for able learners at the middle school level. A curriculum for the study of technology has five major components: technology and society, technology to empower learning, technology-related skill development, and the history and evolution of technology.

By studying technology's impact on society and its economic implications, students begin to develop global awareness of its critical importance to the success of individuals and communities. One teacher asked a group of his most able learners the following question: "Would simply inundating an impoverished community with advanced technology be sufficient catalyst to improve their situation?" The students spent the next two weeks conducting research and preparing for a stimulating and productive debate on the question. Is providing technology to third world countries a logical first step to economic and social stability, or is the perceived *need* for technology prerequisite to acquisition if it is to truly transform the life of individuals and communities?

Questions like these, posed by teachers who are willing to facilitate research and debate, form the basis for technology literacy instruction that will capture the interest and enthusiasm of able learners. It also serves as the perfect opportunity to engage students in basic social science research.

Able learners also need to understand how technology can enhance their learning power. Able learners often grow to be professional students who spend 8 to 10 years in postsecondary education, and an important prerequisite to academic success is a thorough mastery of academic computing. Students who can conduct electronic searches for information, use word processors, spreadsheets, and other utilities, and create multi-media presentations have a decided edge in the competition for admission to postsecondary education, financial resources and support and, ultimately, jobs in the next century.

For students to fully understand the potential for technology to increase their learning potency, they should be guided through an analysis of their own learning strengths and needs and introduced to the technology that can enhance their strengths and strengthen their areas of need (Johnston and Johnston, 1996).

As with every advancement in our society, technology brings with it substantial ethical problems. Able students are fascinated by and have the capacity to understand and deal with complex ethical questions. They need to be aware of problems ranging from security of information and laws governing software copyright and hardware security to the rights of underdeveloped countries to have access to advanced technology. A well-designed technology literacy program is the ideal place for able learners to develop a personal code of ethics for technology use that they can take with them as they enter information age workplaces.

Able learners also need systematic instruction in basic computer skills. When teaching able learners in any subject area we run the risk of overlooking basic skills in our zeal to maximize their amazing potential with advanced instruction. Some able learners need to develop basic computer skills ranging from keyboarding and basic telecommunication to fundamentals of electronic searches and technical reading. Since most academic classes focus on reading imaginative or expository material, a technology literacy class is an ideal place for able students to develop the ability to read, understand, and write technical materials, an essential skill for the 21st century workplace.

Finally, a comprehensive technology literacy class for able learners includes instruction in the history and capacity of technological devices. Students require a clear understanding of the development of technology in order to feel comfortable in a society that is too much like the one described in Alvin Toffler's *Future Shock*, which described a society plagued by depression and stress, the result of technology advancing too rapidly—advancing beyond our capacity to understand or assimilate its impact. Without an awareness of the origins of technology and the normal progressions of its development in our society, individuals can become overwhelmed by rapid changes in our daily lives. Able learners should know there is a logical evolution in the development of technology.

Every new design starts when someone sees a need for a tool to accomplish a task. Once the tool is developed, it often creates more need and new tools are designed and produced. This cycle of "need defined - need met - more need created" accounts for the rapid development of hardware and software during the past 10 years.

By introducing such concepts to our able learners we can ensure that they will become masters of technology and not victims of the stress and confusions that befall those who allow technology to master them. And for those of us who may already be experiencing the results of technology's advancement far beyond our own comfort level, what better companions exist than fearless and able students to embark with us on a journey of exploration and understanding?

Technology as a Surrogate Teacher

Just as ATM machines sometimes replace a bank teller, computers with appropriate software can serve as an extra teacher or, in some cases, in place of a teacher. This is a particularly important feature of technology for teachers who need to differentiate instruction for gifted learners within the regular classroom. Able students can use instructional software to develop, practice, and enhance basic skills; engage in problem-solving activities; and enhance understanding of an unlimited range of topics either inside or beyond the regular school curriculum.

Software programs guide students through systematic instruction in math, language arts, science, social studies, and many other disciplines. Since students are able to control the pace at which they work, they are not held back by peers (or teachers) who may need to explore at a slower rate, an all-too-common situation when teaching able learners—and the concern most often voiced by the parents of gifted students who are placed in the regular classroom.

Since more than 14,000 educational software titles are available for classroom computers, choosing software for able learners can be a tedious process and few teachers have the time or resources it takes to develop an adequate classroom software collection. When funds are available for software purchases, it is important to carefully evaluate potential titles before making a selection. Fortunately, criteria exist to help teachers sift through the available programs and choose those that will work best for able learners.

Ideally, instructional software for able learners should:

- Contain adequate and understandable directions
- Serve a wide range of ability and age levels
- Teach, remediate, or extend some aspect of the curriculum
- Challenge students and require the use of high levels of problem solving and critical thinking
- Provoke further thinking and inquiry
- Provide appropriate and timely feedback for students
- Allow users to manipulate the difficulty level to increase or decrease the challenge.

School leaders must ensure teachers have access to appropriate software for able learners. In one Texas middle school, the principal sets aside part of the instructional material budget each year for software. When questions were raised about specific titles and programs, a group of able students came to the rescue by developing a plan to sort and evaluate the titles in the school and preview and evaluate titles being considered for purchase. Students used critical thinking skills in the development of the rating scale and as they judged each piece of software on criteria similar to those listed above. In addition, they added their own "kid evaluation" adjectives: cool, fun, and awesome! In another school, the overall rating for each piece of software was shared on a "coolness" scale: DOA (dead on arrival), uncool, cool, way cool, maximum cool.

Another way technology can serve as an extra teacher for able learners is through the use of Integrated Learning Systems. These comprehensive programs provide pre and post-tests, data banks of instructional materials, and practice exercises. They are illustrated with attractive graphics and many allow students to manipulate the difficulty of the material, the pace with which it is covered, or the instructional materials themselves. Students can test themselves to determine their entry level, choose instructional units, and assess their own performance.

Integrated Learning Systems are often closely correlated to state and national achievement tests, so able learners can prepare for these exams, reduce test performance anxiety, and improve their scores significantly. These integrated systems allow students to take control of their own learning and often motivate students to higher levels of engagement with test preparation materials than is typical in a regular classroom. Because able learners are often competitive, particularly against goals and benchmarks set for their own performance, motivation to use this software is usually high. They can set instructional goals for themselves and receive constant and immediate feedback on their progress toward these goals.

While the initial investment in Integrated Learning Systems may be quite high, the payoff in increased student motivation and performance make them worthy of serious consideration for instructional leaders charged with developing programs for able learners. Beyond that application, they are also very useful in providing intensive instruction for other targeted populations in the school, whether for enrichment or remediation.

Technology as an Instructional Tool

Technology is also a powerful tool that can greatly enhance teaching and learning in the classroom. Just as technology is used in business and industry to increase efficiency and improve finished products, so can it be used to accomplish the same goals in a classroom. Teachers and students can use technology to do the things they've always done in school, only do them faster, better, and with less effort.

Word processing and desktop publishing enable students and teachers to create high quality products that are visually appealing, easily edited for improvements, and simple to reproduce. Students who use word processors write longer and more sophisticated works, produce fewer errors, and are more likely to edit and rewrite their materials (Johnston and Johnston, 1996).

Graphic and clip art programs, as well as image scanners can empower even the most artistically challenged teacher or student to add depth and personality to written work through borders, illustrations, artwork, and photos. High quality, visually appealing letters, reports, and projects send a clear message that the able learners are being challenged and that excellence is expected and modeled by teachers and mentors.

Grade management programs can help teachers maintain accurate and comprehensive records and enable schools to advise parents regularly about student performance. In addition, by setting up individual academic record files, these programs can provide the regular academic feedback that is so important for able learners.

LCD projection and multi-media presentations can help teachers capture the attention and imagination of able learners who are very clearly the products of our highly visual and interactive media-rich world. By training students to use these technologies, their own work, presented in this format, is more engaging, instructive, and easily archived than traditional student products.

Databases and spreadsheets can be used to store, analyze, and manipulate information ranging from the patterns of temperature and rainfall, to bird migration, to infant mortality in a local cemetery. Through the use of these inexpensive "utility" technologies, students are equipped with some of the most powerful analytical and research tools ever developed.

Information resources on CD-ROMs allow able students to access vast volumes of information without ever leaving their classrooms. Add on-line information services, and students have access to almost limitless stores of information on virtually every subject. These simple technologies can be used to provide the engaging interactive and self-directed learning environments in which able students thrive.

By using technology as a tool for teaching and learning, teachers and able learners can accomplish mundane tasks in less time and with greater efficiency, thereby giving them more time to engage in significant instruction, reflective and productive thinking, and independent learning.

Technology as a Catalyst for Transforming Instruction

In its most promising form, technology can be used to transform instruction for able learners. Teachers can use technology to shift the focus of instruction and move beyond teaching information for recall to using information to create authentic and innovative student products. With appropriate technology, teachers can structure real-life problems and simulations that require high levels of student performance. The classroom becomes a knowledge workplace, and students engage in meaningful, product-oriented activities that focus on authentic problems, issues, and opportunities (Johnston and Johnston, 1996).

In a transformed classroom, students tackle problems and projects involving cooperative learning, interdisciplinary research, and authentic assessment. Technology makes it possible for students to work on novel problems or the production of useful products and information while learning to access, analyze, and report information and plan and manage complicated projects.

However, these transformations don't just happen when computers and other instructional technology are delivered to the classroom. The transformation of instruction for able learners requires that judicious changes be made in the way classrooms are organized and instruction is delivered.

Through technology, classrooms for able learners can be transformed into multi-task work environments. Cooperative groups focus on effectiveness and collaboration rather than individual performance and compliance. Students are rewarded for completion of real products in response to real needs in the school or their community. Diversity is respected and rewarded as students are exposed to new and different ideas (Johnston and Johnston, 1996).

To illustrate this multi-task environment, in one middle school classroom, teams of students volunteered to produce a variety of authentic products in relation to their study of *Romeo and Juliet.*

One group wrote and produced a children's version of the play for presentation to the primary grades in a neighboring school; another developed a Hyper-Studio, interactive review and study guide for all students to use; another group used a graphics program to produce a children's book about the story; another used a computer-assisted design program to illustrate the theater in which the play would have been performed; and a final group used desktop publishing (and a lot of on-line research) to produce a newspaper that might have appeared on the day after the debut of the play in the 17th century! In addition to splendid products from each group, it was also clear that this was a classroom for everyone. All students, regardless of ability or talents, had important work to do to make their group's product the best it could be.

Those who doubt the possibilities of a technology-rich classroom need only watch a group of able students as they surf the Internet or use any other high tech tool to complete their work. They are absorbed, curious, and tenacious in securing information. It is quite a different picture from the one we too often see in classrooms: bored students, restlessly inattentive to the labored presentations of frustrated teachers. Intuitively, we know how this generation learns and how to hold their attention. We have to use the same tools that capture their imagination outside school to transform their classrooms and make learning meaningful inside school.

Figure 1 (Johnston and Johnston, 1996) shows a graphic comparison of the traditional and the transformed classroom. It is not difficult to imagine which one is more likely to capture the attention and full participation of able learners.

Figure 1

The Traditional Classroom	**The Transformed Classroom**
Information given by the teacher.	Information comes from a variety of sources in response to problem situation.
Students store and retrieve information on demand.	Students create, manipulate, and use information to solve real-life problems.
Teacher, text, and local resources are available to students.	Students have access to global resources through on-line services and CD-ROM technology.
Students expected to master information as given.	Students expected to employ information in solution of novel problems or completion of authentic work tasks.
Students solve assigned problems designed to illustrate basic content concepts.	Students solve problems which come from real life in the community, nation and world.
Curriculum shaped by logical progression through discrete content area materials.	Curriculum shaped by the knowledge necessary to solve real-life problems or complete real learning and work tasks.
Assessment based on teacher-constructed tests, teacher judgment, standardized tests.	Evaluation based on quality of solutions, portfolios documenting student performance, self and teacher assessment, and standardized measures.
Teacher is authority: source of knowledge, tasks, correct responses.	Teacher is mentor and guide, often learning material at the same time the students do.

Supporting Instructional Technology for Able Learners

Create a team of experts

Because technology resources are limited, school leaders need to practice a form of triage in allocating them: They should be allocated to the teachers who are most likely to use them. That sounds somewhat ruthless but, to quote one sage, "technology is like clothes, not like fire." You can get warm standing beside a fire, but for clothes to work, you must put them on. Likewise with technology: You can stand beside a computer all day, but unless you interact with it, it cannot do much to improve your work or life. Distributing the resources equally (i.e., placing one computer in everyone's class, whether they use it or not), will not produce the critical mass of technology needed for truly transforming instruction by teachers who are willing to do so. By equipping teachers and students who are already enthusiastic about instructional technology, schools can create "model" technology classrooms that serve as demonstration and training sites, a place for technology inservice training, and an infectious environment from which enthusiasm for technology can spread.

Because they enjoy high credibility in the school and "speak the same language" as their peers, technology-using teachers provide the best source of expertise about what actually works in a classroom, and they make the best teachers of other teachers. Indeed, trainers who are "too expert" can intimidate and frustrate novice users. Model technology teachers, on the other hand, can lead workshops, strategic planning, and other technology projects designed specifically for the individual school site. School leaders need to find creative ways to free up these pioneers so they can assist colleagues who are just beginning to use technology. In most schools the use of instructional technology spreads one teacher at a time.

Involve parents

Often the parents of able learners are skilled in the use of computers, word processing, telecommunications, multi-media, and other forms of information technology. Parent volunteers can provide the support that is necessary for teachers to manage instructional technology projects in regular classrooms or assist in technology-oriented classes. Parents can teach keyboarding skills, demonstrate the basics of desktop publishing, assist with instruction and supervision for multi-media project development, and help conduct Internet searches.

Having technically literate adults on campus will encourage teachers and students to use available technology. Spending 30 minutes with a volunteer skilled in the use of a particular hardware or software product can do more for a technical novice than a day at an expensive workshop or institute.

The parents of able learners who assist with the instructional technology program, by virtue of their presence and involvement, will send the message to teachers that they expect their students to have access to the technology tools they need to be 21st century scholars and information workers. Who better than your most vocal parent advocates to encourage teachers to take the technology plunge?

Showcase technology initiatives and projects

Further the use of technology by providing ample opportunity for teachers and students to share projects and ideas. One school has able students develop hyper-media programs for use during open house. When parents arrive, they find multi-media displays in each classroom. The programs provide background on the teacher, explain classroom rules and procedures, and give information parents usually find written on a chalk or bulletin board. Another school publishes an electronic student newspaper that is distributed on disk to each classroom. For more sophisticated users, the paper is also posted on the school's website, so teachers and students are motivated to use the computer to access the latest news and information about their school. Other ideas for sharing technology include:

- Display finished work in the office, lunchroom, and other common areas
- Broadcast audio and visual creations via the school's intercom or closed circuit system
- Ask teachers to share ideas and celebrate success during faculty meetings
- Devote a portion of parent newsletters and teacher bulletins to showcase technology in your school
- Create a website and let the able learners maintain it

By showcasing technology, school leaders send a clear message that they expect technology to be part of day-to-day academic life.

Provide technical support

One constant when dealing with instructional technology is the axiom that if anything can go wrong, it will. Screens will freeze, printers will jam, programs will fail, mice will stick, and data will disappear. For all its practical value and potential to transform instruction, technology can be terribly frustrating and infinitely fallible. School leaders should expect the best, but plan for the worst. Identify staff members who can assist others when things go wrong. When problems are quickly and easily solved, teachers are encouraged to continue to try out new equipment and software.

Finally, when developing an instructional technology plan for able learners, Barron and Orwig (1993) say it is essential that there be a balance between "high tech" and "high touch." The integration of technology will not replace teachers because technology cannot provide a teacher's compassion or ability to analyze an individual student's learning needs. Instead, teachers can use technology as another tool for presenting and providing access to knowledge. Human beings remain the essential factor for providing high touch in an increasingly high-tech world.

For those who work with able learners, it is technology's ability to liberate them and their students from drudgery and mundane intellectual activity that is the greatest gift of all. By freeing creative teachers to actively mentor able students through challenging intellectual tasks, technology provides the very foundation for a successful program for able learners: committed teachers working with curious and interested learners to promote learning and continued engagement with schooling.

References

Barron, A., and Orwig, G. *New Technologies for Education: A Beginner's Guide.* Englewood, Colo.: Libraries Unlimited, 1993.

Johnston, J. H., and Johnston, L. J. "Technology: Bringing Our Present and Future into the Classroom." *Schools in the Middle* February/March 1996.

Toffler, Alvin. H. *Future Shock.* New York: Random House, 1970.

CHAPTER 6

The Principal's Role in Establishing an Agenda of High Achievement

Ronald D. Williamson, University of North Carolina at Greensboro

Across the nation, principals are confronted by parents and community members demanding improved student achievement. The news media report declines in test scores. Employers decry the lack of skills among employees. Parents recount the experiences of their children in navigating the maze of public education.

Nowhere are the challenges greater than at the middle level, for it is in the middle grades that the balance between student development and academic achievement is most questioned. It is here that children and their parents most often confront the specter of graduation requirements and standards for college admission. It is also when schools most frequently begin to distinguish children and their educational experiences based on academic skill and potential.

Conflicting demands emerge at the middle level. On the one hand, there are calls to respond to the dynamic nature of early adolescent development. On the other, there are shouts for more rigorous and challenging educational experiences. These competing expectations create a cauldron of discontent that, left unattended, envelops and emasculates the middle level school.

This melee begs for responsive leadership. Middle level leaders have a vital role in creating a climate that supports student achievement, and at the same time is responsive to diverse student needs. The importance of leadership has consistently emerged:

Almost without exception, the major studies and reviews of school effectiveness, regardless of the operational definition of effectiveness that is employed or the theoretical orientations of the researchers, have identified the principal as a strong performer in achieving educational excellence. (Johnston and Markle, 1986, p. 12).

The Importance of Leadership

Leadership and effective schools go hand in hand. The work of Brookover and Lezotte (1977), and Edmonds (1979) revealed that effective schools shared a number of characteristics among which was appropriate instructional leadership. Leadership was characterized by a passion and zeal for student learning, a willingness to examine data and information to promote student success, and a clear mission focused on high levels of achievement for all students.

An earlier examination of middle school leadership identified several roles principals assume—inspirational leader, human resource developer, and change agent—each affecting the leaders' ability to shape and influence their school's program (Williamson, 1991).

The first role, that of inspirational leader, described the importance of possessing a clear educational philosophy and actively working to promote and implement that philosophy. The school leader, in collaboration with constituent groups, guides the examination and refinement of school programs.

A midwestern middle school illustrates this skill. A banner draped over the entrance to the school proclaims unequivocally that at this school "the success of every student is our only goal." While the principal and many faculty members are committed to the goal, school activities occasionally reflect a quite different attitude.

Some faculty members accepted as the norm attitudes that detracted from the school's stated mission. When a group of teachers stood around the school office and discussed deficiencies of individual students or groups of students they were not confronted. When harsh grading practices were applied to student work no questions were raised. When individuals read newspapers or graded papers during staff development sessions they were not challenged. While 35 percent of students got at least one failing grade each marking period it was considered the students' problem.

The new principal rallied the faculty. He quietly but firmly let faculty members know his expectations for teacher deportment. He engaged teachers and other staff in conversations about the merits of students. He found ways to recognize and reward staff for efforts to promote student achievement.

Through these quiet efforts the culture of this middle level school changed. One senior teacher remarked: "Without [his] leadership I'm not sure we would have made the progress we did. It wasn't by berating us for our faults, but by quiet, inspirational leadership that [he] set the new standards for how we work together. It's really made a difference."

In the human resource development role, principals selected and utilized strategies that "bring out the best" in school constituents (teachers, students, parents). This role, essential to creation of a climate that provides faculty comfort with curricular and instructional change, is evident. For example, one principal in southeastern Michigan described the early days of his school's middle school program:

Teachers were afraid to try new things. They were anxious. What if it doesn't work? What if it comes off poorly? What will students, parents, colleagues think?

My role was to minimize their anxiety. So I told them. What is most important is try some things. If they work, great. If they don't, the key is what did you learn from that experience and how will you use that to guide planning.

Not taking risks and being innovative is the problem. Too often we see lack of success as the issue. That's just not it.

Being attentive to this human dimension is critical when modifying a school's program. Motivation theory espoused by Maslow (1954) has been applied to such change initiatives. Maslow saw human needs as a hierarchy. Higher needs, such as esteem and a desire for knowledge, arise only after the lower needs, such as food and shelter, have been met. The most basic needs were composed of safety and survival issues—food, water, shelter.

Middle level reform is much the same (Williamson and Johnston, 1991). For people involved in implementing substantive changes, such as curricular and instructional reform, the leader must attend to the most basic needs—security and survival. Clearly this does not require attention to the same basic needs suggested by Maslow. It does, however, imply that school leaders remain sensitive to the need for teachers and other school personnel to feel safe and comfortable in modifying their practice, in engaging in innovative behaviors, and even in being less than successful in some of these ventures. To be less than attentive places reforms in jeopardy.

When a middle level principal in Michigan raised difficult questions about the services her faculty members provided to their most able learners, she encountered resistance. Teachers rejected any notion that able students were not being challenged, refuting both test score data and anecdotal reports from students and parents.

A study group of parents and teachers was established to examine the data, and prepare recommendations for action. In convening the study group the principal ensured that key stakeholder groups were represented: teachers, parents of able learners, parents of less able learners, counselors, curriculum staff. She found it was important to have all key players "at the table," participating in the discussion, and offering their perspectives.

Including stakeholders is essential to the success of any planning initiative. While including "known dissenters" will often provoke some initial skepticism about the project, it frequently serves as a catalyst for lively and engaging discussion, discussion of core beliefs and values—an essential first activity in any planning effort (Williamson and Johnston, 1991).

For this planning group, as for many, it was important to establish a set of ground rules to guide their meetings. They found that clear guidelines and procedures alleviated some of the natural tension that arose regarding controversial issues and varying perspectives. Their adopted ground rules included:

- Have a prepared agenda for each meeting
- Prepare minutes from each meeting and distribute them prior to the next meeting
- Follow an informal version of *Robert's Rules of Order*
- Define a quorum
- Consensus will be the preferred decision-making method
- If consensus cannot be reached provisions will be made for recording and distributing minority reports or dissenting opinions
- Unless it is an emergency situation, no item will be formally agreed to at the same meeting in which it was introduced.

A middle level school principal in a southeastern state found that when working with parents and teacher groups to examine school practice, conflict occasionally arose. The principal developed a set of strategies to ensure more "open" communication when conflict was present. His suggestions included:

1. Share data and descriptions, not value judgments or interpretations
2. Use active listening skills
3. Focus on the present, not what has been or might be
4. Agree when those of a different viewpoint are right
5. Own your ideas and feelings; use "I" as much as possible
6. Guard against too much openness
7. Make constructive use of silence; provide (and demand) time to think
8. Delay making judgments or decisions
9. Explain, do not defend
10. Be sensitive to nonverbal clues and messages
11. Recognize and request rewording of questions that have no answers, are rhetorical, or include commands or directives
12. Avoid use of superlatives and absolutes (most, best, always, never)

13. Assume the motives of others are "honorable"

14. Discourage preaching and teaching behaviors.

At a middle level school in southeastern Michigan an approach to solving complex school reform problems such as initiating programs to more effectively challenge able learners was developed. The school designed an eight-step problem-solving process. Its value was described by the principal: "We had a problem with individuals or groups suggesting ways to change our program. They would identify one strategy and advocate its merits. Others discounted the suggestion, believing it was self-serving. This model, once agreed upon, served as a road map for how we would solve problems. It forced us to look at alternatives, and consider both advantages and disadvantages."

Problem-Solving Model

Step 1: Identify the problem

Step 2: Prepare an analysis and discussion of the problem

Step 3: Identify alternative solutions

Step 4: Discuss the advantages and disadvantages of each alternative

Step 5: Select an alternative for implementation

Step 6: Implement the proposed alternative

Step 7: Gather data and assess the success of the alternative

Step 8: Identify new problem or refine strategy

Each of the components of this problem-solving strategy contributed to its success. First, it required analysis and discussion of more than one alternative for each identified problem. This focused discussion on "problem identification" rather than "solution selection." Second, the process included identification of advantages and disadvantages. It recognized that all solutions are encumbered with disadvantages and thus sanctioned those who dissented—legitimized alternative viewpoints, and affirmed difficult questions. Third, the approach required a process for measuring the success of any implemented change. This provided another venue for examining their effectiveness and discussing refinements and enhancements. The principal described its impact: "At first some of us wanted to skip parts of this process—to move quickly to solutions. Thankfully, some faculty members slowed us down, held us accountable to our process, made us be much more thoughtful and reflective. This resulted in better decisions, decisions that have the support of most faculty."

The third role suggested was that of change agent. It consists of helping stakeholders continually look for ways to strengthen and refine their programs, being sensitive to individual and group concerns about change, and addressing the varied needs of each group.

A middle level principal from Colorado described this role: "My job is to help my community—teachers and parents—see that it is possible to change our practice and still deliver a quality, rigorous program." To deliver on that commitment, middle level principals do whatever it takes to challenge, inspire, support and develop their schools.

Another middle level principal from the midwest, confronted by a faculty and community unbothered by declining achievement scores, drafted eight questions for their consideration. Each raised provocative issues about the school's program and together with a collaborative decision-making process served as a vehicle for engaging his teachers and parents in modifying that school's practice:

What Is the Status of the Achievement Agenda in Your School?

1. How does the achievement of our students compare with the achievement of students in our district/county?

2. What is the distribution of achievement among students based on gender, ethnicity, or socioeconomic status?

3. What is the perception of achievement in our school among students, parents, faculty, community?

4. What specific activities take place in our school to promote conversations and discussion of achievement?

5. What professional development is provided at our school to ensure improved student achievement?

6. What groups or individuals participate in making decisions about achievement activities or programs?

7. Who is accountable for improved achievement in our school?

8. What is the achievement "bottom line" in our school?

A recent study of reform in urban middle level schools identified leadership as an essential component. It found that when reform was most effective the principals "act as levers of change" (Lewis, 1993, p. 114). Principals balanced "time-consuming daily routines against whatever it takes to fulfill the vision the staff has agreed upon. They (the principals) make time for change" (p. 114). Summarizing the importance of leadership, the report stated, "where systematic change is most visible, good leadership ripples through the system" (p. 111).

The Multifaceted Leadership Role

Middle level leaders must have a framework for acknowledging their multi-faceted role. One organizing tool was suggested by Bolman and Deal (1991). It consolidates the major theories of organizational and leadership theory into four perspectives or frames—structural, human resource, political, and symbolic. Each frame, they suggest, provides interesting and unique insights into the work of leaders. The importance of the frames is described: "Frames are both windows on the world and lenses that bring the world into focus" (pp. 11).

The structural frame, built around the formal roles and relationships of an organization, suggests that the purpose of organizations is to accomplish goals, and that leadership should strive to find the right organizational pattern, the appropriate reporting relationship, the correct job description to achieve organizational goals. This perspective depicts organizations as relatively closed systems existing to achieve explicit goals. Coordination and control are seen as essential to effectiveness and that organizations are most effective when order and rationality prevail.

The human resource frame reflects an understanding that organizations and the people who work in them are inextricably linked and suggests that leaders must examine the "fit between individual and organization" in order to assure effectiveness. This conception of the leadership role is built on the assumption that "a good fit between individual and organization benefits both" (Bolman and Deal, 1991, p. 121). It allows people to engage in meaningful and satisfying work while employers benefit from the talent and energy unleashed by employees in such a setting.

Competition for power and resources is central to the third frame—political. It suggests that conflict among constituent groups is inevitable and that the quest for power and the related control of resources is a constant organizational dynamic. Bargaining and negotiating among interest groups in such a setting reflects the struggle for power and control.

Bolman and Deal suggest that each constituent group brings distinct values, preferences, beliefs, and perceptions to any discussion and that these differences are modified slowly. Furthermore, the most critical decisions in organizations involve the allocation of resources—human and financial. These two dynamics—differences in basic underlying principles and competition for resources—create an environment in which conflict prevails and where control and power emerge as the greatest of all resources.

The fourth and final frame in Bolman and Deal's model is the symbolic frame represented by organizational culture—symbols, rituals and ceremonies, stories and tales, rewards and reinforcements. This frame departs from traditional views of organizational theory because it assumes that understanding the meaning behind these indicators is the key to understanding organization effectiveness. The statement "what is most important about any event is not what happened, but what it means" (p. 244) exemplifies this frame. The symbolic frame also suggests that most organizations are ambiguous and uncertain. In the face of such ambiguity people use symbols, cultural indicators, "to increase predictability and provide direction" (p. 244). Furthermore, events and processes are important not for what they accomplish but for what they express.

Bolman and Deal suggest that leadership effectiveness is increased where leaders understand and respond in each of the four frames. Integrating the four perspectives into a coherent and viable leadership style allows the contemporary leader to navigate the world of complex and competing issues and demands. They suggest that: "The truly effective manager and leader will need multiple tools, the skill to use each of them, and the wisdom to match frames to situations" (p. 12).

Principal's Role in Establishing a Culture Supportive of Achievement

How then do middle level principals promote high levels of achievement for all students? How do they challenge accepted practice, provide for greater curricular and instructional innovation, create a sense of membership, and promote teacher efficacy and student engagement?

Bolman and Deal's leadership model (1991) provides a useful way to examine the principal's role. Each frame offers insight into the role of the school principal in improving student achievement.

Attention to the Human Dimension (Human Resource Frame): Principals understand that refining and strengthening their school's program requires attention to those who must implement the changes. They encourage teachers to take risks and understand when success is not imminent. One Michigan principal described it this way:

> I want my teachers to try new things. Sometimes they work. Sometimes they don't. When it doesn't work out the only question is what did you learn? What will you try next? It's the only way to promote continued innovation.

Principals also provide opportunity for reflection. They use regular meetings to discuss and debate curricular and instructional practice. They support staff members in their own professional development. They secure resources so teachers may attend conferences and workshops, or work collaboratively to develop new units or materials. They encourage thoughtful practice.

Other Suggested Leadership Activities

- Ensure time for teachers to talk with one another about curricular and instructional issues
- Provide staff development focused on meeting the needs of all learners
- Model thoughtful and reflective consideration of alternatives
- Communicate effectively and often with all constituent groups
- Work with staff to develop high expectations for staff performance
- Support staff members who use new or innovative instructional, curricular, or assessment practices
- Model the use of appropriate interpersonal strategies when working with students, staff, parents, and community
- Recognize staff and students for academic achievement
- Use recognition to ensure the maintenance of high achievement standards for all students
- Provide teachers and parents with books, articles, and other materials about promoting student achievement and curricular and instructional change
- Ensure staff development programs that are needs-driven and responsive to staff priorities.

Understand the Importance of Cultural Symbols (Symbolic Frame): Principals also understand how to use school culture to shape school practice. They recognize staff for their work on behalf of students. They allocate resources to support innovation rather than maintenance of the status quo. They talk about the heroes and heroines among the staff who work diligently to ensure high levels of achievement for all students.

The principal of a middle school in Michigan established opening school activities that reinforced the school's focus on achievement. In September, prior to the Olympic Games, the school assembled all students on the athletic field to hold an "Opening Day" spectacular. Classes marched onto the field by team, each with a banner similar to those carried by national teams at the Olympics. Students carrying the banners were selected for their accomplishments—service to the school, improvement in academic achievement. The principal spoke to the assembled students and faculty about the importance of their success in school and introduced a former Olympic athlete who exemplified the importance of education and school success.

As students and staff left the ceremony, a renewed enthusiasm for schooling emerged—a commitment to the success of every student, and belief among students that "achievement was the most important product." Such a ceremony or extravaganza served to illustrate, with great visibility, the importance of student success and achievement.

Other Suggested Leadership Activities

- Modify school routines to reinforce achievement (e.g., announcements, use of staff meetings)
- Create new school symbols that embrace high achievement for all students as a school goal
- Talk with teachers and the community about student success
- Recognize staff members who promote high levels of achievement and/or use innovative instructional practices
- Reward students for all types of achievement (e.g., academic, community service, athletic)
- Speak to community groups (e.g., service clubs, church groups) about student success and teacher innovations

- Arrange ceremonies (e.g., assemblies, festivals, parent meetings) that support achievement as a priority

- Ensure alignment between stated goals and the actions of teachers and administrators.

Pay Attention to Organization (Structural Frame): Providing for the achievement needs of all students requires that the principal create an environment supportive of change (Mizell, 1995). The principal creates an organization that emphasizes academic performance. They are not apologetic for this emphasis but rather see it as the highest priority of their school.

Principals enthusiastically involve faculty and community in school governance in support of an achievement focus. Parent insights are welcome. Criticism is seen as a vehicle for school improvement. Dissent and diverse points of view are valued. Debate clarifies thinking and purpose. Such schools value shared decision making and believe that such participation improves the quality of decisions.

Achievement-focused schools possess clear indicators of student success. There is agreement about measuring and assessing school effectiveness. Leaders of such schools are comfortable talking about its success or failure. Achieving goals is cause for celebration. Failure is seen as an opportunity to redesign and recommit instructional resources. Principals believe that together, teachers, parents, and principal can commit to plans that result in improved student achievement.

Other Suggested Leadership Activities

- Develop a plan to involve constituents in school planning

- Design a clear statement of school mission

- Establish a focus on student achievement as the school's first priority

- Identify explicit indicators of student success

- Routinely gather and study student achievement data

- Discuss student achievement during performance evaluations of all staff

- Provide for the effective use of time

- Ensure productive and purposeful classroom activities

- Build accountability for student achievement into every aspect of the school's program.

Recognize That Politics Plays a Role (Political Frame): Principals focused on improved student achievement are also aware of the political dimension. They are not shy about discussing student achievement. They engage parents and the community in assessing the school's effectiveness and in developing plans for its improvement. The principal openly acknowledges areas of needed improvement. One principal described the political role:

I must be seen in my community. I attend community events. I speak at civic and church groups. Wherever I go I talk about student achievement as the number one priority of our school. Our commitment can't be challenged. It's so very visible.

Principals also play an important role mediating and moderating competing forces. When confronted with difficult and complex issues, they are comfortable exploring a range of alternatives, analyzing the advantages and disadvantages of each, and gathering data and information to guide decision making. In this role, principals work with constituents to develop mutually agreed upon problem-solving strategies.

One principal in North Carolina, when faced with strongly held opinions on both sides of the grouping issue, established a study group composed of faculty, parents, and students. The group first agreed on ground rules for their work (e.g., prepared agendas, no final votes at the same meeting when a topic is introduced, quorums). Then they proceeded to identify important questions to guide their work (e.g., Is there a decline in the number of students taking AP courses at the high school?) and gather data and information (e.g., review test score data, conduct interviews with students and parents, look at high school data). During each of these activities a cohesiveness developed among the work group. People with strongly held points of view learned to work together, developed shared interests and, most important, developed an appreciation for diverse points of view.

Other Suggested Leadership Activities

- Be prepared for conflict between constituent groups
- Engage teachers, parents, and community in school governance
- Allocate school resources to support an achievement focus
- Establish a mutually agreed upon process for analyzing and solving school problems
- Involve teachers and parents in study groups to analyze achievement data and identify areas for improvement
- Secure resources to support your school's achievement agenda
- Work with faculty and parents to gather, analyze, and report achievement data
- Speak to school and community groups about the achievements of students and teachers
- Keep superintendent and other key leaders informed about student achievement in your school and plans to address identified issues
- Welcome and involve those who raise significant questions about the school's program and who challenge current programs and operations.

Conclusion

The continued success of the middle level school requires that leaders commit to a renewed emphasis on high levels of achievement for all students. Schools modify curriculum, organize into teams, and modify grouping practices not as ends but as a means—greater success for all.

Somehow the importance of student success at the middle level has been distorted and the function and purpose of the middle level school has been misinterpreted. Reestablishing the connection between middle level reform and heightened student achievement is essential.

No one plays a more pivotal role in making this connection than the school principal. Leadership is essential to modify school culture and critical curricular and instructional practices. The middle level principal must be comfortable challenging accepted norms, advocating for high levels of student success, and using all the levers available to engage faculty and community in refining and strengthening their school's program.

References

Bolman, L., and Deal, T. *Reframing Organizations*. San Francisco, Calif.: Jossey-Bass, 1991.

Brookover, W. B., and Lezotte, L. W. *Changes in School Characteristics Coincident With Changes in Student Achievement*. East Lansing, Mich.: Michigan State University, College of Urban Development, 1977.

Edmonds, R. "Effective Schools for the Urban Poor." *Educational Leadership* 2(1979): 15-27.

Johnston, J. H., and Markle, G. *What Research Says to the Middle Level Practitioner*. Columbus, Ohio: National Middle School Association, 1986.

Lewis, A. *Changing the Odds: Middle School Reform in Progress 1991-1993*. New York: The Edna McConnell Clark Foundation, 1993.

Little, J. W. "The Persistence of Privacy: Autonomy and Initiative in Teachers' Professional Relations." *College Teachers Record* 4(1990): 509-36.

Maslow, A. H. *Motivation and Personality*. New York: Harper & Row, 1954.

Mizell, H. *The New Principal*. New York: The Edna McConnell Clark Foundation, 1995.

Williamson, R. "Leadership in the Middle Level." In *Middle Level Education: Programs, Policies, and Practices,* edited by J. Capelluti and D. Stokes. Reston, Va.: NASSP, 1991.

Williamson, R., and Johnston, J. H. *Planning for Success: Successful Implementation of Middle Level Reorganization*. Reston, Va: NASSP, 1991.

CHAPTER 7

Evaluating Programs for Able Learners: A Model for Collaboration and Consensus

J. Howard Johnston, University of South Florida
Ronald D. Williamson, University of North Carolina at Greensboro

At a recent school board meeting, a principal was first surprised and then dismayed to hear a litany of complaints about the program for gifted and talented students in her school. No one seemed satisfied. The parents of students in the program thought it was not challenging enough for their children; other parents found the program too exclusive, particularly with respect to its service to racial or language minority students. Board members asked about the performance of able learners on the state's standardized achievement test, but the principal had little to offer except her impression that the students did quite well. One parent waived the district's curriculum guide and pressed the principal to explain why her child was not receiving either the content or the instruction specified for able learners; another asked why, if the program was to be individualized, his child's Individualized Education Plan (IEP) looked exactly like that of his neighbor's child. The principal could answer none of these questions with specific information. Finally, to bring this grilling of the principal to a merciful end, the board called for a full evaluation of the school's program for able learners. A committee was created, including a number of the angry parents, and yet another program evaluation was launched amid incrimination, accusations, and defensiveness.

This scene is hardly unfamiliar to educators. Too often, evaluations are begun because someone sees trouble with a program and its operation. When program managers are asked for answers, they often lack even rudimentary data about the program, its operation, its outcomes, or the satisfaction of its clients. Citizens and district leaders lose confidence in the program and, with increasing frequency, in the manager's ability to run it. Programs are often modified or even terminated based on what people *believe* about it rather than what they *know* about it.

By the time a program review is begun, the program is often in such deep trouble with its constituents that the process is long, convoluted, painful, and enormously time and energy-consuming. Mention "program review" to most administrators and teachers, and they imagine hours of meetings, reams of paper, days of wrangling over what the data really mean, and thick reports that are stored out of sight and mind until the next round of questions is raised.

It need not be this way. A carefully planned, ongoing evaluation of able learner programs provides information that is important for a number of purposes:

- It can be used to answer specific questions from the district and the community about the program's operations, outcomes, and user satisfaction.

- It provides information for routine program monitoring and adjustment, thus avoiding wrenching changes at unpredictable times.

- It provides a longitudinal data base for use in strategic planning, budgeting, and grant solicitation.

- Most important, it indicates an "accountability stance" on the part of the program and the school—an acceptance of responsibility for monitoring and maintaining program effectiveness and efficiency.

This chapter outlines a model for evaluating programs for able learners, a process for building consensus and securing participation from program stakeholders, and recommended methods for gathering information that is responsive, credible, and accessible by professionals and lay people alike. It is a plan for getting the information needed to be accountable to the school's many publics, and for avoiding the painful scene outlined in the opening of this chapter.

Accountability and Program Evaluation

Ultimately, all program evaluation is conducted to document the achievement of its goals. Typically, program evaluations are seen as being formative or summative. *Formative* evaluations are designed to provide information that will be useful in making routine modifications, monitoring progress toward meeting goals, and adjusting program elements to improve performance. *Summative* evaluations are designed to render a judgment about the overall effectiveness of the program, and are often conducted to determine if the program should be continued, substantially modified, or terminated.

Overarching these general purposes, however, is the critical issue of accountability. Accountability is simply school professionals' acceptance of responsibility for operation and ultimate success of the program in facilitating learning for gifted and talented students. That is often a pretty intimidating thought! How can a school accept responsibility for what a student learns when children come to school with so many problems about which the school can do nothing? Impoverished communities; families affected by poverty, alcohol, or drugs; and neighborhoods wracked with violence and disorder all mitigate against the success of even the most well-intentioned and well-executed programs. But that is why a thoughtfully developed and carefully planned program evaluation is so critical. It clearly outlines the program's scope of accountability and provides a comprehensive picture of the program's achievements. Instead of using a single measure to assess the effects of a program (standardized test scores, for example), a systematic program evaluation plan can identify multiple sources of evidence to use for a complete picture of the program and its operations.

To begin a program evaluation, school leaders must identify the types of accountability that will drive the evaluation, and articulate the questions to be answered in each area. Five important types of accountability need systematic attention and consideration:

Coverage Accountability: The extent to which the program serves the individuals, locations, or groups for which it is intended. To respond to this type of accountability, the program evaluation must answer questions such as these:

- Are we serving the students we intend to serve? How have we identified them? Are the methods of identification comprehensive? Have we failed to identify significant numbers of eligible students?

- Is there any bias operating in our identification process that excludes certain groups of eligible students?

- Are the identification process and standards clear, logical, and explicit? Do they conform to state and federal regulations? Does everyone know them?

Program Fidelity: The extent to which the program conforms to its original design and plan of operation and the reasons for any deviation from original designs. Fidelity assessments are driven by questions such as:

- Do curricula, instructional methods, materials, and other support components of the program exist as planned in the original design?

- Is the program staffed as planned, both in number and qualifications of personnel?

- Is the program's budget as planned? Have hidden costs arisen or savings been realized?

Impact Accountability: The extent to which the program meets its stated goals and objectives, and any unanticipated outcomes, positive or negative, that might be produced by the program. Impact accountability is often one of the most difficult to address, particularly if the program has global aims (e.g., improving student's attitudes toward advanced classes in mathematics) rather than specific ones (e.g. ensuring completion of algebra I by the end of the eighth grade). Impact questions resemble these:

- Have we met our stated goals and objectives? To what degree? Which of them have been met? How many students have met them? Did we meet the standards set for the program?

- Are there any unanticipated outcomes of the program? Are they positive? Negative? Were they accidents or can they be attributed to the program? Can they be planned into subsequent programs of this type? Do these unanticipated outcomes conflict with or offset any of the other program goals?

Cost-Benefit Accountability: The extent to which the program achieves its goals in a cost-effective manner, achieving maximum performance from each dollar spent. In an era of declining budgets in education, this form of accountability is most critical. Expensive innovations that produce little tangible result are unlikely to be continued, nor should they be. These bottom line questions are:

- How much did the program actually cost? Was it within projected budgets?

- What were the indirect costs of the program? Did it place demands on other units of the school or district that were not anticipated in the initial budget? Can those costs be absorbed or must they be budgeted?

- What were the opportunity costs of the program? By doing this program were we prevented from doing another that might have produced similar or greater benefits? Who was affected by this lost opportunity?

- Did the program realize savings in other areas? By doing this program did we save money somewhere else? Can costs be shared by another non-district agency?

- Did the program generate revenue, or does it have the potential for doing so (through grants, the sale of program materials, training of other professionals)?

Satisfaction: The degree to which the program's constituents feel it met their needs, and the acceptance of the program by others not served directly by it. As schools accept greater responsibility for meeting the needs of their clients and consumers, it becomes crucial to determine how satisfied those customers actually are with the program. Just as important as the opinions of people served by the program are the views of those who are not served directly but whom it affects in some obvious ways. For programs aimed at able learners, strong opinions are often held by the parents of students in the program as well as the parents of children not selected for participation. These questions illustrate important issues in assessing satisfaction:

- Are enrolled students and their parents satisfied with the program's operations and outcomes? Are segments of this groupless satisfied? Who are they? Why are they dissatisfied?

- Are non-enrolled students and parents satisfied with the program and its selection criteria? Do they feel they are included in the decisions affecting their children? What is the nature of their dissatisfaction?

- How is the program perceived by the school staff and other students? How is it perceived by the school board and the community at large?

- Are the teachers who "receive" the program's graduates satisfied with their performance? Does it meet standards established in the original program design?

Comprehensive program evaluations usually seek information about each form of accountability. Increasingly, different constituents demand different kinds of information: Boards may want information on parent satisfaction and costs and benefits; parents will want to know about the impact of the program on their child's learning; student advocate groups will need assurance that the program serves all eligible children to the fullest extent possible; teachers will be concerned about the fidelity of the program to its original intents and its impact on students. For the program review to be effective and informative, it must address all these information needs.

Engaging Stakeholders

For an evaluation to be credible and useful, it must be accepted by all the program's stakeholders. If one group distrusts the evaluation information, the individuals who produced it, or the manner in which it is reported, school leaders can be pretty sure that group will lobby against any program changes recommended by the evaluation process. To ensure all stakeholders accept the results, it is important for each group to be represented in planning and conducting the evaluation. Careful planning at this stage will help ensure the results of the evaluation can be used with confidence in planning for program change.

First, it is important for the school to identify the program's stakeholders, recognizing that some people have a much more highly vested interest in the program than others. Problems arise when either low-interest stakeholders are over-represented or high-interest stakeholders under-represented in the evaluation process.

In a recent case, a district created a 34-member committee to examine the middle school gifted program. The panel included representatives from the parents, the non-parent community, the media, the board, the district office, local clergy, the student body, the PTA, non-school agencies, local government, the chamber of commerce, a local university, and two nearby private schools. Notice who was missing? In their zeal to be inclusive, they neglected to include teachers on the original committee listing. Although the situation was hastily corrected, the teachers remembered throughout the process that they had been added as an afterthought.

In securing stakeholder participation, it is essential for school leaders to differentiate among primary and secondary stakeholders and provide for appropriate levels of participation by each group. The 34-member evaluation committee was not inherently bad, it just failed to differentiate between those people who were highly vested in the program and those with only marginal interest.

A more effective organization would have called for a different form of organization with different levels of participation. The model shown below seeks to engage as many stakeholders as possible, but at a level that is appropriate for their interest in the program.

Primary Stakeholders	Secondary Stakeholders	Tertiary Stakeholders
• Teachers • Parents • Building administrators • Students • District gifted coordinator	• Board members • Parents of students not in program • District office personnel • PTA representatives	• Non-parent community • Non-school agencies • Local government • Chamber of commerce • University faculty • Private school faculty

Primary stakeholders have direct, regular contact with the program and the students in it. They are the most affected by program changes, and the most heavily vested in the operation and outcomes of the program. These groups should be well-represented on the working group that will actually conduct the evaluation.

Secondary stakeholders have either legal, policy, or resource interests in the program. These individuals, although not involved in daily program operations, are accountable to larger groups for the program's effectiveness. They are individuals who form district policy, who represent the larger parent community, or who have broad program management responsibilities that include the program under review among others. This group needs to be fully informed about the program review process and supplied with evaluation plans and other relevant documents as the evaluation proceeds.

Even at this level, however, differentiations might exist. In large districts, board members probably will not want to receive material directly from all of the operating committees. However, it is important that district officials keep board members briefed on these activities so they can respond intelligently to their constituents.

Tertiary stakeholders an interest in the school's performance in have general, although they may not have investments in specific programs. This includes the larger community of taxpayers and business people, other child-serving agencies, and other advocate or watchdog groups. Because these individuals are usually the most distant from the daily operations of the school, they are often inclined to be the most critical of it. Involving this group early and keeping them informed of the program review at planned, strategic points is important for the ultimate success of the evaluation.

Clearly, there are not always distinct divisions among these groups. University faculty members may be secondary stakeholders if they run a teacher education program in the school; other child-serving agencies may be secondary stakeholders if they provide parallel services to children in the program. Local conditions always determine who is involved in the different aspects of the program evaluation. Two fundamental principles are central to determining involvement:

• Ensure participation by those with the most to lose or gain in the program. This will guarantee an attentive, responsive, and responsible core of individuals to perform the evaluation task.

• Conduct the evaluation as an open process, assuring that those who are often excluded from participation have every opportunity to participate.

Often, schools must make special efforts to include participation by people who are often excluded, particularly poor or language minority parents. Such efforts might include scheduling meetings at times these individuals can attend, providing interpreters or other bilingual representatives, paying a small stipend to parents who must travel or pay for child care in order to partic-ipate. Participation by all central stakeholders is essential for evaluation success, so participation should not be limited to those with the time or other resources necessary to endure any inconve-nience of doing so.

Once the district noted earlier identified primary, secondary, and tertiary stakeholders, it was able to identify appropriate forms of participation for each group. The model they used may be helpful to other districts planning an evaluation.

The Task Force. The task force was composed of all stakeholders, anyone with any interest in the program. It included the primary, secondary, and tertiary groups identified above.

When it was created, district officials realized they had excluded parents with limited English proficiency. To remedy this situation, they contacted clergy from churches that served this largely Hispanic population and asked if they could provide representatives for this important parent group. In some cases, clergy served as representatives; in others, they identified bilingual church members who were able to serve. In this way, a large segment of parents, often overlooked, was represented in the process. The role of the task force was threefold:

1. *Focus and Issues.* The task force met for half a day to identify the focus the program evalua-tion should take and the primary issues it should focus on. An important question for this group to answer is, "What does success look like? What will we accept as evidence that this is a successful program for this community and our children? " In this way, the district could be certain the evaluation would respond to the questions and issues that were important to the stakeholders, thus ensuring the relevance of the evaluation's results to local concerns.

2. *Sounding Board.* Because the group was broadly representative of the community and its chil-dren, it provided a perfect setting for presentation and discussion of initial results, findings, conclusions, and recommendations. By reporting the results of the evaluation to this group, the evaluation team could gauge the level of understanding, acceptance, and credibility they might expect in the larger community.

3. *Information Gathering and Dissemination.* This group can be central to data collection and dissemination efforts. People tend to believe information that comes from friends, colleagues, acquaintances, or trusted members of their own community. They are also likely to give can-did information back to these people. By seeking advice from the task force on the best way to gather and disseminate information in their communities, the district can help to ensure that information about the program will be understood and widely used.

The Steering Committee. This group was composed of secondary stakeholders, with represen-tation from the Evaluation Team. The role of this steering committee was to provide linkages between the goals and interests of the district, its partners, and the evaluation plan itself. The pur-pose of this committee was twofold:

1. *Congruence.* This group helped evaluators maintain a broader view by placing the evalua-tion in the context of the district's mission, goals, and policies. In this role, steering commit-tee members reviewed evaluation plans, instruments, and preliminary reports to ensure they addressed issues that were congruent with the school district's aims.

2. *Communication.* Members of this group must first identify the different audiences for the evaluation's results and determine the information needs of each one. (There is little point in giving people with marginal interest huge reports they will never read.) They are in a partic-ularly strong position to convey news of the evaluation to their constituent groups and to solicit feedback and information. The board member kept her colleagues informed of the

evaluation, the PTA representatives conveyed information to that group, and so on. This ongoing system of communication helped ensure no one was surprised by the evaluation's results—or, as is often the case, that it was done in the first place. A dissemination plan that is tailored to the information needs of all stakeholders is central to the success of the evaluation, and this group is the one best equipped to develop such a plan. It is critical that they do not overlook community resources: the media, business and professional groups, church congregations, social clubs and groups, and all the other groups and gatherings to which adults in the community belong.

The Evaluation Team. This team was made up of teachers and students in the program, parents of enrolled students, and the district's able learner coordinator. This working group actually conducted the evaluation by engaging in the following activities:

- Outlining the goals of the program, determining indicators that would provide evidence of goal attainment, and identifying data sources to be used in the evaluation.

- Selecting or developing surveys and other data-collection instruments, managing or directing the data collection, reducing and analyzing the data, and reporting findings, conclusions, and recommendations.

- Maintaining contact with the steering committee and the task force, as appropriate, throughout the process.

- Reporting findings, conclusions, and recommendations to the steering committee, task force, and other appropriate audiences.

The evaluation team's job is a big one. For it to be done effectively, but without placing undue burdens on its members, the team should spend the first hours of its planning identifying helpful resources. District research and testing offices may already have much of the data they need; student groups may help with data collection as a school-service project; parent volunteers can code, enter, or help analyze data. Although it will assume most responsibility for the evaluation, the evaluation team should be seen as a management team, not necessarily the sole source of labor for the project.

The Evaluation Plan

Once the school or program has completed the first, critical steps of identifying stakeholders and planning for their meaningful involvement in the evaluation, the evaluation is ready to program. A useful model for this plan that can be easily adapted for assessing programs for able learners is found in the NASSP Council on Middle Level Education's publication, *Assessing Excellence: A Guide for Studying the Middle School* (NASSP, 1988). The model consists of several distinct steps, each of which is represented by a question.

1. *What are we evaluating?* It may sound simple, but it is critical to specify, in advance, the precise program or program element being evaluated. This allows the evaluation to be clearly focused on that program and its outcomes, not on other issues.

Being specific will make the evaluation more meaningful and more manageable. Rather than evaluating the program for able learners, it is best to focus on the specific level (e.g., the middle school), a specific component of the program (e.g., the International Baccalaureate program of the high school), or a specific group affected by the program (e.g., minority gifted, or gifted students with learning disabilities). Such a view will yield more specific insights about the program and will permit more specific recommendations to come from the evaluation.

Even when more general evaluations are called for (as in the example in the opening paragraphs of this chapter), it is best to identify as precisely as possible the school components to be studied such as achievement, instruction, climate, or curriculum. If a task force meeting reveals that the major issues focus on achievement and instruction, those would be the best places to start.

As the Council says, "Schools are very complex institutions, and must be studied in pieces, even if you study all the pieces at once. Labor must be divided, and the most efficient way to accomplish such a division is to give responsibility for each piece to one of the interested parties" (p. 17).

2. *What are the aims, goals, or intended outcomes of the program?* Most programs for able learners have specific goals or outcomes specified in their original design. Certainly, a large portion of the evaluation must focus on those goals. However, it is also important to examine the program's performance in other areas of interest or concern that did not appear in the original planning. This is best accomplished in the task force meetings by asking this large group of stakeholders what information they need about the program. Several sources of information are important in specifying goals.

- The original goal statements of the program, probably as they appear in the curriculum or program planning document.

- The goals suggested by the task force in response to the questions, "What do you expect of this program? What outcomes do you see for it?" This is a particularly critical discussion if some time has elapsed between the original program plan and the evaluation. Communities change, so their expectations for the programs in their schools often change as well.

- New mandates, research, or policies from the state, district, or profession. Looking at changes in policy or professional knowledge about a field may suggest goals that were not considered in the original design of the program for able learners. Guidelines from the Council for Exceptional Children or other learned societies may be particularly helpful.

At this stage, it is important to state evaluation questions. Such questions force the group to be succinct, direct, and clear about what they want to know. For example, questions such as these are much easier to answer than are vague statements of purpose:

- Does the program have an effect on the attitudes of students toward mathematics?

- Does the program improve algebra achievement for students enrolled?

- Does the program increase the likelihood of student enrollment in subsequent, advanced math courses in high school?

During this exercise, it often becomes obvious that little consensus exists on the goals for the program for able learners, or the goals are badly out of touch with the state of the profession or community expectations. If so, that is the first and most important finding of the evaluation. It is best to interrupt the evaluation at this point to build consensus on program goals and aims before trying to assess how the program is meeting those goals.

3. *What will indicate attainment of our program goals?* It is normally almost impossible to measure program goals directly. "Increasing student achievement in algebra" may be quite easily assessed through a standardized test, but a less specific goal, such as "improving student attitudes toward the study of mathematics," is more difficult to assess with a single measure. This situation requires that we use several indicators to determine if each goal has been achieved.

For example, if the program for able learners is to promote positive attitudes toward the study of advanced mathematics, an attitude scale might provide information about the current state of student attitudes, but it does not tell much about the effect of the program on subsequent mathematics performance. It would be necessary to look at enrollment patterns to determine if students actually opt into higher level math courses or pursue college majors with a mathematics emphasis.

In selecting indicators for each goal, evaluators need to keep several criteria in mind:

- **Ease of assessment.** The indicators should be measurable in ways that do not disrupt the program. The measures might be quantitative (attitude or opinion surveys, tests, frequency counts of students in advanced classes) or qualitative (interviews with teachers, students, or parents), but they are more likely to be useful if they can be conducted during normal school routines. If the measurement is too demanding of time and energy, people simply will not do it.

- **Clear and Convincing.** Indicators should be directly, logically, and clearly related to the goals. An achievement measure may not tell much about attitude. Conversely, students who love math class (or the teacher) might do poorly on standardized tests. Be certain that the measures selected are obviously connected to the goal being assessed.

- **Comprehensive.** Generally it is not possible to specify a single indicator that can do the whole job of determining whether a goal has been met. Taken together, the indicators should provide clear and convincing evidence that the program goal has or has not been met.

The specification of indicators is a crucial step in program evaluation. It is the clearest possible expression of what the group will accept as evidence that the program is or is not working as expected. By giving sufficient attention to this process at this stage, program evaluators can avoid a great deal of confusion over "what do these data mean" when it is time to draw conclusions and make recommendations.

This is an excellent time to have the discussion suggested earlier, "What does success look like for each goal of our program? What will we accept as evidence that this goal is being met?" A strategy for this discussion is to ask the team to think about someone who has already met the goal...a real person they know. (Do they know someone who has a positive attitude toward advanced mathematics?) Then, brainstorm a list of things this person says or does that lead us to that conclusion. Embedded in that list will be good, intuitive, concrete ways of measuring some of the most ephemeral program outcomes. As in other preliminary stages of the planning, the extent to which consensus is achieved on specifying these indicators will affect the confidence stakeholders will have in the outcome of the evaluation.

4. *What kind of data can we gather about each of our indicators?* Data collection can be an daunting task. To make it both meaningful and efficient, evaluators should plan to collect only data that clearly linked to program goals and indicators. To maximize efficiency, the evaluation team should begin its data collection by identifying existing data that can be used to answer their evaluation questions. By carefully identifying indicators for each goal, only the most essential and most convincing data will be collected, thereby eliminating much wasteful effort and confusion.

Evaluators must consider the use of many types of data, both quantitative and qualitative. Quantitative data normally consist of tests, surveys, frequency counts...virtually anything to which a numerical value can be assigned. Quantitative data consist of observations, interviews, diary or journal entries, and other forms of "personalized" data. Both are important. Quantitative data allow us to make comparisons across groups, times, and settings. They provide a useful measure of student achievement that is standardized and, thus, shows change over time. Qualitative data are useful to "illuminate" the program and to track the very important human dimension of the school experience. How do students and families deal with certain conditions? How do teachers and students relate to one another? What kind of behavior does the school's climate and culture support? All these are important questions for program evaluators that can be answered most clearly by qualitative data.

The most important criteria for the data to be used in the evaluation are as follows:

- They must be clearly related to the indicators and goals of the program.
- They must be relatively easy to collect and analyze.
- They must be likely to be convincing to the stakeholders.
- They must be collected accurately and reliably.

5. *How are the data to be analyzed?* The purpose of data analysis in a program evaluation is make things clear to people—not to muddle or confuse them. The primary objective is to provide information on which good program decisions can be made—not to demonstrate our statistical prowess. In short, the analysis must communicate to people answers to the questions they want answered. Complicated analysis often breeds distrust, and the concomitant belief that "you can prove anything with statistics." Three standards should guide analysis:

- Analysis should be in a form that is understandable and useful to the audience. (The analysis should be explainable by any member of the evaluation team; if they don't understand it, no one else will, either.)
- The analysis should be driven by the evaluation questions. Only analysis that is required to answer the questions should be conducted. Other complicated analysis often obscures or confuses the main questions and issues.
- The analysis should be used to illuminate issues, concerns, and problems, not conceal them. Care must be taken to be sure that the real status of the program is uncovered. Often, this requires disaggregating scores that might otherwise conceal a problem. In one district, achievement data were very high for students in gifted programs, until the district disaggregated the scores of minority children. At that point, they found that minority children were not being well-served by the program; their scores were substantially and consistently lower than those of their peers with similar ability. An uncomfortable finding? Certainly. An essential finding? Absolutely. Without such information, the district could not begin to make the program changes necessary to support high achievement by minority students.

Data analysis is hardly the most glamorous part of an evaluation, but it is a key element in answering important questions. For those questions to be answered clearly and convincingly, the analysis must be clear and convincing to all the stakeholders—professionals and lay people alike.

6. *How do we build consensus on findings, conclusions and recommendations?* Often the most contentious part of an evaluation is the discussion about "what do all these data mean?" If the goals of the program are clear, the indicators explicitly linked to the goals, and the data clearly related to the indicators, the results of the analysis should be quite clear. Even the best-planned evaluations, though, can lead to differing interpretations and conclusions. To build consensus, it is important to begin by distinguishing among findings, conclusions, and recommendations.

- Findings are actual outcomes of the data analysis. Normally, they are quite clear and explicit: "35 percent of students in the able learner algebra program report very positive or positive attitudes toward their mathematics class, 39 percent report negative or very negative attitudes," "89 percent of able learners in algebra I complete pre-calculus mathematics prior to high school graduation," or "68 percent of girls and 96 percent of boys in the able learner algebra I program complete pre-calculus math prior to graduation." These are simply statements about the data and typically do not convey any judgment.
- Conclusions are inferences about the data. They can be relatively simple ("More boys complete pre-calculus mathematics than girls") or may be combined to produce somewhat more complex conclusions ("Students tend to complete the entire mathematics sequence, despite relatively neutral to negative attitudes expressed in algebra I." Or, "Negative attitudes toward

mathematics lead more girls to abandon the mathematics sequence than boys.") Conclusions are arguable. Because they rely on inferences, and often assume cause-effect relationships, they can easily debated. This is the point at which people are most likely to rely on their own experiences, biases, and feelings about the topic or the program. The wise evaluator attempts to keep the conclusions as concrete and defensible as possible by continuing to link them clearly to the data. ("Both males and females express predominantly neutral to negative attitudes toward algebra I, but more males than females complete the entire math sequence.) In this case, no causal relationship is inferred, although the gender differences are clear.

- Recommendations are suggested actions that are based on conclusions. Again, consensus is more likely when they are clearly linked to the data and the conclusions. If we conclude (quite inappropriately) that "girls' attitudes are like boys' in the eighth grade but they drop out of math in higher numbers before the end of the sequence because there is a genetic propensity for them to do so," we will make a very different (and probably illegal) recommendation than if we conclude, "we are doing something between ninth and twelfth grade to discourage girls from continuing in mathematics." In the first case, we might accept the higher dropout rate for girls; in the other, we would recommend an intervention to keep them in the program and support their achievement.

Legal, Ethical, and Moral Issues

In making recommendations, it is essential that evaluators consider both the conclusions they have drawn and the legal and ethical dimensions of educational programming. It is illegal and unethical to treat girls differently from boys with respect to academic programs; therefore, we must recommend an intervention that preserves those moral principles. Often the distinctions are not so clear cut, however. Once the data have been analyzed and conclusions drawn, it is essential for all members of the evaluation team to think carefully about their own values and beliefs and how they might affect their view of the evaluation results. Decisions must be based on conclusions that are supported by data and on good faith commitments to do what is best for students in a democratic society.

An Example

The following example shows how an evaluation plan might be constructed for an assessment of the mathematics program for able learners.

Evaluation object:

A program to improve able learners' mathematics achievement and attitude toward mathematics and related studies.

Goals of the program (from original documentation):

- To improve student attitudes toward the study of mathematics
- To improve student achievement in mathematics in algebra
- To increase student enrollment in advanced mathematics courses.

Evaluation questions:

1. Are student attitudes toward mathematics better after participation in the program than before participation?

2. Do students in the program score higher on mathematics achievement tests than students not in the program? Does student achievement improve from the beginning to the end of the program?

3. Are students who complete the program more likely to enroll in advanced mathematics courses in high school or college?

Stakeholders:

- Primary: Students, parents, mathematics teachers, able learner program teachers.
- Secondary: Board members, non-program parents and students, district math and able learner coordinators.
- Tertiary: Community members, school partners.

Audience for reports:

Parents and students, math and able learner teachers, district office, board of education.

Evaluation Team: (11)

Two middle school math teachers, one high school math teacher, one able learner teacher from each school, two parents, two students, district able learner coordinator, district mathematics coordinator.

This example shows how measures and analysis procedures can be linked, clearly and succinctly, to the evaluation objectives and questions that are driving the project.

Goals/Indicators/Data Sources

Goals	Indicators	Data Sources	Analysis
Improve attitudes toward mathematics	Change in attitude toward math. Change in subject preference (e.g., math preferred).	Attitude survey, locally produced. Subject preference inventory.	Compare pre-test and post-test scores collected at beginning and end of program. Compare attitudes and subject preference of program and non-program students.
Improve student achievement in algebra I.	Change in mathematics achievement scores for algebra I content.	Standardized algebra achievement test.	Compare pre-test and post-test scores from beginning and end of program. Compare program and non-program student achievement, controlling for prior math performance.
Increase student enrollment in advanced math courses.	Enrollment in advanced high school math courses. Enrollment in advanced math courses in college.	Number of students enrolled. Number of students enrolled.	Compare program and non-program student enrollment. Compare program and non-program students (long term study).

Findings and Conclusions

What does it all mean? After the data are collected and analyzed, how can the team and the task force make sense of them? How can the group members avoid imposing their own biases on the data? How can the group achieve consensus? These questions point to one of the most challenging segments of the evaluation process: making meaning from the information that was gathered.

To identify findings and conclusions that enjoy consensus in the group, effective planners develop a systematic method for "making sense" of the data. Normally, it includes these steps:

Stating findings and observations that come directly from the data.

Such statements are supported directly by the data and make no inferences, offer no explanations, and intimate no judgments. If post-test scores on the attitude scale are higher than pretest scores, the finding is that "attitude scores collected at the end of the program were higher than those collected at the beginning." If more boys than girls enrolled in second and third year math in the high school, the finding is stated exactly that way. The purpose of the statement is to explain what the data say, not to explain why or how they turned out that way. Since there is little inference being made, agreement at this point tends to be quite high. This is a task best performed by the evaluation team.

Drawing conclusions—Stage 1.

Conclusions come from patterns that emerge in the findings. They require a higher level of inference, because they often attempt to establish cause-effect relationships between the program and the data.

An example of findings and conclusions follows.

Findings	Conclusions
• Attitude scores collected before the program were lower than scores collected at its conclusion.	• The program improved student attitudes.
• On a subject preference inventory conducted after the program, math was rated one rank higher than on an inventory conducted before the program.	• The program improved math's ranking with students in comparison with other subjects.
• Scores of students in the program on the algebra achievement test improved significantly between pre and post-test.	• The program improved algebra achievement for enrolled students.
• Scores of enrolled students improved significantly more than scores of non-enrolled students.	• The program was more effective than standard programs in raising student achievement scores.
• More students from the program enrolled in second and third year high school math than students not in the program.	• More boys than girls enrolled in second and third year high school math.
• The program increased the likelihood of enrollment in advanced mathematics courses.	• Girls in the program were no more likely to enroll in advanced high school math than girls not in the program.
• The program did not affect the enrollment patterns of girls as much as boys.	
• The program had no effect on girls.	

Usually, findings are pretty clear and the conclusions pretty obvious. However, there is always the danger of assuming the program had an effect when, in fact, something else was affecting the outcome. In the fourth conclusion, for example, it may be that students were selected for the program on the basis of their interest in mathematics. While interest has little effect on achievement (oddly enough), it does affect the willingness of students to approach or avoid the subject in the future. Therefore, the evaluators would have to be very careful they are comparing apples to apples for these kinds of conclusions to be valid. The last three conclusions are clearly arguable, so it is essential to use a clarifying process to reach agreement.

Drawing Conclusions—Stage 2.

In cases where the conclusions are not indisputable, the evaluation team, and ultimately the task force, need to have an open, candid discussion of plausible reasons for the finding that was produced. While this discussion is constrained by the data, it is something akin to a brainstorming session. The process looks like this:

- Brainstorm all possible explanations for the finding.

- Eliminate those that are simply outrageous or are not supported by the data.

- After the list is shortened, create smaller discussion groups and charge them with the task of drawing conclusions that respect the data and incorporate as many of the group's explanations as is feasible.

- Allow the entire group to review the subgroup's work and edit for agreement.

  Generally, this process takes care of most disagreement. However, if agreement cannot be reached, make sure to adhere to these principles in drawing accurate conclusions:

- Draw modest conclusions rather than dramatic ones. Be sure not to go beyond the data collected. In the last finding on the table above, it is more accurate to say, "The program had a differential effect on the enrollment patterns of boys and girls." Based on the data collected, the team cannot be sure the program had "no effect," but it is pretty clear it had a differential effect.

- State multiple, plausible conclusions with the note that the data were not sufficient to answer the question. Then, either gather more information or try to incorporate both, competing conclusions in subsequent program planning.

Answering Evaluation Questions

Once findings and conclusions have been drawn, it is time to answer the evaluation questions that drove the inquiry in the first place. To do so, a process that calls for discussion and consensus building is essential.

1. Form subgroups of the evaluation team. Assign each team to answer the evaluation questions that were used to organize the study.

2. Require that each team state its answer and *provide a rationale based on the findings and conclusions from the study.* (The following form may be helpful in structuring the task.)

3. After each subgroup has prepared their responses to the questions, they present them to the entire team to develop a joint statement for the report to the task force and, ultimately, the board and other audiences.

Question	Answer	Rationale
Does the program improve student attitudes toward mathematics?	Yes...for both boys and girls.	Both boys' and girls' attitude scores improved from pretest to posttest.
Does the program improve student achievement in algebra I?	Yes...for both boys and girls.	Post test scores were higher than pretest scores for both boys and girls in the program. Achievement gains were greater for students enrolled in the program than for students not enrolled.
Does the program increase student enrollment in advanced high school math classes?	Yes...for boys.	Boys in the program enrolled in advanced mathematics courses with greater frequency than girls in the program and students not in the program.
	No...for girls.	Girls enrolled in the program took advanced math courses with the same frequency as girls not enrolled in the program.

Making Recommendations

Ultimately, all evaluations result in recommendations about the program under study. In making recommendations, leaders must consider the following:

1. *Priority.* How central is the issue to the goals and mission of the school? No one may care that students are less than enthusiastic about mathematics; however, people will care deeply if the program is not affecting the aspirations of girls as well as boys. Recommendations should be directed toward those areas that are most important to a community.

2. *Resources.* How much will it cost? Recommendations that place few demands on money, time, personnel, or facilities are more likely to be implemented than those which are more demanding. If a high-demand recommendation is to be made, it is also important to make its importance clear and suggest how resources might be reallocated or generated to pay for it.

3. *Feasibility.* Feasibility is an eminently practical consideration. It asks, "what is the chance this recommendation will be accepted?"

- First, what will be displaced or modified by this recommendation? If a program to enhance positive attitude formation among able learners threatens to displace an honors music program, it probably won't be implemented. On the other hand, recommending a program to promote girls' interest in mathematics and math-related careers because none exists will probably be met with great support.

- Second, does the recommendation conform to the existing political climate of the school or district? Recommending a self-concept enhancement program in a school where achievement scores are plummeting won't garner much support. An achievement enhancement program that contains a self-concept dimension probably will be accepted.

- Third, people will ask, "What's in this for me?" So, the evaluation team might as well ask that question, too. How will this change affect the teachers, the community, the children, the nature of the job, or the quality of school life? If people see no benefit, they also see no reason to change.

Disseminating Results

Dissemination is a simple matter if the audiences for the evaluation were clearly identified in the planning stages. The ultimate purpose of dissemination is to get the information into the hands of people who need it. The manner in which this is achieved, however, will have a major effect on the confidence that stakeholders have in the evaluation and its recommendations. Dissemination plans must address several issues and questions.

1. *Who needs to know and what do they need to know?* Avoid burying people with a casual interest in the topic with volumes of data and reports. Secondary and tertiary stakeholders (remember them?) need relatively succinct information that is clear, unambiguous, and not obfuscated by large amounts of technical detail.

2. *Disclose everything.* While this sounds like a contradiction to the first recommendation, all relevant information should be available for inspection by anyone who needs to see it. It should be accessible in the school library, the public library, or other public information systems. If the public feels that data are being concealed, they will distrust the *entire* evaluation.

3. *Provide for discussion.* Make sure that all stakeholders have a chance to question and discuss the evaluation and its recommendations. Arrange for discussions in schools, among parent groups and with board members. Offer to present a seminar on the study for other civic groups. Few will accept, but the offer conveys a sense of openness that inspires confidence in the result.

4. *Engage the press.* Get help from the local education reporter in sharing the essence of the evaluation with the public. Invite members of the public to comment on the conclusions or call evaluation team members with questions.

A Final Note

Good evaluations can be time-consuming and complex. However, the information they provide not only improves programs but also convinces the public that the school and its programs have adopted a quality performance stance and are committed to continuous improvement. That is a form of public confidence that cannot be purchased in any other way.

References

Council on Middle Level Education. *Assessing Excellence: A Guide for Studying the Middle Level School*, Reston, Va.: National Association of Secondary School Principals, 1988.

Rossi, P. H., and Freeman, H. E. *Evaluation: A Systematic Approach,* 4th ed. Newbury Park, Calif.: Sage, 1989.

CHAPTER 8

Building Strong Parent Support

Susan E. Galletti, Director of Middle Level Services,
National Association of Secondary School Principals

Ten years ago, during my first principalship, I was involved in detracking a 6–8 middle school in an affluent community in the state of Washington. It was often said, facetiously, that parents in this community tracked their children from the womb to attend Harvard; many of these successful parents were products of a tracked system themselves. Parents and educators in this community saw their students achieve the highest results on state standardized test scores each year, and students had many diverse talents in such areas as academics, music, athletics, leadership, and citizenship.

During my first two years in the principalship in this school, I was immersed in the addition of the sixth grade to a 7–8 program, along with implementing several effective middle school practices such as interdisciplinary teaming. During this time, I also became aware that there were many very bright students who did not feel good about themselves because they were not accepted into the one "gifted" class offered at each grade level. These same students were often not accepted into the algebra track and the foreign language program. Entry into these three classes essentially "tracked" students and, in the perception of the students and their parents, gave them an advantage for entry into accelerated high school courses.

I became increasingly disturbed by what I felt was an immoral situation—limiting access of students to opportunities, high quality content, and engaging instruction, for reasons I could not justify. This realization led to my efforts to detrack the school.

Staff members favored detracking and were prepared to meet the needs of high achieving students once we implemented modified grouping patterns. However, I quickly discovered that this idea did not find favor with parents of "gifted" students. As I began to share information with these parents about the reasons to detrack, they, in turn, found and distributed articles about all the reasons to provide "gifted" programs. These parents began to exert pressure on the board of directors (school board), other parents, and teachers to continue the "gifted" program as it then existed. In their eyes, I was an enemy of bright children.

I learned some important lessons that helped me gain the parent support necessary to detrack *and* provide more opportunities for high quality content and engaging instructional experiences for all students. A key was inviting about 30 parents of "gifted" students to meet in the library to help me select the students for the "gifted" program. Parents were given the sixth grade test data used to select students (without student names attached) and asked to identify the 26 students for the gifted program using the district criteria of an I.Q. score of 130 on the California Test of Basic Skills (CTBS) plus achievement scores on sub-tests to arrive at a total score.

The parents discovered that although 55 of the students had an I.Q. of 130 or above, only 25 of these students would qualify. One student had an I.Q. of 150 and would not qualify because of his achievement scores. One student who *would* qualify with achievement scores could not because of her I.Q. score of 129. When I told parents I knew the names attached to the scores, and that some of their own children would not qualify for the "gifted" class because of the exercise they were completing, the entire tenor of the room changed. When they asked if we could expand the gifted program, I explained that even with an expanded program, some of their children still would not qualify.

We then had an hour of serious conversation and parents left the meeting with an understanding that what they needed was a "gifted" program for 100 percent of the students. For this school, that meant a humanities program with integrated instruction, cooperative learning, and a focus on thinking skills. These parents went on to gain the support of other parents, and when the idea of "expanding" the gifted program to include all students was presented to the school board, the proposal was embraced and then implemented.

We still used criteria to identify "gifted" students for the purpose of receiving state funding; however, instead of placing these students in the same class, we distributed them throughout all classes. All humanities teachers began to implement instructional strategies and teach content previously reserved for the "gifted" students. At the end of the year, students evaluated the program as a great success.

As a result of this process to expand opportunities to more high achieving students and the study that followed, I learned a number of lessons about parental involvement in issues related to high achieving students:

1. Parents of high achieving students make a point of being involved in their child's education and are, therefore, generally more influential about school practices.

2. Detracking a school involves as much or more political skill than technical and educational skills.

3. To successfully detrack a school, the fears of parents of high achieving students (fears such as their children will be "slowed down" and curriculum will be "watered down") must be addressed.

4. The goal of any detracking efforts should be to expand the gifted program, NOT eliminate it. The goal of detracking is to provide more students the opportunity to access high quality content and instructional strategies.

5. Parent support is necessary not only for the advocacy and nourishment of each student's potential, but also for the expansion of school opportunities to provide *all* students with enriching educational experiences.

The Need for Strong Parent Support

Adults need to nurture students' talents, to open doors of opportunity, and to encourage them to use their talents constructively. When parents value education, students' motivation to achieve increases. Parents can also encourage high achievement by nurturing the physical and emotional health of their children, answering questions, modeling task commitment, and directing children to resources that provide stimulation and enlightenment. If parents are aware of opportunities that will help "maintain, sharpen, or advance" the children's abilities, and if they encourage their children to participate, in addition to providing a supportive environment, they can stimulate student achievement. If children perceive that their parents value their talents, the resulting positive attitude can, in itself, stimulate those children to move forward (Schwartz, 1994).

Parent support to encourage the high achievement of all children is vital. Parents can be powerful allies or powerful opponents in the process of "detracking." Parents of children who have been placed in "special" programs are especially sensitive to changes in grouping and may fear that changes will undermine their children's chances to excel (Wheelock, 1992).

Clark and Clark (1989) point out the need for administrators to "check out" the expectations of parents: "Knowledge of parent and community expectations of the school is vital in restructuring the middle level school. Too often, administrators assume they know what parents and community members want from their school. With all the emphasis on 'back-to-basic' and standardized testing, it is easy to believe that all the American public wants is a narrow content-based curriculum. This assumption is erroneous." Clark and Clark go on to suggest that administrators must ascertain the expectations of parents and community members as a part of any restructuring effort because "the success of any middle level school is determined by the extent to which it is supported and valued by the community and by the parents of the students who attend" (pp. 4–5).

Wheelock (1992) suggests that constituencies must be developed and need to involve parents from all socioeconomic groups and represent all current track placements in order for schools to successfully "detrack." She points out that:

If, in principle, all parents need to be informed about school grouping practice, too often only a few of them are familiar with unspoken norms that are unremarkable but may have enormous impact on the future of their children. For example, many parents believe that math 8 is the only eighth-grade math course, whereas in reality, it may be the lowest track in a particular school's math sequence. Other parents may not realize that enrollment in certain 'gate keeping' courses, such as pre-algebra and algebra in the middle grades, predetermines later access to enrollment in higher-level courses at the high-school level (p. 79).

There is increasing evidence that schools will not be able to detrack until the attitudes of those involved in making decisions about school practices are changed. The importance is described:

Alternative practices must make sense to educators and their communities before they can be fully implemented and sustained in schools. This making sense occurs when the values and beliefs at the core of tracking are challenged and replaced with new norms—norms that support heterogeneous grouping and classroom practices that such grouping requires (Oakes 1985; Wheelock, 1992).

Parent Attitudes About Tracking

What attitudes do parents have about tracking and do those attitudes differ depending on their child's track? In conclusions about parental expectations, Clark and Clark (1989) quote Goodlad: "I do not know of serious studies that come up with a narrow list of parental expectations of schools. When it comes to education, it appears that more parents want their children to have it all" (p. 5).

It also appears that parent attitudes about tracking practices have remained about the same for the past 60 years. In 1935, Walter Sauvain, in a study entitled *What Parents Think of Ability Grouping* discovered the following:

- The parents most heartily in favor of grouping, raising least objections to it, were those who knew their children were in bright classes.

- The parents who were most opposed to grouping were those who knew their children were in slow classes.

- Most parents seemed to feel that their children did better when grouped homogeneously (this was especially true of parents who had children in bright classes).

- Parents exert much pressure to get their children into higher ability groups.

- Little opposition is likely from parents where homogeneous or ability grouping is used, particularly from parents of children in the bright sections.

In 1954, the *Ladies Home Journal* sponsored a symposium focusing on the question of ability grouping. The participants agreed that ability grouping was necessary if academic standards were to be maintained while providing for the entire range of abilities present in any large school. The *Journal* also reported that during the same year, a Gallup poll showed that approximately three-fourths of those surveyed favored some form of ability grouping, and 8 percent favored a program difficult enough so some students failed and were retained in the same grade. There was also strong support—approximately 66 percent—for excluding from school students who did not work or who were behavior problems (October 1954, pp. 56-57, 184).

Sixty years after Sauvain's study and 40 years after the *Ladies Home Journal* symposium, parent attitudes have remained relatively the same, according to a report published by Public Agenda entitled *First Things First: What Americans Expect from the Public Schools* (Johnson and Immerwahr, 1994). This study found that only 34 percent of Americans think that mixing students of different achievement levels together in classes—heterogeneous grouping—will help increase student learning. They also found that people remain skeptical about this strategy of mixing students even when presented with arguments in favor of it. Eighty-seven percent of those opposing heterogeneous grouping remain doubtful even when told that one of the benefits of heterogeneous grouping is that more accomplished students serve as good role models for underachievers.

Focus groups on heterogeneous grouping conducted for yet another Public Agenda research project, *The Broken Contract* (Immerwahr 1994), suggest that other evidence in favor of detracking is equally unconvincing. Some proponents of heterogeneous grouping have suggested that parental opposition to detracking is camouflage for racial prejudice—the fear of white parents that their children will be put in classes with "underachieving" African-American students. This study found that opposition to heterogeneous grouping is as strong among African-American parents as among white parents, and support for it is equally weak.

The Broken Contract (Immerwahr, 1994), a survey of schools in Connecticut, revealed a wide difference in attitudes about tracking practices between educators and the public, with 27 percent of the public, 35 percent of educational leaders, and 59 percent of educators agreeing that fast learners and slow learners should be mixed in the same class so slower kids learn from faster kids and academic achievement improves.

A recurrent theme among proponents of heterogeneous grouping is that "tracking" of students stigmatizes low achievers, whom they fear are routinely under-served in public schools. Significantly, the public's concern may be somewhat different from that of the experts. *The Broken Contract* asked which students receive the most attention in school—fast learners, slow learners, or average learners. The overwhelming majority (72 percent) are convinced that average learners get less attention than either fast learners or slow learners. The public's concern, in other words, seems to be that average students don't get the attention they need because the teacher is distracted trying to deal with the youngsters at the extremes. Many Americans believe separating students by ability may be the way for average learners to get just as much attention as fast and slow learners.

So, tracking continues in public schools despite research that indicates it is not a beneficial practice. The public's attitude about tracking is often based on their own experiences in schools and their recognition of differences in the needs of their own children. "In short, heterogeneous grouping makes no intuitive sense to people and seems to fly in the face of their real-world experiences" (Immerwahr, 1994, pp. 18–19).

Parents and teachers defend tracking for the following reasons: education has become more complex, content more broad, and students more heterogeneous; guidelines for federal funds require grouping of students; tradition supports tracking; homogeneous groups are easier to teach; there is a better match between the learner and the environment; there is a better attempt at providing for individual differences; and socioeconomic status, learning disabilities, and experiences account for differences in students, not schools (Nevi, 1987).

Three predominant reasons emerge from the literature about why tracking practices persist:

1. Tracking is systemic, stemming from the "factory model"

2. Tracking is value based, where classification and sorting based on observable and measurable data, and efficiency make sense

3. Politically active parents apply pressure to ensure programs in which their children will receive educational advantages (Bellanca and Swartz, 1993).

Simply, tracking seems to be an easier way for teachers to plan and deliver instruction, tracking makes good common sense, and parents of a small group of students who benefit are skillful in influencing decisions about programs that benefit their children (George, 1988).

In my own study (Galletti, 1996), I analyzed comments and other statistical data from 691 questionnaires returned by parents of seventh and eighth grade students in three tracks in two large school districts (one urban and one suburban). I found attitudes about tracking to be similar to those found in the studies published by Public Agenda:

- More than half the returns were from parents of students in the fast track (55.6 percent).

- Of the parents who responded, 58.5 percent checked that they *do* support tracking, 14.4 percent indicated they *do not* support tracking, and 27.1 percent checked that they *do not know* whether they support tracking or not.

- A majority of parents who support tracking indicated that they do so because it allows gifted students to be challenged (24.9 percent). The second most popular response supporting tracking was that it best meets the individual needs of students (17.9 percent).

- Respondents also support tracking based on the experience(s) of their own child (12.1 percent) and because tracking allows extra help for the "slow" student (10.4 percent).

- Less frequent comments included feelings that tracking is best for the teacher, sorts out discipline problems, raises students' self-esteem, raises standards for all, reduces class size, challenges all and raises expectations for all, and fits with their own experiences of schooling.

- A small percentage of parents (3.6 percent) indicate they support tracking for some but not all grade levels; 1.7 percent volunteered they do not like peer tutoring and cooperative learning experiences.

- Among parents indicating they *do not* support tracking, 24.8 percent believe it damages self-esteem (the most common response). The next highest responses from parents indicated they believe tracking creates low expectations and perceptions for students (16.8 percent), discriminates and segregates (14.9 percent), favors fast track students (12.9 percent), and labels and promotes elitism (9.9 percent). Some of these parents (12.9 percent) volunteered that they believe all students should be given the same opportunities.

- Among the parents who are unsure about their position on tracking, a fairly similar percentage of comments indicate that these parents believe tracking is good for the fast track students (22.5 percent) and bad for the average and slow track students (17.9 percent). Only 4.3 percent of these parents indicated they believe tracking to be good for slow track students. A significant percentage of parents (14.6 percent) indicated they don't know enough about the topic and a slightly smaller percentage (11.8 percent) indicate they favor mixed groups of students.

I found no significant difference in parent attitudes about tracking with respect to community type (urban or suburban), race/ethnicity, or socioeconomic status.

Parent Influence About Tracking

Parent influence on tracking decisions could include a range of activities to promote, contribute to, or reduce tracking practices or policies that relate to their child's placement in classes, course offerings in their child's school, or policies or procedures in their school district. For example, a parent-initiated meeting with a principal or counselor that either results in placing a child in a desired track or in the principal's decisions to continue or change school practices, such as continuing a "gifted" program or opening algebra classes to all students.

According to Bellanca and Swartz (1993), the influence of parents is described as follows:

When it comes to the tracking issue, politically active parents have the edge. They can ensure that the school starts a gifted program and that their child gets placement in the right sections taught by the best teachers with the best resources. Because these parents have worked inside the school political power base, they are well positioned to ensure that threats to their child's program are fended aside. In the meantime, the less active parents have no say when their low-performing child is assigned the newest teacher's class, is relegated to the back row, sent to the principal for discipline purposes, or is taught the same watered-down curriculum year after year (pp. ix–x).

George (1988) suggested that: "Parents of the top 10 percent of students in American public schools tend to be sophisticated in their understanding of the politics of school district decision-making, and skillful in their ability to influence those decisions."

An example of parent influence is cited in the October 4, 1989 *Journal American*. (Johnson, K.). Twenty-five parents of gifted students convinced the Bellevue (Wash.) school board to direct administrators of Tyee Middle School to modify changes that the school had made in their gifted program. The middle school site council, composed of parents, staff, and administrators, had decided to distribute gifted students throughout the school's classes. The parents of the gifted students convinced the board to keep gifted students homogeneously grouped for part of the day.

Parents can also positively influence detracking efforts. For example, in *Crossing the Tracks*, Wheelock (1992) describes the work of the Albany (N.Y.) Citizens for Education, who joined with the Urban League of the Albany Area, the Albany NAACP, and the City School District of Albany to reduce the number of tracks, adopt a transitional math curriculum, and introduce a model that encompasses curriculum enrichment in heterogeneous classes.

Recently, it was pointed out that: "In some school districts, parents of high achievers have used their political power to stop detracking efforts and, indeed, many schools continue to provide special activities for high achievers either within the classroom or after school" (Barendse, May/June 1992).

Not surprisingly, during my research I found a significant relationship between parent attempt/success at influencing track placement and practices, attitudes, and track placement of a student in this study. Of the 27.5 percent of parents who had some influence on tracking placement and practices, a significantly large number ($p < .005$) are parents of students in the fast track. Parents of students in the fast track also had the most influence. Parents of students in the average track who had not attempted nor had success at influencing tracking practices were the most against tracking, and parents of students in the average track who did make attempts to influence tracking practices were least in favor of detracking efforts.

Communicating with Parents

Schools should let all parents know about educational options available to their children and suggest possibilities, depending on the talents and interests of the student. Parents should be advised to encourage all their children to excel in areas that are most congruent with their natural abilities and interests while avoiding the expectation for perfect performance at all times.

It is also helpful to offer workshops for parents on techniques to help them deal with high achieving students in the larger contexts of school, friends, and family. When parents realize that the school is supporting and encouraging their efforts to nurture *their* child's talents, they will be more interested in being involved in efforts to develop programs to nurture the talents of *all* children. When communicating with parents to gain parent support for detracking, some guidelines should be considered:

1. Communicate with all parents, not just the parents of "gifted" students, or the parents who are perceived to be supportive, or the parents who are on advisory committees. All parents need to receive information about tracking practices and the consequent implications for their children and others' children.

2. Communicate factual, honest information to parents in a comprehensive way. Include information about the number of sections/levels of different classes, such as math, and the differences in curriculum and instructional methods in the various levels. Let parents know how many students receive differentiated experiences and why. Share with parents any assessment results your school has that indicate positive (or negative) assessments of detracking efforts—particularly academic and social results and surveys of students and staff.

3. Include teachers in the presentation of information to parents, especially to describe staff development in instructional strategies to help teachers challenge all students in heterogeneous classes (i.e., cooperative learning, interdisciplinary curriculum, use of technology, higher level thinking skills, etc.); describe challenging assignments for students of diverse abilities; explain how assistance will be provided to students without "holding back" other students; and describe flexible and alternative grouping practices that can occur within the heterogeneous classroom.

4. Provide parents the opportunity and time to express their concerns and ask questions in a manner that will lead to productive results. Anticipate who will want to "attack" and how you can plan meetings so parents feel they have been heard, their concerns have been acknowledged and are respected, and that they are invited to be involved to develop the best program for all students.

5. Focus on anticipated outcomes for all students as a result of detracking. Include advantages to all students such as exposure to a rich and challenging curriculum, the opportunity to interact with diverse backgrounds and points of view, the opportunity to take risks, greater confidence and more positive self-esteem, and the reduction (if not elimination) of labeling.

6. Communicate in many different ways: letters, newsletters, open houses, one-on-one conferences, PTSA meetings, through teachers, through students, through fellow principals and central office administrators. Always be clear and consistent about your message, no matter who your audience is.

Promoting Parent Knowledge and Understanding of Detracking

All parents are entitled to know the facts about tracking practices in their schools. Yet, in many school communities, parents find out about tracking practices—both accurate and inaccurate information—via conversations with other parents and/or in informal ways, often because principals, counselors, and teachers don't want to share that information so they can avoid parents knocking on their doors to challenge their child's placement. In fact, such information needs to be shared honestly and thoroughly so there can be a common base of understanding about detracking.

In *Making the Best of Schools: A Handbook for Parents, Teachers and Policy Makers,* Jeannie Oakes and Martin Lipton (1990) suggest information that ought to be shared with all parents. It includes:

- The scope of the tracking policy, whether determined by the district or defined within the school
- How decisions are made about track placement
- How teachers are assigned to classrooms
- The number of classes in which subjects and grades are tracked
- All curriculum choices available in each subject
- The kinds of material in each curriculum
- The number of children moving from low tracks into higher tracks each year
- The percentage of students enrolled in each track by race and grade compared with those percentages overall
- Expectations for the future of students in each curriculum and track.

Sharing this information is an important step toward initiating conversations about the issue of educational inequity resulting from tracking.

Information can and should be shared any number of ways, including printed material, open houses, newsletters, special workshops, and conferences. Once the information is shared, it is important to invite parents to ask questions, and to provide honest, frank, accurate answers about the current practices and the desired practices. I have found inviting parents to visit classrooms that are detracked, where teachers are providing challenging classroom experiences in heterogeneous settings, to be particularly effective. Teachers can explain specific strategies they use in the classroom to meet a wide range of student needs and respond to the concerns of parents that their children will be "slowed down," "lost," or "forgotten."

The Political Dimension

Jeannie Oakes (1985) has suggested that there are deliberate efforts to limit the educational experiences of some students and augment those of others. She states that "reformers must address pressures from the social-political milieu that hold tracking in place," and implies that this pressure comes from parents, among others:

The pressure placed on educators by savvy parents who want their children enrolled in the 'best' classes is no doubt the most obvious such political factor. In most communities, middle-class white parents, in particular, better understand the inequalities in a school's structure and know how to pressure the school into responding positively to their children. Parents of high-track students are clearly advantaged—both in terms of educational opportunities and status—by the current arrangement. And in a competitive system that offers only a small percentage of students slots in the high-track classes, these parents have few options but to push to have their children better educated than other children. Administrators rightfully worry that attempts to do away with tracking will lead to a loss of support from these involved parents and a lower enrollment of children from the most advantaged families. The pressure from more affluent and better educated parents to keep schools tracked and to have their children placed and kept in the highest-level courses certainly reflect a competitive, individualistic attitude toward the purpose of schooling (Oakes, in Wheelock, 1992, pp. xiii–xiv).

Parents' involvement in decision making varies dramatically according to their child's placement. For example, "where a school district fails to provide adequate and appropriate educational opportunities for gifted children, their parents have often become forceful advocates. About half of the states mandate special education services for gifted children to parallel those provided to handicapped children. Parents of gifted students are informed through literature and advice from 'gifted advocates' that it may be necessary to take a district through due process hearings and to court to obtain the most appropriate instruction within the district's existing, regular, and special education curricular offerings" (Karnes and Marquardt, 1988, p. 52).

It has been suggested that without significant shifts in the distribution of economic and political power, school reform toward equity is impossible, since "the elite groups who now control schools would never permit these reforms to occur. As long as education is tied to government support and its political structure favors certain groups over others, education will serve the needs of those with the most political power" (Spring, 1989, p. 185).

Often, parents who serve in influential positions on school improvement teams or site-based decision-making teams have high achieving students. These parents also often feel it is their responsibility to represent the interests of high achieving students. Sometimes, it is necessary to engage these parents in discussions outside the arena of the school improvement team meetings to share your expectations that the parent serve as an advocate for the interests of *all* students in your school.

Tracking *is* a public policy issue that deals primarily with the issue of opportunity and raises fundamental questions that go to the heart of public policy and raises concerns about the purposes of schooling.

Implications for School Leaders

Initiating reforms such as detracking requires that school leaders attend to a range of community needs—students, faculty, parents. Providing such attention provides greater assurance that the reform will proceed successfully.

First, educators must recognize and acknowledge that detracking and expanding enrichment opportunities to all students has a political dimension and requires political skills.

Second, educational leaders must fully understand the context within which arguments are presented by thoroughly understanding the view of both those who support and those who oppose student tracking and sorting.

Because of the political nature of providing a school atmosphere that is rich in opportunities for all students, experienced principals often cite the importance of 'vision and courage,' as well as 'persistence, patience, and willingness to risk,' and note the need for 'strong-willed, persuasive principals with a sound sense of timing.' As schools adopt innovations to provide more opportunity for all high achieving students to access rich education settings, principals may be called on to develop and communicate strategies for school-based decision making and planning, to incorporate the concerns of dissenters into plans for change, and to diffuse tension with humor and sound judgment. (Wheelock, 1992, p. 26)

Being open to negotiation, being willing to proceed slowly, providing accurate and complete information, honestly acknowledging pitfalls, ensuring high quality classroom experiences through staff development, and involving all parents in discussions goes a long way to developing the trust necessary to move beyond the political dimensions of sorting. Even the most carefully thought-out action plans, however, still may not reduce all resistance. Personal conviction and courage are required. School leaders who find themselves in this position should seek a network of supporters and principals who have successfully detracked and seen the benefits for high achieving students throughout the school.

Gaining Parent Support

Many of the arguments supporting detracking suggest benefits to all children, with the least benefits (but no adverse results) to "gifted" students. But, parents want to know how detracking will affect *their* child. Moreover, as was discussed earlier, many parents have attitudes about tracking based in large part on their own experiences, or what they perceive to be "common sense" ideas. Parents of students with disabilities want to be sure their children won't be "lost" or intimidated; parents of academically high achieving students want to be sure that their children aren't "held back" and subjected to curriculum that is "watered down," geared toward "the middle," and lacking in stimulation and challenge. Parents of "average" students want to know that their children will not "fall through the cracks" and lack teachers' attention because of the needs of the students at the two extremes.

One method of gaining parent support is to openly address these concerns and provide specific, concrete examples of how the school will be active in eliminating these concerns. For example, explain how students will get extra assistance in understanding directions for homework, if needed, while still providing homework that is exciting and challenging.

One of the best ways to eliminate these concerns is to invite parents to visit and observe in the classroom of a teacher who is successfully meeting the needs of all students. Another technique to allay concerns of parents is to have a diverse group of students meet with parents to share their perceptions of benefits and drawbacks of a heterogeneous classroom. Prepare (do *not* prompt) students for such a meeting, just as you would adults, by letting them know what you hope to accomplish, what to anticipate, and what your expectations are for their delivery of their responses. Do not tell them what you expect the content of their responses to be. Teachers can help select students who will provide a range of responses and represent the diversity of the classroom.

Guidelines for Involving Parents

Discussions such as these lead to certain guidelines for involving parents in promoting the achievement of their own child and all children:

- Inform parents of educational practices in the school that challenge and enrich their child and all children.

- Invite parents to see classrooms that are detracked and engaging students in high quality content in a heterogeneous setting.

- Invite parents to share their knowledge of their child's strengths, talents, and attributes with teachers who then incorporate this knowledge into their lessons and interactions with the students.

- Involve parents in the change process, including everyone who is going to be affected. It is especially effective to meet with key parents (identify a diverse group of formal and informal leaders who represent different viewpoints) in small groups prior to hosting a large meeting.

- Work with teachers prior to involving parents to ensure that you and they can clearly explain the benefits of new grouping practices for all children; be sure that teachers have the skills to deliver these benefits.

- Be prepared to "phase in" alternatives to tracking if there is a great deal of resistance; for example, instituting "pilot" programs in a skilled (and if possible, helpful, popular) teacher(s) classroom(s) or in a grade level where there is a high predictability of success.

- Focus all discussions and activities on maintaining a high level of instruction and strengthening curriculum and instruction for all students. Assure parents that students will not be experiencing a "watered-down" curriculum in a mixed-ability class where the teacher "teaches to the middle," but rather that students will be experiencing a richer, more engaging curriculum and instruction where teachers teach "to the top," have high expectations for all students, and provide strategies that allow all students to be successful without slowing down the highest achieving students.

- Keep parents informed through progress reports; sharing results of evaluations; assessments by students and teachers; academic successes and changes in discipline, attendance, and attitudes. Be sure to include the problems as well as the successes and how you are addressing the problems.

- Invite parents to raise questions and make suggestions. Let parents know how you incorporate their suggestions. Prepare to answer tough questions and understand the different viewpoints of parents.

Wheelock (1992) answers tough questions like: "Won't mixing groups of students hold back the learning of the smarter students?" "Won't 'slower' students feel overwhelmed by their 'smarter' counterparts in heterogeneous classes?" and "I've read all the research documenting the harms of tracking, but I'm still not sure whether it's tracking itself that harms students or the inferior teaching and curriculum offered in the low track. Couldn't we just work harder to make the lower tracks better?"

Conclusion

New research on ways students learn suggests that all students have the capacity to be high achieving students. The involvement and support of parents in nurturing the talents and potential of their own child(ren) is beneficial and contributes to the achievement of individual students. As Schwartz (1994) suggests: "One cannot say that these factors (of parental support) are essential, however, for gifted children have succeeded without such parental behaviors, though they might have reached even greater goals had they had the appropriate support" (p. 54).

Likewise, evidence of successful efforts by schools to detrack and create greater opportunities for all students to become high achievers through high quality content and engaging instructional practices suggests the need for parent support of such programs. Principals and schools have succeeded in detracking without such parental support, but, like the degree of achievement individual students acquire, schools have found they could reach even higher achievement for even more students if parent support is cultivated.

References

Barendse, D. M. "Evidence Against Tracking Grows." *Educational Research Newsletter* 5(1992):1-8.

Bellanca, J., and Swartz, E. E., eds. *The Challenge of Detracking*. Palatine, Illinois: IRI/Skylight Publishing, Inc., 1993.

Clark, D. C., and Clark, S. "School Restructuring: A Leadership Challenge for Middle Level Administrators." *Schools in the Middle,* 1989.

Galletti, S. E. "The Relationship Between Track Placement of Middle Level Students and Their Parents' Attitudes Regarding Tracking and the Functions of Public Schooling." Doctoral dissertation, University of Washington, 1996.

George, P. "Tracking and Ability Grouping." *Middle School Journal* 1(1988): 21-28.

Immerwahr, John, (with Jill Bose and Will Friedman). *The Broken Contract: Conneticut Citizens Look at Public Education*. New York: Public Agenda, 1994.

Johnson, J., and Immerwahr, J. *First Things First: What Americans Expect from the Public Schools*. New York: Public Agenda, 1994.

Johnson, Kathy Bunnell. "Parents Fault Class for Gifted." *Journal American*, October 1989.

Karnes, F. A., and Marquardt, R. G. "The Pennsylvania Supreme Court Decision on Gifted Education." *Gifted Child Quarterly* 32(1988): 360-61.

Ladies Home Journal. October 1954, pp. 56-57, 184.

Nevi, C. "In Defense of Tracking." *Educational Leadership* 1987: 25-26.

Oakes, J. *Keeping Track*. New Haven, Conn.: Yale University Press, 1985.

Oakes, J., and Lipton, M. *Making the Best of Schools: A Handbook for Parents, Teachers, and Policymakers*. New Haven, Conn.: Yale University Press, 1990.

Sauvain, W. H. "What Parents Think of Ability Grouping." *Nation's Schools,* 1935: p.36.

Schwartz, L. L. *Why Give "Gifts" to the Gifted?* Newbury Park, Calif.: Corwin Press, 1994.

Spring, J. *The Sorting Machine Revisited*. New York: Longman, 1989.

Wheelock, A. *Crossing the Tracks*. New York: The New Press, 1992.

CHAPTER 9

Minority Students and Gifted Programs

Gwendolyn Cooke, Director of Urban Services
National Association of Secondary School Principals

Minority advocacy groups like the Children's Defense Fund, National Council of LaRaza, National Association for Asian and Pacific American Education, and the National Black Child Development Institute articulate a vision that "every child has the right to achieve academically, regardless of income or family background, and the right to a quality education in a public school setting" (Tollett, 1995). This vision is consistent with most state charters and locally developed school districts' mission statements. In short, this vision mandates that all children have the advantages of the highest quality education the system can provide.

Despite such support, this vision of educational equity is seldom realized because of complex issues, including but not limited to institutional racism (as evidenced by school tracking), teachers' beliefs in deficit theories, socioeconomic stratification, income-based housing patterns, mother's education, limited English proficiency, school districts' strategies to increase efficiency and reduce costs, and higher levels of poverty among minority students (Pallas, 1989; Schwartz, 1994; Oakes, 1995).

Getting a high quality education has always been seen as one of the best ways to improve one's social and economic prospects, especially for those socially or economically disadvantaged. However, when examining programs for the gifted, minority students—African Americans, Hispanic Americans, and Asian Americans—are at a disadvantage relative to White children. Minority children are less likely to have gifted programs in their schools and, even when the programs are present, are less likely to be selected for inclusion.

Definition of Terms

In this discussion, "minority students" refers to African-American, Hispanic, and Asian-American students. For this discussion the following ethnic identifiers are used:

a. African-American refers to individuals of African heritage, most of whom were born in the United States, making up the largest ethnic group in America.

b. Hispanic is a generic term that includes such diverse communities as persons of Mexican descent, Puerto Ricans (both in Puerto Rico and on the mainland), Cuban Americans, and persons from Central and South America, the Caribbean, and other locations. Other labels include Latino, Latin American, Spanish Origin, Spanish Surname, or Spanish Speaking.

c. Asian-American refers to those persons whose origins are Asia (Japan, China, The Philippines, Vietnam, Korea, Guam, Laos, Kampuchea, Taiwan, Burma, Thailand, Malaysia, Indonesia, and others) or the Indian subcontinent including India, Pakistan, Bangladesh, Sri Lanka, Bhutan, or Nepal. These groups differ in sociocultural traits, but subgroups within each group often differ as well (Huang, 1993).

Myths About Minorities

The images are familiar. Asian Americans are our nation's "model minority." Asians are hard working, cooperative, subservient, respectful citizens who are economically successful. This seductive and attractive proposition reinforces the American dream that if one works hard, one will be successful. But, it also has damaging consequences, because it causes people to ignore the real problems facing the nation's fastest growing minority group. The stereotype suggests that all Asians are the same because they all experience success, thus denying the poverty and illiteracy in Asian American communities (U.S. Commission on Civil Rights, 1992).

In addition to ignoring the wide range of Asian-American experiences, the stereotype overlooks the fact that Asian Americans experience racism (Lee, 1996). Moreover, according to Lee, within the model minority discourse, Asian Americans represent the "good" race and African Americans represent the "bad" race. Asian Americans represent the hope and possibility of the American dream (p. 5).

In the context of schooling, this myth translates into Asian-American students being labeled as over-achievers, "whiz kids," who are over-represented in programs for the gifted (Barstow, 1987), or as docile children (Huang, 1993) who are hurt by the stereotype and do not qualify for programs that address equity issues or specific cultural needs. Asian high school students, however, question the widely held myths. Consider the following observations of achieving Asian students in an interview titled, "In Our Own Words."

Khanh: One of the frustrating things about being Asian is that there's a myth that you're intelligent, and if you're not, if you're just average, you can be condemned. People always look at you like you're some kind of rocket scientist, and I knew that I wasn't. I was capable of doing work, but I was no Einstein (p. 56).

Genevieve: One teacher I had distrusted Asians — she said that Asians would all study together and cheat. My sister—who was in the same class with this teacher—and I talked about it, and we really emphasized our Americanness or our "Whiteness" so that this teacher wouldn't associate us with the stereotype that she had (p. 55).

The stereotype held about some Hispanics, especially Mexican Americans, Puerto Ricans, and people from South America, is that they are members of limited English speaking families of seasonal workers with poverty-related problems: adults with few long-range goals and little interest in their children's schooling, alcoholism, domestic violence, despair, and pressures on children to drop out of school to contribute to household income. This stereotype results in low expectations by too many teachers for Hispanic students. Such attitudes demand attention, because Hispanics are expected to become the largest minority in the United States by 2010 (Claiborne, 1994).

African Americans are frequently connected with social problems that many Americans regard as the result of moral depravity: illiteracy, drug use, teen pregnancy, and unemployment. Moreover, African-American youth who do not achieve often face being labeled as "acting White," a popular topic for the mass media. Worse, achieving African-American youth are frequently showcased to the extent that it becomes clear the public views them as oddities. In view of these stereotypes, too frequently, achieving black youth ask themselves why they *should* achieve (Gilliam, 1996).

Sadly, these myths frequently translate into negative teacher attitudes about the achievement potential of minority students (Ford, 1996). Clearly, these attitudes, and the stereotypes that spawn them, must be addressed and overcome.

Identification as Gifted and Talented

Demographers project that for the next 20 years the minority population will continue to increase, rising to 4 of every 10 school age children early into the next century (Claiborne, 1994). In 25 of the nation's largest cities, people of culturally diverse and non-English-speaking backgrounds are in the majority. These demographics call for changes in curricula, learning resources and materials, instructional techniques, communication strategies, methods for parental involvement, and identification of gifted students.

With the many challenges facing school districts, it would be easy to give the identification of gifted students a low priority. To do so, however, would demonstrate a lack of vision and leadership. An aggressive initiative in this area can propel a school district to focus on an education of high expectations, high content, and high support, resulting in excellence and equality of opportunity for all students.

Examining definitions of giftedness is the first step. While there is no consensus about the definition, the federal government has adopted five definitions since 1970. The three most recent definitions appear in Table 1.

TABLE 1

Federal Definitions of Gifted and Talented Students

1978 The term "gifted and talented children" means children and, whenever applicable, youth identified by professionally qualified persons and who, by virtue of outstanding abilities, are capable of high performance. These abilities, either potential or demonstrated, include (1) general intellectual ability, (2) general and specific academic ability, (3) creative or productive thinking, (4) leadership ability, and (5) ability in the performing arts (USDE, 1978).

1988 The term "gifted and talented" students means children and youth who give evidence of high performance capability in areas such as intellectual, creative, artistic, or leadership capacity, or in specific academic fields, and who require services or activities not provided by the school in order to fully develop such capabilities (USDE, 1988).

1993 Children and youth with outstanding talent perform or show the potential for performing at remarkably high levels of accomplishment when compared with others of their age, experience, or environment. These children and youth exhibit high performance capacity in intellectual, creative, and/or artistic areas, and unusual leadership capacity, or excel in specific academic fields. They require services or activities not ordinarily provided by the schools. Outstanding talents are present in children and youth from all cultural groups, across all economic strata, and in all areas of human endeavor (USDE, 1993).

Source: Ford, Donna Y. *Reversing Underachievement Among Gifted Black Students*, 1996, p. 10.

The most recent federal definition (Ford, 1993) offers much promise for increased equity in identifying minority students. The definition moves beyond an academic definition, and there is specific reference to the fact that no racial, ethnic, or socioeconomic group has a monopoly on giftedness. It challenges educators to identify all gifted students and provide challenging curricula and enrichment experiences.

What existing frames of reference or theories about intelligence are culturally sensitive and might increase the pool of potentially gifted students from which to choose? Three recent theories that offer hope are Howard Gardner's theory of multiple intelligences, Joseph S. Renzulli's three ring conceptualization model, and Robert J. Sternberg's triarchic theory of intelligence.

Gardner (1983) provides a means of mapping the broad range of abilities that humans possess by grouping their capabilities into seven comprehensive categories or "intelligences": linguistic, logical-mathematical, spatial, bodily-kinesthetic, musical, interpersonal, and intrapersonal.

Renzulli (1986) defines giftedness as task commitment coupled with above average intelligence and creativity. Thus, attention should be given to all three when identifying students. Renzulli further recommends that giftedness be assessed in a natural setting, a real-life situation, and broadens the identification percentages from the traditional 3–5 percent of the population to 15–20 percent.

Sternberg's (1990) theory focuses on social intelligence and competence. He identifies three kinds of intelligences—componential, experiential, and contextual—and suggests they must be understood in a sociocultural context; are purposeful, goal-oriented, relevant behavior; and depend on information-processing skills and strategies.

A study by VanTassel-Baska, Patton, and Prillaman (1989) revealed that nearly 90 percent of states rely primarily on standardized, norm-referenced tests to identify gifted students, including those from economically and racially diverse groups. Cultural differences are not considered. Minority and economically disadvantaged students must demonstrate their giftedness the way White middle class students express theirs. Deviations from these norms usually go unidentified, contributing to the under-representation of minority students in gifted programs (Baldwin, 1987; Frasier, 1987; Ford, 1993).

National Report on Identification

In 1982, Susanne Richert, James Alvino, and Rebecca McDonnell completed *The National Report on Identification: Assessment and Recommendations for Comprehensive Identification of Gifted and Talented Youth,* a study commissioned by the U.S. Department of Education (1985). The report endorsed several principles that should underlie identification of gifted students:

1. *Advocacy.* Identification should be designed in the best interests of all students.

2. *Defensibility.* Procedures should be based on the best available research and recommendations.

3. *Equity.* Procedures should guarantee that no one is overlooked (e.g., disadvantaged children).

4. *Pluralism.* The broadest defensible definition of giftedness should be adopted.

5. *Comprehensiveness.* As many gifted learners as possible should be identified.

Schools serious about inclusivity would do well to adopt these principles to guide their policies and regulations for programs for the gifted. Sample identification instruments developed by Ford (1996) encompass a multidimensional and multimodal framework in keeping with the spirit of these principles. (See Table 2.)

Teacher Expectations

Negative attitudes and expectations about the capabilities and talents of minority students persist among educators. Teachers communicate their expectations of students through both overt and covert behavioral cues (Ford, 1996). (See Table 3.)

Teachers tend to evaluate minority students' behavior and academic performance in a biased manner (Harvey and Slatin, 1975; Marwit, Marwit and Walker, 1978; Heller, 1985; Matute-Bianchi, 1986). Minority and working class students are frequently assigned to lower ability groups than their achievement test scores warrant. When work is identical, or of equal quality, teachers judge the oral work of students who speak in Black or working class dialect to be poorer than that of students who

TABLE 2
Sample Identification Instruments: A Multidimensional and Multimodal Framework

QUANTITATIVE
Traditional
Weschler Intelligence Scale for Children—Revised (1)
Stanford-Binet Intelligence Test (1)
Otis-Lennon Mental Ability Test (2)
Iowa Tests of Basic Skills (2)
Comprehensive Test of Basic Skills (2)
Peabody Individual Achievement Test—Revised (2)

Nontraditional
Raven's Coloured, Standard, and Advanced Progressive Matrices (1)
Kaufman Assessment Battery for Children (1, 2)
Matrix Analogies Test—Expanded and Short Form (1)
Torrance Test of Creative Thinking (3)
Torrance Creativity Tests for Children (3)
Tests of Creativity in Movement and Action (3)
Vineland Social Maturity Scale (4)
California Preschool Competence Scale (4)
Basic Motor Ability Test (5)
Developmental Test of Visual and Motor Integration (5)
Purdue Perceptual Motor Survey (5)

QUALITATIVE
Portfolios and performance-based assessments (e.g., writing samples, artwork, audio or visual taping of classroom discussions, journals, projects) (1–5)

Biographical inventories (1–5)

Nomination forms and checklists (completed by parents, teachers, peers, self) (1–7)

Transcripts (e.g., to explore strengths in certain subjects and areas or look for inconsistent performance) (1–5)

Learning styles and inventories (6)

Motivational and attitudinal measures (7)

Promising instruments for developing profiles:
   Baldwin Identification Matrix
   Frasier Talent Assessment Profile
   Potentially Gifted Minority Student Project
   Program of Assessment Diagnosis and Instruction
   System of Multicultural Pluralistic Assessment

Note: 1 = intellectual; 2 = academic; 3 = creative; 4 = leadership; 5 = visual and performing arts; 6 = learning styles; 7 = sociomotional (e.g., motivation, self-concept, self-esteem, attitudes toward school, anxiety, peer relationships).

Source: Ford, Donna Y. *Reversing Underachievement Among Gifted Black Students*, 1996, p. 37.

TABLE 3

Factors Affecting Teacher Expectations of Students

Factor	Teacher Expectations
Gender	Lower expectations for elementary boys and for older girls; expectations are often related to subject areas and vocational choices.
SES	Lower expectations for lower SES students (including parents' level of education, types of jobs, place of residence).
Race	Lower expectations for racially and culturally diverse students.
Test scores; permanent records	Belief in "fixed ability" keeps one from recognizing progress, especially small successes.
Negative comments about student	Lounge talk, other teachers' or principal's evaluation results in lower teacher expectations.
Type of school	Lower expectations for rural and inner-city (urban) students; higher for suburban.
Oral language patterns	Lower expectations for anyone who speaks nonstandard English or English as a second language.
Neatness; appearance	Lower expectations associated with general disorganization- poor handwriting, dress, and so forth.
Halo effect	Tendency to label a child's overall ability based on one characteristic (e.g., teacher lets child's giftedness, rather than effort, motivation, and actual performance, play a major role in evaluations).
Teacher training institutions	Perpetuation of myths and ideologies of limitations of certain groups.

Source: Ford, Donna Y. *Reversing Underachievement Among Gifted Black Students*, 1996, p. 141.

---

speak standard English; and unlike the preferential treatment many teachers give to their brightest White students, they give bright African Americans, especially females, the least attention. If minority students identified for gifted programs are to achieve, professional development for teachers, counselors, and administrators must address these critical issues of equity and access.

Tracking

Tracking, the "practice of dividing students into instructional groups on the criterion of assumed similarities in ability or attainment" is widespread. Criteria generally used for placement in tracked classes include standardized tests, teacher or counselor recommendation (including grades), and parent or student choice. Fairness in placement of minority students in classes remains a concern for educators, parents, and other student advocates.

According to Oakes (1985), tracking systems are cumulative, beginning in elementary school. They are designed to help prepare students to reach their fullest potential relative to their contribution to society. From the first grade, students begin to get tracked into faster or slower classes, as well as being sorted within each class. When students are tracked at such an early age, the chance of changing their track position becomes increasingly difficult with each succeeding year. Once students are tracked into a curriculum, they take classes that ensure they will remain in that track. Consequently, by the time students enter the middle level school, their track has pretty much been determined, and by the time they enter high school, their educational future has long since been chosen for them.

Oakes (1995) further documents school-by-school and districtwide tracking practices in two school systems—Rockford, Ill., and San Jose, Calif.—with school desegregation court cases. She found that neither of the two systems clearly applied criteria to assign students to particular tracks. Both school systems honored parent requests for students' initial track placements and for subsequent changes. Not all parents were informed about tracking practices or about parents' right to influence their children's placements, and African-American and Hispanic parents had less access than others to this knowledge.

In Rockford, White students whose scores fell within a range that would qualify them for participation in either a higher or lower track were far more likely to be placed in high track classes than were African-American students whose scores fell within that same range. High scoring African Americans were found in low track classes—seldom the case for high scoring Whites. Among several striking examples of skewed placements in Rockford's junior highs was a school where the range of reading comprehension scores among eighth graders enrolled in basic (low track) English classes was from the 1st to the 72nd percentile. Of these, 10 students scored above the national average of 50NP. Six of these high scoring students were African-American, including the highest achieving student in the class; a seventh was Hispanic.

Some studies consistently suggest that African-American and Hispanic students in racially mixed schools are discriminated against in the tracking process, even when differences in academic performance (e.g., test scores) are controlled. White and Asian students appear to have a clear advantage in gaining admission to high track classes.

Oakes and Guiton (Oakes, 1995) analyzed interview, observation, and transcript data about student placements in three diverse comprehensive high schools over a two-year period. Differences in tracking at all three schools appeared to flow, in some cases, from educators' perceptions about race and social class difference. Most striking were commonly held beliefs in high ability and motivation of Asian students, and the lack of support and value for education among Hispanic families.

Recent data concerning African-American and Hispanic students' access to advanced courses further illustrates the gravity of tracking. According to the National Center for Education Statistics (USDOE,1995a), African-American high school graduates are still less likely than White graduates to take advanced science and mathematics courses or study a foreign language. In 1992, these students were twice as likely as White graduates to have taken remedial mathematics and were less likely to have taken higher level mathematics. They were also less likely to have taken chemistry, physics, or the combination of biology, chemistry, and physics. Furthermore, Black college-bound graduates were far less likely than White graduates to have taken at least two years of a foreign language in high school (59 and 75 percent, respectively), which could affect their chances of attending a selective college. (See Table 4.)

TABLE 4

Percentage of High School Graduates Taking Selected Courses

Mathematics and science courses	1992		
	White	Black	Hispanic
Any mathematics	99.7	99.1	NR
Remedial mathematics	14.6	30.9	24.2
Algebra I	94.0	NR	92.5
Algebra II	59.2	40.9	46.9
Geometry	72.6	60.4	62.9
Trigonometry	22.5	13.0	15.2
Algebra II, geometry, and trigonometry	15.9	6.8	NR
Calculus	10.7	6.9	4.7
Biology	93.5	92.2	91.2
AP/honors biology	6.5	3.2	NR
Chemistry	58.0	45.9	42.6
AP/honors chemistry	4.2	2.3	NR
Physics	25.9	17.6	15.7
AP/honors physics	2.9	1.4	NR
Biology, chemistry, and physics	22.6	15.5	12.8

SOURCE: NCES, 1987 and 1990 NAEP High School Transcript Studies, High School and Beyond Transcript Study, and National Education Longitudinal Study Transcripts, 1992.

Combined tables, by author, appearing in NCES *Findings from the Condition of Education, 1994, No. 2 and No. 4. The Educational Progress of Black Students and Hispanic Students, 1995.*

In 1992, Hispanic graduates were more likely than White graduates to have taken remedial mathematics, just as likely to have taken algebra I, and less likely to have taken geometry, algebra II, or trigonometry than were White graduates. Although similar percentages of Hispanic and White graduates took biology, Hispanics were less likely to have taken chemistry, physics, or a combination of biology, chemistry, and physics. However, Hispanic college-bound graduates were just as likely as their White peers to have taken at least two years of a foreign language in high school (72 and 75 percent, respectively). (See Table 4.) These patterns evolve from middle level grouping patterns.

An African-American mathematics educator's experiences illustrate the magnitude of the challenge facing gifted minority students seeking access to advanced courses.

I understand the importance of the research on tracking. Staying on the college preparatory track was a difficult act for me to negotiate in my school experience. For example, as a high school senior, my counselor and a school administrator attempted to remove several African-American classmates and me from a physics course. No attempt was made to remove any White students from this special physics course. This particular physics course was being taught by a scholar-in-residence from MIT. The administrators justified their actions on the basis of our average grades in a chemistry course. My counselor argued, "This course is not for you. A section of non calculus-based physics can be arranged for you."

We were able to remain in the course on the basis of three arguments. First, our chemistry teacher never returned a single examination to us. We argued that our grades were determined by how this teacher perceived us as scientists, rather than our achievements. Second, each of us had earned above average grades in prerequisite courses: biology, algebra, geometry, and mathematical analysis. Finally, each of us had near perfect scores on the science portion of the ACT examination. We knew this information about each other because we all attended the same school counseling and advising sessions over the previous three years.

Reluctantly, the school administrator and my counselor allowed us to return and continue the course. However, it took years to overcome the psychological scars associated with this degradation. Part of the healing process has included reexamining my dilemma and the response at the time. Creating a physical space for ourselves in the physics course was only part of our dilemma. A larger battle should have been waged against the philosophical tenets embedded within the school's administrative framework: elitism and dysconscious racism. Allowing my classmates and me to enter the physics class did not change the school administration's philosophy of governance (Tate, 1994).

Promising Initiatives

In recent years, several projects have addressed the issues of minority participation in programs for able learners and have enjoyed promising results. Among these, the Javits program is, perhaps, the most comprehensive and well-known.

The Javits Program

The Jacob K. Javits Gifted and Talented Students Act of 1988 marks the culmination of the efforts by gifted education proponents to ensure equity for minority and economically disadvantaged students. This Act funds local initiatives that focus on the development of talent among students who have been traditionally under-represented in gifted and talented programs.

During a five-year period (1989–94), the Javits Program funded 75 projects at all levels: elementary, elementary through middle school, middle/junior high, middle and high school, and kindergarten through high school. Table 5 summarizes projects that targeted middle level students. (Comprehensive descriptions of the projects are available from the U.S. Department of Education, Javits Gifted and Talented Students Education Program Office.)

Javits Results

Javits projects sought to promote talent development among minority children by:

1. Familiarizing administrators and teachers with historical perspectives of giftedness

TABLE 5

Javits Middle Level Project 1992–93

Project	Grade Levels	Targeted Population	Identification	Teacher Training	Parent Involvement	Key Decisionmakers Training	Curriculum Development	Guidance Course	Summer Program	Gardner's Multiple Intelligences
Language Arts, Dissemination, Training, Research	K–8	verbally gifted		✔			✔			
Science Curriculum for Highly Able Learners	K–8			✔			✔			
Project Mustard Seed	K–8	small and rural districts economically disadvantaged minority students	✔	✔		✔	✔			
Project Spring II	3–8	rural Appalachian, Black, Hispanic, Native American	✔	✔	✔					
Challenging Upper Elementary School Gifted Students by Integrating Course Curriculum w/Law	4–8	selected materials will be translated to Vietnamese and Spanish			✔	✔	✔			
Project High Hopes	5–10	high ability students with disabilities (hearing impaired, learning disabled, emotional or behavioral disorders)	✔	✔			✔		✔	
Urban Scholars	6–9	urban disadvantaged and ethnically diverse students		✔			✔	✔	✔	
Cherokee Nation Summer Program for G/T Students	6–9	economically disadvantaged Native Americans of the Cherokee Nation		✔	✔				✔	
Project Reach	7–12	economically disadvantaged twice exceptional learners (e.g. physical disabilities, learning disabilities, communication disorders, or behavioral disorders)	✔	✔						
DISCOVER III	K–12	Navite Americans, Hispanic, Black	✔	✔			✔			✔
LEGACY	K–12	economically, disadvantaged, limited English, disabled		✔			✔			
Breaking Traditional Barriers	K–12	economically, disadvantaged, limited English proficiency, culturally diverse (56 languages)	✔		✔		✔			

SOURCE: U.S. Department of Education, OERI, Javits Gifted and Talented Students Education Program, Grants Projects Abstracts, 1992, 1993.

TABLE 6

Javits Middle Level Project 1994–96

Project	Grade Levels	Targeted Population	Identification	Teacher Training	Curriculum Development	Parent Involvement	Key Decisionmakers	Guidance Course	Enrichment Institute
Project CUE (Creating Urban Excellence)	Pre K–8	urban, economically disadvantaged, learning disabled	✔	✔		✔			
Ohio Javits Project	K–6	economically disadvantaged, urban, rural, and Applachian parents	✔	✔		✔	✔		
Project CCA: Creating A Community of Achievement	6–8	African American, economically disadvantaged			✔	✔	✔		
Urban Scholars (refunded)	6–9		✔	✔	✔	✔		✔	
Project Critical	K–12	urban economically disadvantaged Black, Hispanics			✔	✔			
Major Achievement Program	K–12	ethnic minorities, economically disadvantaged	✔			✔		✔	

SOURCE: U.S. Department of Education, OERI, Javits Gifted and Talented Students Education Program, Grants Projects Abstracts, 1992, 1993.

2. Providing professional development opportunities for administrators and teachers to sensitize them to evolving conceptions of giftedness

3. Developing curricular units and activities to enhance student learning

4. Organizing and implementing workshops for parents to heighten their awareness of potential talents of their children.

Callahan (n.d.) reviewed data provided in the individual evaluation reports collected through on-site visits to Javits projects. Site visits consisted of observations and interviews with students, parents, staff, and community representatives. Three projects dealt with the middle level grades: Discovery III, Cherokee National Summer Program, and the Urban Scholars Program. This analysis revealed several significant findings:

Student Outcomes—Teacher Ratings and Focus Group Approaches

Students interviewed in focus groups from the Urban Scholars Project reported they improved their performance and sense of self. One intervention strategy that seemed very effective at modifying students' self-perceptions and behavior was working with a mentor. As a result of the mentoring experience students felt that "Somebody thinks I am important. Somebody thinks that I am worth their [sic] time." Students' attendance and behavior in general improved while they participated in the program.

Student Outcomes—Observations

Students and teachers reported increased creative productivity among students participating in classes in math, science, and the social sciences. Students routinely provided unique responses to classroom questions and applied their learning to projects such as production of a robotics model of the human arm, creation of a car alarm that functions like a telephone beeper, and creation of a fantasy drama.

Recommendation for Placement in the Gifted and Talented Programs in the Schools

One of the concerns about using non-traditional procedures for identifying high ability students is that the students would not remain "identified" for participation in the enhanced program once the Javits program ended or they moved beyond their current grade. Results from the Urban Scholars Program refute this concern. Forty-six percent of the students completing the programs were selected for one of three exam schools in the Boston Public Schools. One hundred percent of those completing a follow-up survey were enrolled in algebra I or a higher level math course and all but four were enrolled in either biology or earth science. (Callahan, n.d.).

Unanticipated Outcomes

Goal Setting. One of the students in the Urban Scholars Program commented on a survey form: "Now that I have seen students graduate, I think I can make it too." Another said, "I know I am going to college." A third, "I'm capable of anything."

Participation in Other Activities. Twenty Native American students involved in Explorations formed the Oklahoma White House Conference Youth Committee, creating their own document outlining the problems they found with American education and offering solutions to those problems. Two students were selected to serve on the Oklahoma White House Conference Committee and participated in the conference in Washington, D.C. (Callahan, n.d.)

Javits Projects: Essential Elements for Promoting Talent Development

In a second report of Javits Projects, Gubbins, Callahan, and Renzulli (December, 1995) reported on 60 projects funded between 1989 and 1992. They conducted 44 non-participant classroom observations and 126 semi-structured interviews to assess and elicit their findings. Their findings focused on the impact of professional development opportunities, curriculum as a tool for eliciting and nurturing talents, and heightening parents' awareness of their children's talents.

Professional Development Key Findings

Several findings identified critical components of staff development programs:

* Teachers were introduced or re-introduced to knowledge about developing the gifts and talents of students from historical and contemporary perspectives.

* Teachers shared their newly acquired or re-oriented knowledge with others, as they developed curricular activities for students independently or with colleagues.

- Teachers observed and critiqued their peers and viewed themselves on videotapes as they experimented with curricular approaches.

- Teachers remarked how effective it was to see themselves and to watch how others approached lessons.

- Flexibility in the classroom stretched beyond pedagogical techniques to include flexibility in thinking.

- Teachers became more and more skilled in their observations using lists of characteristics, behavioral anecdotes, or video clips.

- Training sensitized teachers to the types of behaviors they should elicit through involvement with curriculum.

- Teachers changed their instructional styles. This was evident at all grade levels.

Curriculum Findings

Administrators and teachers involved in the Javits Projects became familiar with one or more models for developing curricular options for students. These models, excluding the two large-scale curriculum projects, included the Enrichment Triad Model, Cognitive Domain of the Taxonomy of Educational Objectives, Taba Teaching Strategies Program, Theory of Multiple Intelligences, and Curriculum Development Model.

Gubbins, Callahan and Renzulli (December, 1995) found that the curricular activities varied in the extent to which they adopted a model as a theoretical or organizational framework, addressed the strategies of curriculum differentiation, connected the instructional activities to the model's components, or focused on skills to promote and elicit advanced-level skills. Many times the curricular units and activities were intended for local use only. Other curricular developers field tested the curricula, made revisions, and used formal and informal dissemination techniques to share curricula with others.

Heightening Parents' Awareness of Their Children's Talents Findings

Several Javits projects emphasized the importance of helping parents understand, encourage, and nurture their children's giftedness. Of the 60 projects reviewed, 62 percent offered parents training/workshops, 38 percent prepared print materials specifically for parents, and 15 percent developed audiovisual materials with parents as the primary audience.

These activities link school and home in talent development initiatives. Both parents and children benefited from the strategies. Specific benefits for parents included:

- Receiving data on their children's characteristics not readily available from other sources
- Communicating frequently with school staff
- Learning how to encourage and nurture their children's talents by attending workshops, meetings, and conferences, and learning strategies to support and extend their children's learning opportunities.

Case Descriptions and Cross-Case Analysis of Three Javits Projects

The Urban Scholars Program focused on student performance on standardized math or reading tests administered at their respective schools, students' grade point averages, students' understanding of basic elements of scientific methodology, students' participation in the local science fair competitions, students' logic and word problems ability, and students' increased awareness of science and math careers. By the third year of the project, all objectives were met (Gubbins, Callahan, and Renzulli., December, 1995, pp. 25–26).

Several themes emerged from the analysis of the these cases:

- The leadership teams for each project held a shared vision.

- The projects were part of a mosaic of educational opportunities available in the system or district.

- Talent development, not just talent identification, was a major focus.

- Administrators, teachers, and students shared an ambivalence about recognizing and developing talents.

- Professional development opportunities guided teachers in program implementation.

Montgomery County's Gifted and Talented Policy and Regulations

The Montgomery County (Md.) public school system is a large suburban school district with a diverse student population: 18 percent African American, 10 percent Hispanic, 12 percent Asian, and 59 percent White. In November 1995 the district revised its policy and regulations concerning gifted and talented education to explicitly address equity and excellence issues. The policy embraces much of the U.S. Department of Education's recommendations. Gifted and talented students are defined by Montgomery County as follows:

1. Children and youth with outstanding talent who perform or show the potential for performing at high levels of accomplishment when compared with others of their age, experience, or environment. (These talents are present in children and youth from all cultural groups, across all economic strata, and in all areas of human endeavor.)

2. Children and youth who exhibit high performance capability in intellectual, creative, and/or artistic areas, possess an unusual leadership capacity, or excel in specific academic fields. (They require services or activities that may go beyond those ordinarily provided by the schools.)

In the policy's identification section, broad-based screening of all students in second grade and a rescreening of all students in late elementary grades is required. The policy states:

Recognizing there is a range of abilities among gifted and talented students, this screening will identify gifted and talented students using multiple indicators of academic and leadership potential, including tests of academic achievement, aptitude, and creativity and use of testing strategies designed for students of other languages; samples of student work; and nominations obtained from teachers, counselors, peers, parents, subject area experts, community members, and the students themselves (p. 4).

Specific attention is given to identification in grades 6 through 8, the middle level:

Schools will recommend students for classes of gifted and talented or for gifted and talented cluster groupings on the basis of mastery of course prerequisites, willingness to complete challenging assignments, previous grades, teacher recommendations, or other appropriate measures (p. 5).

The prescription for underachieving and traditionally underrepresented students states explicitly that these students will be nurtured through a variety of efforts, including informal identification in primary grades; working with teachers, parents, and mentors on ways to nurture potential; distribution characteristics of gifted/learning disabled and/or underrepresented groups and adaptive techniques that assist these students in mastering challenging instruction; and planning programs for long-term nurturing.

Desired outcomes of the policy speak specifically to diversity: "The classroom, school organization and instructional strategies will be designed to accommodate diversity in student backgrounds as well as their abilities and interests."

The policy also suggests implementation strategies. For example:

1. The assessment tools may include criterion-referenced tests, checklists, portfolios, exhibitions, demonstrations, work products, and journals.

2. Montgomery County Public Schools will report by grade for each middle school the number and percentage of students who complete algebra I each year.

3. Students will be encouraged to participate in academic competitions.

Montgomery County also disseminates a program handbook that mandates grouping, differentiation, and curriculum intervention strategies that support the policy. Accountability for the policy culminates in an annual progress report, including recommended policy changes, submitted to the board of education.

Montgomery County Public Schools policy and regulations are one example of how a district addresses the U.S. Office of Education's recommended principles of advocacy, defensibility, equity, pluralism, and comprehensiveness.

Talent Development: The AVID Model.

San Diego's Advancement Via Individual Determination program (AVID) for low-income students who are underrepresented in postsecondary education is another model recommended for talent development. AVID is a secondary school program that supports restructuring the entire school to meet students' educational and motivational needs. Options to full school implementation include development of a pilot program using AVID strategies focused on instructional methodology with a rigorous curriculum.

AVID is used to identify an ethnically and culturally diverse group of students who have the potential to excel academically. A preparatory class is developed to replace an existing elective. The class uses instructional methodology focused on teaching students how to think, how to study and use the Cornell method of note taking, along with extensive writing experiences. The class is supplemented by use of college tutors, field trips, guest speakers, and other enrichment experiences.

Data from implementing the AVID program model show a reduction in dropouts, increased enrollment and completion of high school honors and Advanced Placement classes, as well as increased college enrollment. In San Diego County, AVID graduates compare favorably to national trends:

- African-American students: two and a half times the national average
- Anglo students (low income): twice the national average
- Hispanic students: three times the national average
- Pan-Asian students: one and a half times the national average (AVID Handbook, n.d.).

Such a program, resulting in such success with underrepresented groups, provides one option for middle level educators concerned with talent development among all students.

Conclusions

The changing demographics of American schools requires that identification and assessment of high achieving students be modified so that all groups are appropriately represented. Use of non-biased tests and use of other practices advocated by Baldwin and Fraiser, Gardner, Renzulli, and Steinberg will also be useful for identifying students from groups who have been traditionally under-served by conventional identification procedures.

Further, professional development for teachers and principals is essential to change behaviors and beliefs. Such training is critical to developing the capacity among educators to strengthen and refine their programs for high achieving minority students and to foster and nurture the gifts of all able learners, regardless of their ethnicity, language, or cultural background. To do less than that will squander one of this nation's most valuable resources.

References

AVID (Advancement Via Individual Determination). Mary Catherine Swanson, director. San Diego, Calif.: San Diego Avid Center, n.d.

Baldwin, A. Y. "I Am Black but Look at Me, I Am Also Gifted." *Gifted Child Quarterly* 4(1987): 180-184.

Barstow, D. "Serve Disadvantaged and Serve All Gifted." *Gifted Child Monthly* 10(1987): 1-3.

Callahan, C. M. "What We Have Accomplished with the Jacob K. Javits Gifted and Talented Students Education Act Innovative Programs" U.S. Department of Education, ED Contract #RP921147001, Javits Grant Study, Undated.

Claiborne, W. "Fighting School Failure Among Hispanics." *Washington Post*, October 12, 1994: p. A-1.

Ford, D. Y. *Reversing Underachievement Among Gifted Black Students*. New York: Teachers College Press, 1996.

————. "Support for the Achievement Ideology and Determinants of Under Achievement as Perceived by Gifted, Above Average, and Average Black Students." *Journal for the Education of the Gifted* 3(1993): 280-98.

Ford, D. Y., and Harris, J. J. III. "Promoting Achievement Among Gifted Black Students: The Efficacy of New Definitions and Identification Practices." *Urban Education* 29(1994): 202-38.

Frasier, M. M. "The Identification of the Gifted Black Child: Developing New Perspectives." *Journal for the Education of the Gifted* 3(1987): 155-80.

Gardner, H. Frames of Mind: *The Theory of Multiple Intelligences*. New York: Basic Books, 1983.

Gilliam, D. "The Dilemma at Capital High." *The Washington Post*, April 27, 1996, p. B-1.

Gubbins, E. J.; Callahan, C. M.; and Renzulli, J. S. "Case Analysis of Three Javits Projects." U.S. Department of Education, ED Contract #RP921147001, November 1995.

————. "Javits Projects: Essential Elements for Promoting Talent Development." U.S. Department of Education, ED Contract #RP921147001, December 1995.

Harvey, D., and Slatin, G. T. "The Relationship Between Child's SES and Teacher Expectations: A Test of the Middle-Class Bias Hypothesis." *Social Forces* 1(1975): 140-59.

Heller, E. J. "Pupil Race and Elementary School Ability Grouping: Are Teachers Biased Against Black Children?" *American Educational Research Journal* 4(1985): 465-83.

Huang, G. "Beyond Culture: Communicating with Asian-American Children and Families." *ERIC Digest* 94(1993): 1.

"In Our Own Words." *Teaching Tolerance*, Fall 1996.

Karp, S. "Rich Schools, Poor Schools and the Courts." *Rethinking Schools* 2(1991): 1-15.

Lee, S. J. *Unraveling the Model Minority Stereotype*. New York: Teachers College Press, 1996.

Marwit, K.; Marwit, S.; and Walker, E. "Effects of Student Race and Physical Attractiveness on Teachers' Judgments of Transgressions." *Journal of Educational Psychology* 70(1978): 911-15.

Matute-Bianchi, M. E. "Ethnic Identities and Patterns of School Success and Failure Among Mexican-Descent and Japanese-American Students in a California High School: An Ethnographic Analysis." *American Journal of Education* 1(1986): 233-55.

Oakes, J. *Keeping Track: How Schools Structure Inequality*. New Haven, Conn.: Yale University Press, 1985.

Oakes, J. "Tracking Diversity and Education Equity: What's New in the Research?" Paper prepared for the Common Destiny Alliance Consensus Panel meeting. Graduate School of Education and Information Studies, UCLA, revised July 1995.

Pallas, A. "Making Schools More Responsive to At-Risk Students." *ERIC Digest* 60(1989): 1.

Renzulli, J. "The Three-Ring Conception of Giftedness. A Developmental Model for Creativity Productivity." In *Conception of Giftedness*, edited by R. J. Sternberg and J. E. Davidson. Cambridge, Mass.: Cambridge University Press, 1986.

Richert, S.; Alvino, J.; and McDonnell, R. *The National Report on Identification: Assessment and Recommendation for Comprehensive Identification of Gifted and Talented Youth*. Washington, D.C.: Education Information Resource Center, U.S. Department of Education, 1985.

Schwartz, L. L. *Why Give Gifts to the Gifted?* Thousand Oaks, Calif.: Corwin Press, Inc., 1994.

Shanker, A. "Succeeding in School." *New York Times* June 9, 1996, p. E-7. (Shanker quotes the research of L. Steinberg, B. B. Brown, and S. Dornbusch.)

Simpson, A. W., and Erickson, M. T. "Teachers' Verbal and Nonverbal Communication Patterns as a Function of Teacher Race, Student Gender and Student Race." *American Educational Research Journal* 2(1983): 183-98.

Sternberg, R. J. *Metaphors of Mind: Conceptions of the Nature of Intelligence*. Cambridge, Mass.: Cambridge University Press, 1990.

Tate, W. E. "From Inner City to Ivory Tower: Does My Voice Matter in the Academy?" *Urban Education* 29(1994): 245-69.

Tollett, E. E. "The Status of African-American Children." *The Black Child Advocate,* Special Issue, No 22. Fall 1995.

U.S. Commission on Civil Rights. *Civil Rights Issues Facing Asian-Americans in the 1990s*. Washington, D.C.: Author, 1992.

National Center for Education Statistics. *Findings from the Conditions of Education 1994, No. 2, The Educational Progress of Black Students*. Washington, D.C.: Office of Educational Research and Improvement, U.S. Department of Education, 1995a.

———. *Findings from the Conditions of Education 1994, No. 4, The Educational Progress of Hispanic Students*. Washington, D.C.: Office of Educational Research and Improvement, U. S. Department of Education, 1995b.

———. *Javits Gifted and Talented Students Education Program Grants Projects Abstracts,* 1992-1993. Washington, D.C.: Office of Educational Research and Improvement, U.S. Department of Education, 1994.

VanTassel-Baska J.; Patton, J.; and Prillaman, D. "Disadvantaged Gifted Learners At-Risk for Educational Attention." *Focus on Exceptional Children* 3(1989): 1-16.

Weis, L. "Excellence and Student Class, Race and Gender Cultures." *In Excellence in Education: Perspective on Policy and Practice,* edited by P. Altbach, G. Kelly, and L. Weis. Buffalo, N. Y.: Prometheus Press, 1985.

CHAPTER 10

Two Parents Speak Out:
Able Learners in Middle School

John H. Powell and Janine Shahinian with

J. Howard Johnston and Ronald D. Williamson

Ater parents agree that it is a challenge to raise healthy, well-adjusted, and competent children
in contemporary America. When children exhibit special needs, talents, and gifts, this challenge is heightened by the desire to ensure appropriate educational services. When the
same student exhibits both special gifts and special needs, the demands on parents, teachers, and
the school are complicated and often bewildering. What special services should be provided? How
should they be delivered to minimize disruptions to the student's learning? How do parents judge
whether or not the school is serious about meeting their child's unique needs?

In the stories that follow, two parents share the stories of their own children as they interact
with the school. Both show slices of reality that are familiar to many educators and to virtually all
parents whose children exhibit these special gifts.

Matt's Story

I know that everyone in school is working as hard as they can to do what's right for children, but
if I could sit down face-to-face with the principals and teachers who will be reading this book,
there are some things that I think I could share, as a parent, that would help my son, and other
kids like him, be more successful in school.

Matt is gifted and attention deficit disordered. That combination is both a blessing and a curse,
for the giftedness sometimes helps him "power through" demanding school assignments and class-
work, but the learning disability can render the most mundane tasks almost impenetrable for him.
It's frustrating and exasperating for Matt and me, and I'm sure the combination is just as puzzling
and frustrating for his teachers.

Like most gifted kids, Matt is articulate, highly verbal, and capable of interesting insights, complicated analysis, and bursts of enormous creativity. He has always been an interesting kid—curious about almost everything, able to make unusual and novel observations about people and
events and, because of his verbal ability, something of a raconteur and storyteller. When Matt says
something, I can be pretty sure he will put a novel and insightful twist on whatever topic we are
discussing.

Like most students with attention deficit disorder, Matt is sometimes frustrated, bewildered by
his disability, and doubtful of his gifts and talents. He often has difficulty with the most routine school
tasks, such as remembering assignments or conveying important information from school to home.
It's not that he avoids work; sometimes, he will work on a paper or other academic project for hours,
only to find out the next day that he forgot to do an easy assignment in the same class.

Watching my son in school is like watching a world-class athlete perform with one hand tied
behind his back.

The First Years of Schooling

At first, it is very difficult to figure out what is happening with your child. From his earliest years, it was clear that Matt was bright and articulate. Obviously, he could perform at very high levels. I'm sure my experience is not unique; surely, by the time their kids start school, most parents of gifted children are well aware of their talents and abilities.

But then messages start to arrive home. "Matt can't stand still in line." "He won't stay in his seat." "He doesn't sleep during nap time, but tosses around and talks." That's probably the message we got more often than any other: Matt talks...and talks...and talks.

His academic skills were fine. He was a good reader; his mathematics ability was advanced; he could write as well as much older children. But his behavior was seen as non-compliant, disobedient, and sometimes disruptive. He often played the clown, entertaining other students (and frequently the teachers) with his clever wit.

In most of the interactions with the school, it was made pretty clear to me that the school saw the problem as intentional...an act of will. Teachers told me that he had poor social skills, that he was immature, undisciplined. One implied that the modern child rearing techniques I probably used (since I am a clinical psychologist) produced an undisciplined, unruly child.

At this point, the potential for harm is great. Before the disability is diagnosed, it is easy to blame the child for his behavior. Because he was so competent in so many ways, it was almost inconceivable that he could not exert more control, could not listen more carefully, could not follow simple rules and directions. "Maybe my parenting is flawed," I thought. "Maybe I was too permissive or restrictive, or accepting, or critical, or attentive or inattentive or protective or laissez-faire." I could almost pick any adjective. No matter what I did, I began to think I might be the reason my child was having difficulty functioning in school.

Matt was bewildered, too. People often seemed upset with him, particularly at school. It would have been easy for him to figure out at a young age that he didn't "fit" at school. That school wasn't for people like him.

I suspect that happens a lot with ADD kids. They are often in trouble at school. If they receive no countervailing messages from the school, the logical conclusion is that they are not students...not learners. They need to find some other way of expressing their competence and uniqueness. Because Matt is such an able learner, he received contradictory messages: "You're such a smart boy, such a good learner...don't you care about how you do in school? Why don't you pay attention? Can't you follow simple directions? Are you lazy?" Fortunately, his academic performance helped to offset the other difficulties he experienced.

Even after the difficulty is diagnosed, there is a lot of friction between parents and ADD children. Even though the parent knows better, it is easy to slip into believing that the child is being willfully uncooperative. "What do you mean you forgot your book (or homework, or you-name-it)? We talked about it last night, this morning, and again this afternoon...and you still forgot? What's wrong with you!?!?" Such exchanges are probably familiar to most parents, but they are almost daily occurrences for the parents of ADD children.

After enough argument, it is easy for the child to begin to doubt himself and his worth. "Maybe there is something wrong with me. Maybe it is something I could change if I weren't so lazy (or stupid, or dumb, or a screw-up, or...)." Unfortunately, the list of adjectives for self-recrimination is nearly endlesss.

Middle School

By middle school, the problems are exacerbated by the increasing demands of the school for homework, higher levels of performance, and greater student responsibility. The opportunity for misunderstood instructions; lost, forgotten or misplaced work or materials; and missed deadlines is almost endless.

Many teachers, frustrated by the sheer number of students they have to deal with, ascribe motives and prescribe remedies that simply don't work with ADD kids. "He's just lazy. If he'd spend more time on his work, he wouldn't have these problems." Many ADD students spend countless hours on the simplest tasks; most parents cannot imagine them spending even more time.

"He really just needs to get organized... to think through his tasks." That, indeed, is an essential element of the disability. One of the defining characteristics of ADD is lack of ability to organize information and delineate complex tasks.

"He's just not focused. If you'll just get him to focus on his work, he'll do fine." Right again! Lack of focus is the defining attribute of ADD. They don't focus because they can't!

By middle school, the parents of ADD children have been, in the words of one of my clients, "just-ed to death! If anyone else tells me that my child is just this...or just that...or just needs to do this...or just needs to do that...I think I'll just scream!"

By now, for many students, it's too late. They have developed very negative academic self-esteem—that part of our self-perception which says we are a "student" or "non-student." For many, they have constructed another view of themselves—the class clown or cut-up, the angry rebel, the victim. Once again, the list of non-productive identities is legion.

Many children internalize the messages they get from the school environment and, ultimately, use them to construct their sense of self. If a student hears often enough that he is a goof-off, he is quite likely to accept that persona and live up (or down) to that reputation.

For gifted children, some of these non-productive behaviors can be intensified. Because they are so smart and capable, they can be very challenging if they become oppositionally defiant or passively aggressive.

Unfortunately, the primary strategy for many schools when dealing with the gifted ADD child is to turn up the pressure on both the child and the parents without making even minor adjustments in classroom procedures. Once, when I suggested to a teacher that he walk around the room as he was giving an assignment to check that students were writing it down correctly, he said, "If I do it for your son, I'll have to do it for everyone!" Precisely. Most students probably record the assignments correctly but, if not, it seems to be a skill worth teaching and monitoring. I suspect that the few minutes it would take for a cursory look at student assignment books would save him a lot of time in correcting misunderstood instructions.

Instead, I was told, "you need to assume some responsibility as a parent to see that your son does his work." I agree. If I knew what my son's work was supposed to be, I would ensure it was done.

I don't know all the strategies that have been developed to work successfully with attention deficit students, but I suspect that with advances in education for exceptional students, there must be many. By the time Matt reached middle school, however, I was disappointed by the small number of professionals who seemed willing to make even the most rudimentary adjustments to accommodate my son's disability.

High School

By high school, Matt had developed a number of strategies for coping with his disability. Few of them are directed at accommodating academic instruction; most are aimed at preserving a personal sense of dignity and esteem.

One of Matt's most common strategies is to "blow off" everyday performance in class and rely on his exceptional verbal ability to perform well on tests. As he sees it, it's not so important that he always do exactly what is assigned, provided that his performance on tests and large projects, such as research papers and other major assignments, is strong. So far, that has been true. He has been able to earn respectable grades by selectively attending to the "big" assignments.

The down side of this strategy is that he also deprecates the value of practice and the cumulative nature of learning in certain areas. Conversely, he emphasizes smart, glib, and facile performances, all of which are facilitated by his verbal gifts. Not surprisingly, he does especially well in fields that require verbal performance and insight, such as English, social sciences, and humanities, and struggles with fields that require more dogged practice, such as mathematics and foreign languages.

Like many bright young people who have struggled with certain structural and organizational aspects of the school program, Matt has learned how to "beat the system" at school. His highly developed verbal and social skills allow him to compensate for other, weaker areas of performance. Thus, Matt is charming, witty, and facile. He has also grown to be considerate, kind, and generous, so his wit is never biting or caustic, although it is frequently ironic. Because of these qualities, he is well-liked by his teachers, who are inclined to cut him some slack on routine work because of his exceptional performance on larger assignments and exams. To a large degree, Matt's performance in any class depends upon how he is seen by the teacher: if he is seen as smart and able, he will do very well; if he is seen as non-compliant or lazy, he will do poorly.

Finally, Matt has learned to approach priorities and needs with a degree of flexibility. He can shift priorities and invest less in a particular need because to do otherwise places him at risk of being disappointed by circumstances surrounding his disability. It is important for him to do well in school, but he is capable of "blowing it off" if he sees that something beyond his control will affect his grades. If, for example, a teacher is absolutely inflexible about daily assignments, Matt is likely to make an effort to comply but, if he begins to lag behind, may attribute his declining grade to bad luck or the unfairness of the teacher.

Schools seem to be reluctant to provide services to the gifted-learning disabled student. The attitude seems to be, "Wait a minute! He's so bright and does so well on tests—you want us to give him extra attention and help?" Ironically, because Matt's disability is not profoundly disabling, it appears that many school personnel are willing to accept less achievement than would be possible with even minimal accommodations. The message is that "We have so many students with special needs, we just don't have time to deal with them." Or, "If we treat this obviously bright student in any special way, it will be seen as unfair by other parents and students."

So Matt and some of his teachers negotiate their accommodations. Are these beneficial compromises? Frankly, it works to keep Matt engaged in the school and its program, face academic challenges with a certain confidence, and plan for additional education and, ultimately, an academic career. These accommodations by both Matt and his teachers, while far from ideal, seem to have worked to produce a happy, self-assured young man—an outcome for which I am grateful as a parent because in my professional role, I see daily how laboriously so many people struggle to achieve those precious states.

Lee's Story

My son just started eighth grade and for the first time in his school career he is enrolled in a program for "high achieving" students. At his school, algebra I is an option for eighth graders and is the only program for bright/talented/gifted/what-have-you students that our district offers below the high school level. By taking algebra in eighth grade, my son will be able to take calculus in his senior year, a subject that will help him pursue his goal of becoming an engineer.

Throughout this first month of school, the algebra teacher has been stressing how hard this class will be, impressing upon the students that it is normally a ninth grade class. Granted, it is only the beginning of the school year, but he is still waiting for the material to become merely challenging, much less "hard." I could have told him he'd find it easy.

Being able to say "I told you so" is a running theme with my son's school career.

The Early Years of Schooling

Lee attended a Montessori preschool program from the time he was 34 months old through his kindergarten year. He began writing phonetically when he was 48 months old and was soon producing little stories using "inventive spelling" that I managed to decode. These I proudly filed next to his vocabulary lists. Lee insisted, though, that he couldn't read, feeling that was something only first graders were allowed to do. When I saw him mastering single digit addition and subtraction in his kindergarten year, I no longer had any doubts about his entering first grade with his age peers. If anything, I began to see his being the youngest as a way to ensure that he'd be challenged in school.

HA! (Or as the kids say these days: Not!)

Oh, how I wish the school system would believe that I did not set out with the goal of becoming a "pushy" parent! We bought this house fully believing that the schools were great, the teachers were great, and the kids did well because of that. I had done the whole "first six years of a child's life are the most crucial" routine and frankly, I was more than glad to turn the job over to professionals. Lee was really psyched to start public school. We have a picture of him emerging from his first grade classroom on the first day literally jumping for joy.

He was never again quite that happy.

I began to notice that Lee could make abstract leaps. I never did any kind of formal instruction with him at home, but it was impossible to not have a conversation with Lee without bringing up "academic" concepts as his curiosity held no bounds. For example, in discussing our ethnic heritage, I told him that I'm half-Italian and that his dad is a quarter Italian. In a flash, he announced that it amounted to three-quarters. This was first grade, mind you; fractions are not taught until fourth. Similarly, he could discuss issues that required use of multiplication and division. He also solved simple problems in his head. The more he learned, the more he wanted to learn. Let him within reach of a calculator and he was asking about all the functions. He got a kick from hearing about such things as infinity, googols, and irrational numbers. Meanwhile at school he was counting beans.

It was when his second grade teacher insisted that his students demonstrate their mastery of the addition facts before getting to do multiplication that we began to have problems. Since multiplication was not considered part of the curriculum until third grade, this was considered "bonus" work. Kids could come up to the teacher and rattle off each "table" (the ones, twos, etc.) to earn extra-credit points. Do it up through the tens and they earned the right to fetch "enrichment" worksheets from the back of the class. Oh joy! More worksheets. Lee decided he'd rather not jump through that hoop.

By now it was apparent that being one of the youngest students in his class didn't compensate for being a fast learner. Lee was still at the top of his class when it came to achieving all the "outcomes," but it could hardly be called an achievement at all. Lee was coasting, and I could see this affecting both his self-esteem and his learning skills. To the extent that school offered new information for him to soak up, he was happy. This was the case with science and social studies.

But while Lee was learning new facts, he was not learning how to learn. Nothing (except gym) was hard; nothing took effort. He did not have to put his mind to something and really think about it or study. Therefore he never got that sense of satisfaction one gets from seeing efforts pay off.

So throughout third and fourth grades, I met frequently with Lee's teachers, pleading with them to find a way to speed up the pace of his math instruction. (While Lee also had strong verbal skills, language arts instruction at least involves reading new stories and writing original compositions.) At each meeting, their typical come-back was to show me the results of a pre-test on which Lee had made a few mistakes. (Never more than 50 percent wrong and frequently less than 25 percent wrong.) This, they felt, proved that Lee was best served with the given curriculum to ensure that he wouldn't develop any "Gaps."

Why is it that the mere thought of Gaps strikes terror in the heart of every elementary teacher? In hindsight, it strikes me that second, third, and fourth grades are the perfect time to actually put Gaps to good effect in the case of a mathematically talented child. Let the child experience for once what it feels like to not know something—not even at 50-75 percent mastery. Let them learn how to identify what they don't know and try to come up with their own strategies for rectifying the situation. Children are at the perfect age during that time since they so want to please their teachers. Let them have that moment of panic when they see the big task ahead of them. Better to learn it now, in the safety of elementary school, than later when they are in high school, college, or beyond. Then let them feel the incredible sense of achievement when they work it out for themselves and accomplish mastery.

After all, isn't the real goal of school to learn how to learn? The need for learning doesn't stop at the end of high school and college. Once our formal schooling comes to an end, we're on our own. No one is there to spoon feed facts to us. In a world that is exploding with knowledge, add one more item to the list of life's certainties after death and taxes: *Gaps*.

You know, it's not like each year of elementary math is that different from the prior years. The concepts build on each other and are reintroduced again and again in what is known as the spiral approach. Even the average transfer student can't go for long without having a Gap (caused by different district curriculums) rectified through the normal course of instruction. But for most mathematically talented students, this amount of built-in review is already too much. The algebra homework awhile back involved Order of Operations. My son announced, "We did this in fifth grade!"

What I tried to impress on Lee's teachers is that, while he couldn't "pass out" of an "outcome" in a pre-test (since we weren't drilling him at home), he could master the outcome in far less time than his average classmates. Given that Lee entered each grade already demonstrating from 60 to 75 percent mastery of the entire year's math curriculum, I wasn't asking for more instruction on his part. What I wanted was for Lee to get his fair share of instruction! You know, "one year's learning in one year's time"? Endless review was totally unnecessary and the inappropriate pacing drove him nuts.

Advocacy Initiatives

A couple of years ago, I heard a speaker on the gifted offer a dramatic example of what this slow pacing felt like. Without warning she suddenly slowed the pace of her talk so that you felt like you were one of those speedy beings with buzzing-fly sound effects in a Classic Star Trek episode. It felt very uncomfortable to have to sit and listen to her. No wonder my son came home from school with so much pent-up anger.

My meetings with the teachers got me nowhere. Their patronizing tone made it quite clear that they were the experts and I was just a pushy mom. It was time, I thought, to show them I meant business.

In college, I majored in both psychology and secondary education (social studies). I completed both a teacher's certificate and the knowledge of how to conduct and analyze scientific studies. For the next few years I tackled my own Gap when it came to knowing appropriate methods for teaching gifted students and studied the subject as though I were in graduate school. I read books, attended conferences, tracked down articles, and made a study of the district's policies regarding gifted education. I "networked" my way up from the principal to nationally recognized experts. Along the way, I also started a grassroots organization of other parents of gifted students in the district. I was attending meetings of some sort right and left and writing up a storm: proposals, reports, letters, articles for my organization's newsletter, and essays that appeared in our local paper.

The school district began to take notice. After amassing all the evidence to show that our district was woefully lacking in programs for gifted students, including a two-year-old report from a district study that recommended immediate implementation of a program that existed only on paper, the school board moved unanimously to give this issue all the attention it deserved. They recommended the formation of a committee to study the situation.

On the whole, fifth grade was a pretty good year for my son. He actually had two teachers who swapped students and team taught: one handled the math and science while the other did the language arts and social studies. It was the middle school model brought down to the fifth grade level and put to great effect. Since each teacher only had to prep two subjects instead of four, they were able to offer far more enrichment within each subject. My son loved the simulations in social studies and all the hands-on science projects.

Math, however, was still not challenging. For the most part, the highest students taught themselves, taking pretests, working on those areas where they needed to improve and then moving on. They worked in teams and turned to their partners to discuss a problem. The teacher was always there, of course, to offer assistance and small-group instruction. But acceleration for the brightest students only occurred if the kids were motivated to push themselves harder. In my son's case, he and his friend didn't see the need to move any faster. They were at the top of their class and were getting A's, so they did the minimum amount of work needed to maintain that level. I must say this, though—for the first time in elementary school, Lee wasn't bored with math. That, alone, was a major improvement.

The Middle School Years

Middle school was a whole new venue. It brought so many new things to adapt to that academic challenges took a back seat.

While the larger student body offered a wider choice of friends, it also became fertile ground for more social problems. A week never went by when I didn't hear some instance in which Lee was picked on by some other students. His adviser teacher was very sympathetic, but admitted there was little she could do. Finally, toward the end of the year, she admitted that some group psychology was in effect and the bad behavior was becoming contagious within the whole class. It got so bad that even she was driven to tears on a couple of occasions. Since the opposite class in the two teacher team somehow got all the nicer kids, Lee was allowed to switch and ended his sixth grade year on a more positive note.

Science became a bit more exciting, with more elaborate facilities to learn in. Lee also found the school library and its computers interesting. But I couldn't help feeling that Lee had more opportunities to learn new information in his "exploratory" classes (sort of an introduction to the elective options) than in his academic classes. Lee loved all his exploratory classes: performing arts, computers, tech ed, life skills, languages (a taste of French, German, Spanish, and Latin) and gym. When it came to his core subjects, though, Lee expressed his disinterest by slacking off and forgetting to do his homework. Although Lee's teachers admitted that he knew the material, his grades were only so-so: essentially "A" grades on tests and completed assignments, but too many zeros on incomplete assignments which pulled his grades down.

Meanwhile, Lee's scores on the Explore test for the Midwest Talent Search showed him ranking in the 73rd percentile in English and the 88th percentile in math compared to eighth graders (two grades above). Since the Talent Search model uses the 50th percentile on an above-level test as the cutoff for selecting students for accelerated summer precollege programs, these scores would have easily qualified my son (if we had the money for such things).

Lee and I investigated the possibility of "skipping" into eighth grade algebra during seventh grade, but eventually decided against it. To follow such an advanced sequence of math classes through twelfth grade seemed to invite more hardship than it was worth. As an eighth grader, he would have to travel to the high school extra early in the morning for geometry class, which would then make him late for first period—an elective class. The elective classes are one of the few things Lee enjoys in school. In twelfth grade, he would have to take his math class at the university— again forcing him to travel back and forth and missing out on who knows what opportunities within the high school.

Social issues were also a consideration—not because Lee isn't good at making friends with older students, but because the disruption in the school day and lack of shared experiences would affect his interactions with his classmates. Finally, the ability to maintain high grades became the deciding factor. From what I've heard, colleges make few allowances for lower grades when a student has been accelerated. Seen this way, there is something to be said for getting A's and finding the work easy as opposed to getting B's and finding the work challenging and interesting. The bottom line is that I wanted Lee to enjoy school, not add to his problems.

I can't really say that Lee enjoyed seventh grade, but then it must be a rare middle schooler who will say they like school. The school district made the decision to cut back on one of the elective periods in order to get the core-course teachers to assume responsibility for a fifth hour. I believe Lee found the replacement interdisciplinary block to be easy, boring, slightly fun, or a waste of time depending on the particular unit. Certainly, it didn't compare to his enjoyment in the remaining elective period, where he took a Radio/TV class.

Academically, Lee totally blew off school. He had so many zeros mixed in with his A's that all his report card grades were a C or below, with D's and E's being quite frequent. When confronted with his performance, Lee's response was always one of passivity: "The teacher lost my paper," "I was never given that sheet," "My partner didn't turn it in," "I didn't hear her say that," etc. I was at a loss on how to intervene and not really sure that I should at that point. Maybe he needed a lesson in failure. Maybe he needed to assume some responsibility for himself. Whatever the case, I wasn't about to have our summer ruined with the threat of summer school. Halfway into the year, I asked his teachers if that was a possibility if he didn't get his grades up. I was told that summer school was not for kids like Lee who obviously know the material. They agreed that such a course of action would only hurt his attitude more than help it.

The issue in our case is that here you've got a real smart kid who is not performing to his potential and doesn't see school as a place that is meeting his needs. Unlike the situation in elementary school, I don't blame the middle school teachers. With so many students to teach in heterogeneously grouped classrooms and a specific curriculum they are responsible for following, I don't see how they can be expected to "differentiate" the lessons to accommodate the students who are able to move more quickly. And frankly, I'm not sure it's even wise at an age when kids can't stand being different.

The only solution I see is advanced classes. Not an acceleration option like his current algebra class, per se, just specially grouped classes for the brighter students who are able to learn at a faster pace. However, since the mere mention of anything resembling the dreaded T-word is a stonable offense in this district, I know this will never happen. And as long as kids like my son keep racking up the high scores on standardized tests, which allow the district to pat itself on its back and boast to the world about how wonderful it is, no one sees any reason to treat these kids any differently.

Epilogue

The district is phasing in a new "core" math curriculum with this year's sixth grade class that will (as of this writing) eliminate the eighth grade algebra option. The eighth grade math teachers will differentiate the curriculum so that advanced students will still receive instruction in algebra within a heterogeneously grouped classroom. All I can say is that I'm glad my son will be in high school next year, a school that may meet my son's needs.

A Final Word

These stories give a poignant and articulate view of the challenges and joys of raising children with multiple exceptionalities. At the same time, they are instructive to educators who are serious about creating a child-centered learning environment predicated on strong partnerships between parents and school professionals. Some of the most important lessons to come from these stories are summarized here.

The Power of Conviction. Parent satisfaction is highest when they believe the school is making reasonable efforts to accommodate their child's unique gifts and needs. The surest way to alienate parents is to tell them that accommodations are not possible or not fair. They don't expect perfection, but they do expect that the school will behave reasonably to modify its programs and practices for students with exceptional needs.

It's the Disability, Not the Parent. Parents often report they are made to feel that their child's problems in school result not from a disability but from some failing on the part of the parent or the child. Most often, these messages come during conferences in which parents are told their child is lazy, unmotivated, immature, or in some other way lacking in character or will. It is during this kind of conversation that parents are told that if they "just" do A or B, everything will be O.K.

Blissful Ignorance. Parents of special needs students often report they are astonished by how little school professionals know about the nature of disabilities and the rather minor adjustments to classroom practices required to promote learning for special kids. In some cases, teachers and other school personnel have actively rejected diagnostic results and suggested that such tests are easily faked. This lack of understanding also extends to the laws and regulations covering the provision of services for special needs students in the regular education environment.

Father (and Mother) Knows Best. Parents have watched their children learn and adjust to their disabilities and gifts for years. They are the single best source of information about their child and his or her needs. Often, they can suggest the strategies that their child has used in previous years, or can help support instruction at home. It is critical that parents be consulted, involved in educational planning, and fully informed about the curriculum and instruction their child is receiving. Further, they must be given the information they need to monitor their child's work at home and help him or her meet school requirements.

There are dozens of strategies for working with children who have special needs. Most parents are not concerned which strategies and interventions are being used, only that the school is willing to do *whatever it takes to help their child succeed.*

References

Borland, J. H. *Planning and Implementing Programs for the Gifted.* New York: Teachers College Press, 1989.

Tannenbaum, A. J. *Gifted Children: Psychological and Educational Perspectives.* New York: Macmillan, 1983.

CHAPTER 11

Passageways: Using Gifted Education Policies To Increase Learning in a Middle School

Jay McIntire, Council for Exceptional Children

NOTE: The views expressed here are the author's and do not necessarily reflect positions or policies of the Council for Exceptional Children or its membership.

Both gifted education and middle level education are in a period of transition. From the earliest proposals to reconceptualize middle grades education there has been a perception that middle schools, due to their focus on developmental responsiveness and modified curricular and instructional programs, are inherently in conflict with core beliefs about gifted education.

Rather than search for ways to build bridges between the two approaches, great energy was devoted to documenting and proving that the other approach was inappropriate. As a result of this conflict and the associated tension, a framework for examining policies and programs serving talented middle level youth has emerged.

This chapter will discuss policy development—policies that guide and direct the education of gifted middle grades students. Policy development, while often not seen as a primary function of the principal, is emerging as a key role of the contemporary school leader. Increasingly, states and local school districts rely more on local schools, teachers, and principals to make decisions about their curricular and instructional programs. Making decisions closer to students affords principals and their faculties the opportunity to have greater influence over program development.

The discussion of gifted education policies consists of three parts. The first will discuss the philosophical bases on which both gifted education and middle level education rest. This will be followed by a review of the varied approaches used by schools around the nation to serve their gifted youth. Finally, several implications for principals will be discussed.

Philosophical and Policy Bases for Gifted and Middle Level Education

Middle level education has a clearer and more widely accepted set of core beliefs than gifted education. The struggle among educators of the gifted is to define core beliefs so they are both accepted by experts on gifted education and easily understood by others. Until this is accomplished there will continue to be debate about the role of gifted education in the middle level school.

Comprehensive, cohesive policies at the state and local level are one way to provide a framework for serving gifted students. Policies, however, must be based on an understanding of both the early adolescent learner and effective practices identified by research and practice.

Both gifted education and early adolescent education are in transition. While the transition from a junior high to middle school model has been underway for more than 30 years, it still has not been embraced in many schools. Some schools merely changed names or grade configurations; others made more substantial changes. Regardless of approach, most middle level leaders continue to struggle with achieving the promise of middle level education rather than reverting to practices more commonly associated with a comprehensive high school (Cuban, 1992).

Gifted education is also undergoing a transition—moving from identification and service of a narrowly-defined group of "gifted children" toward a more inclusive model, one that is built on the premise that schools must seek and develop the talents of many (U.S. Department of Education, 1993). Unfortunately, as with middle level education, many schools and states still require and defend the use of practices considered unacceptable by many contemporary gifted educators.

Due to the changes underway in both fields it is to be expected that practitioners in both find it difficult to identify the intersection between the fields—the education of early adolescents who "by virtue of experience or aptitude (have) the ability to identify, attempt to solve, or solve problems in a field of endeavor that is beyond the learning needs of their age peers" (National Association of Secondary School Principals, 1995).

A belief espoused by proponents in both fields is a commitment to the early adolescent learner. To fulfill this commitment and improve educational programs and experiences for these students, teachers and principals must be comfortable discussing and debating the merits of a variety of curricular and instructional strategies. Essential to such discussion is an awareness and knowledge of the philosophical base of each movement.

While many areas of middle level education are being debated (especially curriculum), a series of widely accepted mission statements have been developed. Three documents, prepared by different organizations, offer remarkably similar recommendations. Together they provide guidance to middle level educators about the nature of a strong middle school program. *This We Believe* (National Middle School Association, 1982) provided an early foundation for the movement. *An Agenda for Excellence at the Middle Level* (NASSP, 1985) emerged with a complementary set of recommendations for middle level schools. It challenged middle level educators this way: "Specific attention must be given to the alteration of the culture and climate of the school so that it supports excellence and achievement rather than intellectual conformity and mediocrity"(p.3). The third report, *Turning Points: Preparing American Youth for the 21st Century* (Carnegie Council on Adolescent Development, 1989) prompted a more recent examination and review of middle level programs. Together, these documents provide a philosophical base for the modern middle level school. NMSA recently updated *This We Believe* (1995) and specifically recommended that the learning needs of all students, including those with gifts and talents, be addressed.

There are no comparable position papers for gifted education. This has left principals and other local policymakers to select from a range of definitions, theories, and models. Occasionally this has resulted in state regulations that restrict local options and limit local decision making. Such restrictions often lead to implementation of programs that conflict with what might work best at an individual school.

Federal, state, and local policies provide some guidance in designing programs, but too often these guidelines are developed without active participation of those who must implement them. In some cases policies are out of date, resulting at best in programs of minimal value to students and at worst in discriminatory behavior toward some populations of gifted students.

Developing gifted education programs is a complex undertaking due to the variety of theoretical models available. Until recently the model most often accepted purported that giftedness was a behavioral manifestation of intelligence (IQ), a general characteristic that was consistent across time, across all endeavors, and primarily inherited. Recently, other models have emerged that provide an expanded concept of giftedness. Today, some theorists suggest that it is more appropriate to think about talent development in students than to think of giftedness as an inherent trait.

The Triarchic Model suggests three kinds of intellectual giftedness—analytical, creative, and practical (Sternberg, 1986). These intelligences result in gifted behaviors that are likely to be quite different from one another, even when applied to the same content (Sternberg et al. 1996). Other models applied to education include Gardner's theory of multiple intelligences (1983) and Hong and Milgram's Structure of Giftedness (1996).

Recent models share a common belief that no single measure, such as IQ, can predict the multitude of factors that result in outstanding achievement. This complex view of giftedness led to the development of models that focus less on identification of students who demonstrate potential for giftedness, and more on developing giftedness among students (Renzulli, 1994; Feldhusen, 1995). These models view giftedness as a state that can be achieved rather than a trait, thereby expanding the pool of gifted students.

Despite federal reports touting the importance of educating students who demonstrate outstanding performance or who are predicted to have the capability of such performance (U.S. Department of Health, Education, and Welfare, 1972; U.S. Department of Education, 1993), state regulations to ensure differentiated education for such students (Council of State Directors of Programs for the Gifted, 1991; Coleman and Gallagher, 1992), and school and district policies with the same effect (Batsell and Horak, 1992; Reis and Westberg, 1994), no document has emerged as a generally accepted statement of gifted education's basic values, beliefs, and theories.

Similarly, no model policies have gained widespread acceptance among stakeholders. Due to this lack of consensus, wide variation in state policies is the norm. Despite this inconsistency, local educators are still most likely to find assistance and direction in state legislation, regulations, and guidelines (Passow and Rudnitski, 1993).

The closest equivalent to a clear statement of national goals and beliefs about gifted education is *National Excellence* (U.S. Department of Education, 1993). It provides an overview of gifted education in the United States and calls on educators to address what Secretary of Education Richard Riley referred to as the "quiet crisis" in American education—the underachievement of gifted students. This report does not offer principles, guidelines, or belief statements to guide local programming—that is left to individual states. While the guidance available from state departments of education varies, those with comprehensive policies on gifted education come closest to providing a philosophical framework similar to that available for middle level schools.

Policies guiding gifted education take many forms: legislation, rules and regulations, and guidelines. These terms describe official statements or requirements accepted by an official body such as a legislature, state department of education, school board, or school administrative team. The terms are used interchangeably throughout this chapter and referred to as "policies."

Federal Gifted Education Policy

The most recent federal definition of children with gifts and talents is found in the Jacob K. Javits Gifted and Talented Student Education Act (1988):

Children and youth with outstanding talent perform or show the potential for performing at remarkably high levels of accomplishment when compared to others their age, experience, or environment.

These children and youth exhibit high performance capability in intellectual, creative, and/or artistic areas, possess an unusual leadership capacity, or excel in specific academic fields. They require services or activities not ordinarily provided by the schools.

Children and youth from all cultural groups, across all economic strata, and in all areas of human endeavor have outstanding talents. There are no guidelines from the federal government about the education of highly capable or high performing students. The federal definition, for example, is not accompanied by an obligation to serve, or even recognize students meeting this definition.

There are no federal guidelines assisting states or local districts in identification of students. Perhaps most significantly, there are no federal funds to help schools meet the educational needs of these students. What little federal support is available is used to identify model programs, and provide a handful of leadership activities (Gallagher, 1994).

In *A Nation at Risk,* the National Commission on Excellence in Education (1983) identified the nation's gifted and talented students as among those most at risk. It recommended an expanded federal role in assisting states and localities to meet these students' needs. The National Education Commission on Time and Learning (1994), while not directly addressing the needs of the gifted, did raise serious questions about the barriers that keep students from progressing at an advanced rate. The report stated: "It makes no more sense to put a computer-literate second grader into *Introduction to Computers* than it does to place a recent Hispanic immigrant into *Introductory Spanish*" (p. 31).

The federal role has been limited to issuing reports noting our failures in educating gifted students: resolution of the issues has been left to states and local education units.

State Gifted Education Policy

State departments are most likely to offer guidance to middle level educators developing programs for their students. Guidance from state departments varies widely as to the prescriptiveness of their policies, the assistance they provide in implementing guidelines, and the level of oversight.

While the level of flexibility found in policies promotes the greatest discussion (or complaint), the effectiveness of state policies is also measured by their cohesiveness, completeness, and the degree to which they reflect contemporary theory. Local middle level leaders working with unclear or overly permissive policies face the same struggle with gifted education faced by national leaders—gifted education is so amorphous that it is not easily understood, much less rectified, with middle school tenets.

While policies at the state level vary greatly, they generally have two goals: to increase the likelihood that the needs of gifted students will be addressed, and to assist local education agencies in providing services to gifted students. They most often include a definition of giftedness, screening and identification procedures, requirement for services, teacher certification, funding levels, requirements for local plans for educating the gifted, due process procedures for students, and means of evaluating program effectiveness.

Two states, Montana and Texas, provide an example of the range of guidance provided to teachers and principals. Montana's mandate is understated. Rule 10.55.804 of the state accreditation lays out the requirement for local schools:

Beginning July 1, 1992, the school shall make an identifiable effort to provide educational services to the gifted and talented students which are commensurate with their needs and foster a positive self-image.

It goes on to discuss requirements about program philosophy, identification, curriculum, teacher preparation, evaluation, support services, and parental involvement. In choosing only to require an "identifiable effort," without state oversight, Montana acknowledges the existence of gifted students, but chooses not to noticeably increase the likelihood that the needs of those students will be addressed, or to assist local education agencies in providing services.

Since there is no generally accepted framework or set of beliefs in gifted education, local educators in Montana are left to grapple with an array of possibilities and conceptions to develop their programs. Without commitment of resources—time and staff—quality programs are not likely. Fortunately, Montana provides a resource guide, *Montana's Gifted Education Resource Guide* (Montana Department of Public Instruction, 1994a, 1994b). Otherwise, schools would be left with little or no guidance.

Texas tends toward the opposite extreme. Its plan and guidelines for gifted education require 67 pages of detail and provide an explicit framework for implementing programs. Texas places many requirements on schools and teachers, including requirements in evaluation and planning, identification, program organization, curriculum, staff development, and parent/community involvement (Texas Education Agency, 1990).

In many schools the lack of clarity within gifted education makes it a challenge to link gifted education with middle level education. In Texas, however, the link has been established, perhaps due to the explicit nature of state gifted education policy (Guerrero, 1994).

Combining educational goals from diverse movements requires clear definition of each. Both middle level education and gifted education are in transition. While the two differ on many issues, they are in agreement that early adolescents are characterized by a variety of traits and individual learning styles. Talent development models that seek to maximize strengths of each student seem most appropriate in middle level schools. States without mandates do not require talent development in any children, while Texas and Montana place minimum expectations upon schools in their jurisdictions.

While many states require services and opportunities for some children, local educators are always free to expand these programs to focus on student strengths and the development of individual excellence among a broader and more inclusive population. One reason students identified as gifted seem to be getting something "better" than other children is that too often we focus on the weaknesses of other students.

Several states and localities have developed specific policies that are likely to improve programs for gifted students and could easily be expanded to serve a much wider range of students. The next section will describe the attributes of many gifted programs. In many schools, local educators use these or similar attributes to provide services to an expanded pool of students.

Models and Approaches to Gifted Education

Using state policies as a starting point, principals may wish to consider the following policies. Each could be adapted and used as local policy or practice in your school. All are consistent with the dual goals of increasing the likelihood that the needs of gifted students will be addressed, and assisting local education agencies in providing services to gifted students.

What is most essential is that each school assess local needs and select the strategies that are most appropriate at that site:

- Individualized Education Plans (IEPs) are required for gifted students in Alaska. This ensures that services are based on individual student need, rather than being catch-all programs for "generally gifted" students.

- Objectives of curriculum for gifted students are aligned with core curriculum (N.C.).
- Self-nomination is central to the process of matching students to programs (Harford Co., Md.).
- Due process protections are in place (Pa., Alaska).
- Program evaluation is required (Calif.).
- Multi-age programs are utilized (Cholla Middle School, Phoenix, Ariz.).
- All students must be screened for possible inclusion in programs (Ohio).
- A talent development model is in place. (Harford Co., Md.).
- Program evaluation focuses on student improvement. (N.C.).
- Standardized test scores and grades are used only as supportive information in making placement decisions. (Harford Co., Md.).
- Common planning time is available for creating talent development activities. (Harford Co., Md.).
- Distinctly different programs are available for gifted students with different needs. (Cholla Middle School, Phoenix, Ariz.).
- Multiple services options must be available and utilized based on student interests, needs, and abilities. (Ky.).
- Parent and community involvement is required. (Tex.).
- Evaluation procedures must be free of racial or cultural bias. (Alaska).
- Identified students must receive a minimum of five hours of differentiated instruction per week. (Ohio).
- Identification is "positive, dynamic, flexible, inclusive, and ongoing." (N.H.).
- Normed measures cannot eliminate a student from the "talent pool." (Ky).
- All instructional staff must have basic training in meeting the needs of the gifted. (Va.).
- Screening and selection must be ongoing. (Tex.).
- Students must be educated in the least restrictive environment. (Alaska).
- A scope and sequence of curricular modifications is developed. (Ariz.).
- Eligibility is based upon student's needs, interests, and abilities. (Ky.)

Implications for Principals

Each of these policies or practices may be useful in meeting your needs. Together, these approaches reflect a significant shift in the focus of gifted education. Figure 1 summarizes these approaches to serving talented youth.

The shifts reflect an expanded definition of giftedness—a trend toward greater inclusiveness, less rigid identification criteria, and a broader definition of talent. They also reflect a commitment to tailoring gifted programs to meet the needs of individual students, rather than maintaining practices that assume all gifted students need and thrive on similar programs.

These modifications and their accompanying commitment to seek talented students and to cultivate and nurture talent hold great promise. They provide a common ground on which gifted educators and middle level educators can come together to better serve all students.

Figure 1—Shifts in Contemporary Gifted Education Policy

FROM:	TO:
exclusivity	inclusivity
giftedness as an inherent trait	development of giftedness as a process
giftedness as a general ability	gifted behaviors manifested in different ways, times, types, and content areas
the concern of few	part of overall school and community function multiple qualitative and quantitative sources
single sources of identification data	multiple qualitative and quantitative sources
procedures result in disproportional representation	more equal representation of races, cultures, disabilities, SES groups
general gifted program	program designed for specific needs
arbitrary grouping (tracking, continuous heterogeneous)	flexible regrouping based on learning and social needs
success measured by norm scores	success measured by gain scores
only specialized staff trained	all staff have ownership and training in gifted education
gifts inherited at birth	gifted developed through hard work and interest matched with ability
static	variable, fluid
policies as an end point	policies as a starting point

Three themes arise from these shifts:

First, flexibility emerges as a defining characteristic of gifted programs. It is acknowledged that students manifest their giftedness in a variety of ways, at different times, and in diverse content areas. Multiple measures are used to identify students and to measure their success. Furthermore, programs for gifted students are fluid rather than static. No one program is seen as more appropriate than any other. There is a commitment to match student needs and program options—leading to a range of alternatives and services.

The second theme is recognition that identification and service to talented youngsters is an integral function of the school. Educators, both gifted and middle level, acknowledge a more active approach to find and nurture talent among students, rather than wait for talent to manifest itself. This commitment to identification and service, when combined with a more inclusive and responsive identification process, results in greater likelihood that the needs of all middle level youth will be appropriately served.

Finally, no single policy, program, or approach is appropriate for all gifted students. Those practices identified earlier reflect a range of programs and services. The fundamental issue is service—service to talented students. Increasingly, schools are committing themselves to do "whatever it takes" and to utilize a range of practices and strategies to ensure such service.

Together, these shifts in the emphasis of gifted education provide a framework for expanded discussion and debate about serving the needs of talented middle level students. This Middle level education policy is reflected in *This We Believe: Developmentally Responsive Middle Level Schools* which states, "In essence, every student needs an individualized education plan" (NMSA, 1995).

As educators more closely examine the importance of student achievement as a central function of the middle level school it provides an opportunity for gifted educators and middle level educators to seek common ground—shared beliefs about the importance of maximizing the education of all students, the importance of tailoring educational programs to meet the needs of all students, and a commitment to finding and nurturing the talent of all students.

Policies at the federal and state level offer some guidance to local educators—those charged with serving students. No policy, regardless of its intent or specificity can match the commitment of local educators to serve their students. Both movements, gifted education and middle level education, while in transition, share this commitment.

References

Batsell, G. A., and Horak, L. A. "F.L.E.X. Center: A Middle School Program for the Highly Gifted Learner," 1992.

Carnegie Council on Adolescent Development. *Turning Points: Preparing American Youth for the 21st Century.* Washington, D.C.: Carnegie Council 1989.

Coleman, M. R., and Gallagher, J. J. *Report on State Policies Related to the Identification of Gifted Students.* Chapel Hill, N.C.: University of North Carolina, 1992.

Council of State Directors of Programs for the Gifted. *The 1990 State of the States Report.* Augusta, Maine: CSDPG, 1991.

Cuban, L. "What Happens to Reforms That Last? The Case of the Junior High School." *American Educational Research Journal* 29(1992): 227-51.

Feldhusen, J. F. "Talent Development: The New Direction in Gifted Education." *Roeper Review* 2(1995): 92.

Finn, C. H. Jr.; Manno, B. V.; and Bierlein, L. *Charter Schools in Action: What Have We Learned?* Indianapolis, Ind.: Hudson Institute, 1996.

Gallagher, J. J. "A Retrospective View: The Javits Program." *Gifted Child Quarterly* 38(1994): 95-96.

Gardner, H. *Frames of Mind.* New York: Basic Books, 1983.

Guerrero, J. "Serving the Advanced Middle School Learner in the Heterogeneous Classroom." Paper presented at the annual meeting of the American Educational Research Association, San Francisco, Calif., April 1995.

Harford County Public Schools. "Guidelines: Gifted and Talented Education and Schoolwide Enrichment," 1996.

Hong, E., and Milgram, R. M. "The Structure of Giftedness: The Domain of Literature as an Exemplar." *Gifted Child Quarterly* 40(1996): 31-40.

Levin, B. "Students and Educational Productivity." *Educational Policy Analysis Archives* 5(1993).

Montana Department of Public Instruction. *Gifted Education Resource Guide.* Billings, Mont.: DPI, 1994a.

———. *Learner Goals for Gifted and Talented Students: Strategies for Design, Integration, and Assessment.* Billings, Mont.:DPI, 1994b.

———. Montana State Accreditation Rule 10.55.804. Billings, Mont.: DPI, 1990.

National Association of Secondary School Principals. *An Agenda for Excellence at the Middle Level.* Reston, Va.: NASSP, 1985.

———. Meeting the Needs of Gifted Youth at the Middle Level, Symposium conducted by the National Association of Secondary School Principals, Reston, Va., R. D. Williamson and J. H. Johnston, Chairs. October 1995.

National Commission on Excellence in Education. *A Nation at Risk: The Imperative for Educational Reform.* Washington, D.C.: U.S. Government Printing Office, 1983.

National Education Commission on Time and Learning. *Prisoners of Time.* Washington, D.C.: U.S. Government Printing Office, 1994.

National Middle School Association. *This We Believe.* Columbus, Ohio: NMSA, 1982.

————. *This We Believe: Developmentally Responsive Middle Level Schools*. Columbus, Ohio: NMSA, 1995.

Ohio Department of Education. Rule for School Foundation Units for Gifted Children, 3-4, Columbus, Ohio: DOE, 1988.

Passow, A. H., and Rudnitski, R. A. "State Policies Regarding Education of the Gifted as Reflected in Legislation and Regulation." (CRS93302). Storrs, Conn.: The National Research Center on the Gifted and Talented, 1993.

Reis, S. M., and Westberg, K. L. "An Examination of Current School District Policies." *The Journal of Secondary Gifted Education* 4(1994): 7-18.

Renzulli, J. S. *Schools for Talent Development: A Practical Plan for Total School Improvement*. Mansfield Center, Conn: Creative Learning Press, 1994.

Sternberg, R. J. "A Triarchic Theory of Intellectual Giftedness." *In Conceptions of Giftedness,* edited by R. J. Sternberg and J. Davidson. New York: Cambridge University Press, 1986.

Sternberg, R. J.; Ferrari, M.; Clinkenbeard, P.; and Grigorenko, E. L. "Identification, Instruction, and Assessment of Gifted Children: A Construct Validation of a Triarchic Model." *Gifted Child Quarterly* 40(1996): 129-37.

Texas Education Agency. *The Texas State Plan and Guidelines for the Education of the Gifted/Talented*. Austin, Tex.: TEA, 1990.

U. S. Department of Education. Jacob K. Javits Gifted and Talented Student Education Act. Washington, D.C.: USDOE, Office of Educational Research and Improvement 1988

————. *National Excellence: A Case for Developing America's Talent*. Washington, D.C.: USDOE, 1993.

U.S. Department of Health, Education, and Welfare. *Education of the Gifted and Talented*. Washington, D.C.: USDHEW, 1972.

CHAPTER 12

Twice Exceptional Students: The Gifted Learning Disabled

Karen H. Nathan

J. Howard Johnston, University of South Florida

Among the most baffling of all students are those who are both gifted and learning disabled. No group displays greater contradictions, no group is less understood and, unfortunately, few groups are more frustrated by many of the practices of schooling. For schools to serve this diverse and challenging population, teachers and administrators must address three core issues: identification of gifted students with learning disabilities; the social and emotional impact of these conditions on students and their families; and the programs and interventions that help ensure success for these special children.

Identification

In 1980, Mauser found that 2.3 percent of the learning disabled children he tested in Illinois also fell into the gifted range (Clark, 1983). Until recently, little was done to help these children beyond attempted remediation. Special education teachers who worked with the learning disabled rarely had training in gifted education and, historically, students with learning "handicaps" were considered cognitively deficient and provided with little or no access to creative self-expression or exploration of the sciences and the arts (Clark, 1983).

Testing

According to Nielsen, Higgens, Hammond, and Williams (1993), the gifted learning disabled (GLD) can often be identified with a test called the Wechsler Intelligence Scale for Children (WISC-R). The WISC-R has two subscales: a verbal and a performance assessment. The GLD child often scores two or three standard deviations above average on one subscale, but in the average or slightly above average range on the other. This wide range or "scattering" of scores is a clue that a child is both gifted and learning disabled.

To confirm the initial diagnosis, however, it is essential that the school follow up with a case study that includes interviews with the parents and teachers as well as examining samples of the student's work (Udall, 1991). These steps are particularly important in determining the precise nature of the child's gift and disability.

Characteristics

An estimated 120,000 to 180,000 gifted learning disabled students are in American schools today (Winner, 1996) and the nature of their disabilities is remarkably similar to those students with language-based disabilities. Sally Reis, Terry Neu and Joan McGuire at the National Research Center on the Gifted and Talented found that "all the academically gifted students at the University of Connecticut program for students with learning disabilities had a language-based disability, from spelling problems to severe dyslexia" (Winner, p. 47). Somewhat surprisingly, all these students also had gifts in spatial learning.

Frequently, GLD students go undiagnosed for gifted programs, but are considered too smart for remedial work; the gift conceals the disability and vice versa. Thus, both exceptionalities go undiagnosed and untreated.

When these students are tested, it is often the learning disability that is first diagnosed and treated, usually through enrollment in a remedial program, thereby never allowing the giftedness to be recognized or nurtured. This type of placement often results in tremendous boredom and feelings of despair on the part of students, either of which may lead to disruptiveness or other unproductive behavior. Daniels (1983) describes the impact: "It should be evident that the educational neglect of the gifted/learning disabled has prevented a large number of individuals from making their contributions to society and the world." Indeed, misplacement of gifted students may explain some of the more disruptive events that occur in middle level schools.

Often, parents and teachers are puzzled by a student's extraordinary ability to engage in sophisticated reasoning and the simultaneous inability to perform the simplest of school routines, such as following simple instructions. Studies by Fox, Brody, and Tobin show that GLD students "excel on tasks that require the formation of concepts and manipulation of abstract ideas but often experience great difficulty with tasks requiring memorization of isolated facts and sequencing" (Swesson, 1994 p. 24). Thus, in programs that require students to memorize and recall isolated facts, bits of information, or sequential procedures, gifted/learning disabled students achieve poorly. Winner (1996) concurs with this assessment:

> These children excel at abstract verbal reasoning and seem very bright and motivated outside of school, but they encounter serious problems with school tasks...often develop negative self-images in school...are in as much need of special intervention as the non-gifted learning disabled... It was not until fairly recently that educators and psychologists began to recognize cases of gifted children with learning disabilities (p. 45–46).

Nielsen's studies (1993) identified other defining characteristics of the GLD child. "Twice-exceptional students are often distractible, highly sensitive to criticism, extremely curious and questioning, have difficulty 'getting to the point', are interested in the 'big picture' rather than small details, and/or they have penetrating insights." (Neilsen et al., p. 11)

Daniels (1983) elaborated further on gifted learning disabled students and identified four traits that distinguish them from their regular gifted peers:

- Their vocabulary, although generally developmentally ahead of their average peers, is not as advanced as their gifted peers. This is especially noticeable in spoken language where they often have difficulty thinking of their next word, which results in their language appearing stilted and awkward. In elementary school they frequently do not pick up on puns, satire, sarcasm, plays on words, or jargon.

- Their reaction is slower than their gifted peers and to some extent their average peers. They seem to think for a long time about things that are automatic to most people, such as selecting and arranging learning materials or recalling basic information. This penalizes them tremendously when they take standardized, timed tests.

- They have difficulty being flexible. They learn one way to do something and, if it is successful, they cling to that process and may even repeat it, almost obsessively, even when it is clear it is not working in a new situation. Like the learning disabled in general, without clear and permanent structures, they feel confused and even terrified.

- They adapt poorly to changes, particularly frequent or chaotic ones. Inability to adapt to changes results in a feeling of hopelessness and powerlessness. They feel they are being acted upon by outside forces and have no power to change their situation. It often seems to them that everyone else is in control of what they do, a condition that fosters an external locus of control and resulting passivity and failure.

Unfortunately, placement in an LD resource room may reinforce some of the most undesirable of these traits and prevent the formation of more productive learning behaviors. Such settings, especially if they are strictly routine driven, often eliminate any need to be flexible and adaptable. Thus, students have little opportunity to learn to take initiative or assume control over the conditions that affect their lives. Consequently, the four traits identified earlier, if not addressed directly, tend to result in feelings of negative self-worth (Daniels, 1983).

Social and Emotional Aspects

In general, most GLD children suffer from a loss of self-esteem, self-worth, initiative, and confidence (Daniels, 1983). Maker noted that when the low self-esteem that develops around a learning disability is combined with often unrealistic expectations of the gifted learner, "a level of dissonance between real and ideal self that adds greatly to the handicapped person's inability to relate and succeed can occur" (Clark, 1983 p. 345). In short, the effects of a disability may be magnified for the gifted learner, simply because the discrepancy between their predicted and their actual performance is so great.

Relationships with Others

GLD children usually realize they are different from other children at an early age. They tend to find comfort in solitude. Csikszentmihalyi (Winner, 1996) discovered that teens especially talented in math, science, music, art, and athletics spent an average of five more hours per week alone than their average peers. In a synthesis of other research Winner concluded that although some gifted students turned inward because they are ostracized by their peers, gifted students in general are very comfortable being alone and derive pleasure from solitude. Frequently, it is the solitude that gives them time to develop their special interests and talents.

Partly because of this solitude, GLD children often have difficulty reading social cues and may misinterpret the reactions of other children and adults. They might have difficulty in conversations because their trouble finding the right words will cause them to stammer or pause to think of the proper word or phrase. During adolescence in particular, when belonging to a social group may depend on the quickness of conversation and the ability to gauge the reaction of one's peers almost instantaneously, this can be disastrous.

Often, because GLD students have difficulty reading social cues, they do not fare well in group situations, particularly unstructured ones. Harold Levinson (1994) learned these children are often misdiagnosed by psychiatrists and counselors as being anti-social. However, Levinson noted that bright learning disabled children are not antisocial: indeed, they often like many people, but they can only handle them one at a time.

This misunderstanding of the gifted learning disabled is poignantly related by Abraham Schmitt in his 1992 autobiography, *Brilliant Idiot*. After years of torment, he certainly had many reasons not to like people, yet he liked them very much. However, due to what he called "stimulation overload," he could only handle people one at a time. He was often misunderstood and thought to be anti-social—just like the children in Levinson's study. Projecting Schmitt's plight onto the contemporary middle school environment, imagine how difficult life must be for children like him. In a setting where the peer group predominates, where group cooperative learning is the norm, where the hallways resonate with the quick and sometimes acid repartee of hundreds of young adolescents, stimulation overload, and its resulting social withdrawal and isolation is a virtual certainty.

Beyond isolation, the gifted learning disabled, like the gifted, set extremely high standards for themselves and others. This is often true in ethical, moral, and behavioral as well as academic domains. Thus, they are often disappointed when others do not meet these standards, and may become openly hostile or extremely depressed. In either case, they usually do not enjoy group work in class and would rather work alone.

Other students may reject them as working partners because they are seen as judgmental, patronizing, moody, or critical. Among the fragile egos so often found among adolescents, such behavior is hardly endearing.

Due to their difficulties with directions, (right, left, up, down), and their tendency toward reflective solitude, many GLD children tend to be unskilled at athletics, although there are notable exceptions such as Bruce Jenner. Therefore, when teams are "picked" by other children, the GLD child is often last to be chosen. This has an obvious destructive effect on a child's self-esteem and subsequent willingness to participate in group activities.

Parents and school personnel may be wise to steer away from competitive team sports and encourage individual sports (swimming, skiing, martial arts, gymnastics, dance, weight lifting, diving, running, tennis). According to Nosek (1995), if the child really wants to participate on a team, the YMCA (YWCA in some areas) has the attitude of mainstreaming—everybody learns, everybody plays. The Y's main focus, and that of many enlightened middle schools, is on skill building rather than winning. Regardless of the setting, however, school leaders should never allow gifted learning disabled children (or any children, for that matter) to be humiliated by a coach or another player. If a child joins a team to play a sport, sitting on the bench serves no purpose.

The Toll

To the GLD child, the combination of strengths and weaknesses is puzzling and exasperating. In her studies, Swesson (1994) noted that these stress factors resulted in poor motivation, acting out behavior, depression, anxiety and/or shyness, or withdrawal. Many studies indicate the GLD feel unhappy, frustrated, and helpless. Most often, these feelings are school-related and often do not carry over to their homes or communities where they often "put forth extended effort toward their own hobbies and interests" and "were active problem solvers, analytic thinkers, and showed strong task commitment and effort when the topic was personally meaningful" (Swesson, p. 24). Ironically, it is this very set of traits that makes the child's school behavior so puzzling to parents and community members. How can a child so competent in one setting be so frustrated and ineffective in another?

As with other gifted students, GLD students tend to be highly self-critical and set extremely high goals for themselves. Due to the addition of the learning disability, their high expectations often meet with failure (in their eyes)—resulting in bouts of extreme depression. After years in school they begin to generalize their school failures to an overall feeling of inadequacy and, over time, these feelings can overshadow any positive ones connected with what they accomplish at home. Studies by Whitmore and Maker (1985) showed that when teachers focused on the students' learning disabilities at the expense of developing their gifts, it resulted in poor self-esteem, a lack of motivation, depression, and stress.

As with anyone undergoing extreme stress, the health of the gifted learning disabled often suffers. They are prone to severe headaches, dizziness, anxiety, fatigue, panic attacks, and abdominal pains (Whitmore, 1980; Smith, 1991; Abeel, 1994). This stress can lower their immune system's resistance, making them susceptible to colds and flu. They also are more likely than the general population to have allergies and asthma.

Beyond illness, the stress of the giftedness and the learning disability carries over to the child's family. Smith (1991) describes the effect on the family quite well:

Few people realize how hard the parents of the learning disabled work. Few people know the stress of just getting a person with learning disabilities out of the house in the mornings. There is much strain in being the focusing agent, the memory person, the organizer, and conversation coordinator, day in and day out. Meeting with school personnel, going through deliberations regarding individualized education programs, consulting tutors and therapists—these all cause stress (p. 192).

Not only parents, but brothers and sisters are affected by a twice exceptional child. Bringing siblings into the setting, not as rivals, but as part of the support system "has to be done with the sensitive awareness of an orchestra leader" (Smith, p. 192).

There is, however, an upside to being the parent of a GLD child, although the parent might not realize it until he or she has struggled for a few years. As Sally Smith (1991) puts it, "Parents who have gone through the combat zone of their child's learning disabilities . . . have gained a richer appreciation of life. For the most part, their children have been their finest teachers, teaching them to cherish divergent ways of living and learning" (pp. 200–01).

Tools for Success

Both research and the anecdotal experiences of gifted learning disabled students and adults point to specific resources and strategies that facilitate learning and success. By capitalizing on these resources and employing judicious interventions and strategies, schools and families can promote high achievement.

Personal Characteristics

Curiosity. GLD children are blessed with a high degree of curiosity in pursuing a special interest. John Horner, the most noted American paleontologist of the century and a dyslexic, decided to pursue his career at age eight upon finding his first dinosaur bone. "I thought I was a real idiot, and I'm sure everybody else thought so, too, but I loved digging and I knew one day I would find the remains of dinosaur life that could tell me how they lived, and I wanted to know that" (Smith, 1991, p. 60).

Determination/Resourcefulness. Hugh Newell Jacobson, winner of 90 awards for architecture—including 20 Architectural Record Awards for the best house design of the year—spoke to the Lab School of Washington (for gifted learning disabled) in 1990:

It is particularly joyful to stand in front of all of you after this grief, and I really mean grief. I still smell floor wax and feel scared. The hours of agony, of standing at the blackboard, never coming up with the answers, and everybody else sitting down... and our fathers knew we were lazy, and schools knew we were dumb, and we knew we were neither. I was terrible at math. I failed math time and time again. I never did pass algebra or geometry. I still can't. As an architect, I hire engineers (to do calculations) (p. 60).

Humor. The seriousness of the GLD's school life and life in general requires a healthy dose of humor to get through each day. Nosek (1995) describes the benefit: "Laughter serves as a release for anger, frustration, and helps minimize anxiety" (p. 61). Sometimes puns, or plays on words will have to be explained to young GLD children, but once they catch on, they really catch on and become full participants in the joke. According to Silverman (1989) and Wees (1990), the gifted learning disabled "have an easy grasp of metaphors, analogies, or satire" (in Harris, 1996). They may never appreciate the kinds of jokes others tell in school, but their natural appreciation of satire and irony—upper level humor—will get them through many otherwise painful situations.

Gifted learning disabled students often use humor to lighten a situation when others fail to do so. When one of the authors was deciding on a high school for her GLD son they interviewed at several sites. Her son had his heart set on one particular school because the academic program was intriguing and the students well behaved. During the final interview and without any prior warning, the headmaster blurted out that he would make no accommodations. He looked at the son and with seeming delight said, "I would be your literature teacher. I assign 50 to 100 pages every night, and give a quiz every day because it's the only way to make sure the students have read the work. I don't think you would make it in here." When her son was ready to talk about what happened, he looked at his mother with a grin and said, "I wonder what grade you would have given him for his teaching methods."

Inner Strength. Nelson Rockefeller, a gifted dyslexic, gave this message to children, "Don't accept anyone's verdict that you are lazy, stupid, or retarded. You may very well be smarter than most other children your age" (Nosek, p. 61). When the GLD child comes to truly believe this and internalize it, then he or she can be successful.

Support System

Mentors. Because it is so difficult for GLD students to build relationships in large groups, it is especially important that they be provided with an adult mentor, or at least some exposure to successful GLD adults. Each year at their annual conference, the Orton Dyslexia Society invites a panel of successful dyslexics to discuss their experiences in school and how they overcame their disability. These personal examples are particularly important for students who may find few such models in their school.

Teachers and Tutors. Daniels (1983) describes good teachers of the GLD as resilient. They accept the child's strengths along with their weaknesses, and do not question either. For example, an eight-year-old who can catalogue dinosaurs but does not know the days of the week is not thought to be strange or incompetent by such a teacher. Effective teachers for the GLD must be adaptable and plan according to the children's individual needs, not a standardized curriculum. They must have egos strong enough to understand that an emotional response that appears directed at them or the assignment is usually the result of frustration with the learning disability and an accompanying fear of failure (p. 160).

Nielsen and colleagues (1993) in their Twice Exceptional Child Project, has found many techniques to benefit the GLD students, including self-selected social studies projects, the use of contracts, activities that use high level thinking skills, interviews, and audio recordings. They also recommend that GLD students have access to "a vast array of technology that helps them 'bypass' their disabilities" so they can produce work that demonstrates their giftedness (p. 11).

Parents. Nosek (1995) and Smith (1991) found that support and encouragement from families of GLD students was more influential than the negative influences of peers and teachers. In stories of successful GLD adults it was a parent or parents who helped students develop self-confidence to compensate for their disabilities. Nosek found a direct correlation between modeling by parents and the motivation, doggedness, and determination of the child.

Since the GLD child usually learns more naturally by listening than by reading or trying to read, parents should, whenever possible, read aloud to their child. This may include school assignments. To encourage speaking skills, parents can involve the GLD child in conversations during meals. Siblings must be reminded to be patient and not interrupt while the GLD child is searching for just the right words.

Nosek (1995) tells parents not to forget the importance of well-made movies and TV shows in the life of the GLD. Television documentaries and other programming (e.g., The Discovery Channel, Learning Channel) are a perfect match for the GLD learning strengths. They provide stimulating content and utilize modes in which the child learns best—auditory and visual. Some fabulously creative science fiction movies (e.g., *Star Wars* series, *Star Trek, ET*) are tremendously popular with GLD kids, largely because they resonate so strongly to their "gifts" of imagination, speculation, and analytical thinking.

Smith (1991) tells parents to encourage exploration in whatever their children express an interest. Judy, a GLD adult, became a biologist because her parents helped her raise tadpoles and then took her to the library to learn all she could about frogs.

Mrs. James Totten, daughter of General George Patton, and mother of a Lab School student, said it most poignantly:

> None of us asked for a dyslexic child. The Einsteins, the Pattons, the Edisons did not ask for one, either, nor did they realize that God was giving them a genius, a hero, a great inventor. But all of us will learn, in time, that what we have been given is a very special gift for which, in ignorance, we did not ask (Smith, 1991, p. 68).

Parents need to appreciate the GLD child for all the additional effort required to be successful. Most important, they must say this to their child sincerely and often. Parents need to tell their child they realize he or she has to work two to five times as hard as anyone else in the class and that they are very, very proud of their child. They also need to tell the child's teachers and other significant adults who will listen. Too many significant others in the GLD child's life do not realize the depths of his or her struggle and the price of each and every triumph.

One of the authors recalls with great clarity a moment in which she realized how much she admired her son's struggle for success.

> Once at a conference with the principal and four of my GLD son's teachers, I explained that the hours he spent on homework each night kept him from joining outside activities or spending much time on his beloved computer. The purpose of the conference was to remind them that they had agreed to make accommodations for homework, but were not doing so. I finished by saying that I recently told my son I didn't know how he got through it all. I would have become so angry. Instead of spending all those hours, I'm sure I would have given up long ago and refused to do the work. But he hadn't. He persevered. He never showed his anger. Night after night, week after week, year after year. It was then I realized, and hastened to tell him that for all of that inner strength, he was (and is) without a doubt, the biggest hero I have ever known.

There is much to be learned from parents. They have seen the struggle of their child, observed the strategies that produce success, and witnessed the terrible price of school failure. Parents of GLD students must be included as full partners in the education of their child if the school is to succeed with these challenging students.

Special Teaching/Learning Aids

Due to their poor ability to deal with time and direction, the GLD students need teaching aids that help them in these areas. A clearly printed schedule and a map of the school tucked inside a notebook can be lifesavers. Assignment books that match the sequence of a child's schedule and are monitored daily by teachers and parents are helpful in ensuring tasks are accurately recorded and completed.

As many GLD students have a weakness in language and reading-related areas, special written materials can be helpful. Something as simple as large print books, available in most libraries, can often be useful, because they aid in focusing and tracking.

According to Peter McWilliams, author of *Personal Computers and the Disabled*, the computer has three superhuman qualities that make it an exceptional resource for GLD students:

- Infinite patience. It's nonjudgmental and never gets angry.

- Inexhaustible energy. It remains engaged all day, if necessary.

- Unlimited availability. It's ready whenever the student is (Nosek, p. 59).

The computer's word processing and spell check devices liberate students, allowing them to write and edit with ease. When the final product is printed the student's thoughts are there to be appreciated on the same level as someone with perfect handwriting. The teacher can focus on ideas rather than errors.

The computer, for good reasons, has been called the "great leveler" for the learning disabled. For the GLD, there are no limits on how far one can proceed: travel the Internet, communicate on-line with students in another country, research their favorite subjects—quantum physics, quasars, ancient Chinese history. The computer with a modem has the capability to provide access to any subject the GLD wish to explore—on their level, and through the best learning modes for their disabilities!

For the GLD with more severe language/reading disabilities, there are voice-synthesized reading machines (Kurzweil Reading Machine), and books on cassette tapes (Talking Books, available through libraries and bookstores, and Recordings for the Blind and Dyslexic, accessible for a small membership fee in the local organization). There are also voice synthesized computers and talking and listening computers such as Dragon Dictate and DECtalk.

Nielsen and other researchers (1993) recommend the use of hand-held calculators, spell checkers, and tape recorders. They also suggest that computers with modems, Language Masters, 35-mm cameras, video equipment, and computer software be easily available to all students.

Educational Alternatives

Samantha, a 17-year-old gifted dyslexic, gives the following advice:

> Remember that if you have trouble in school, it might not be because you don't fit the school, it might be because the school doesn't fit you. Be an advocate for yourself. Keep trying. You may not fit in now, but whether you're 7 or 70, one day you will find a place where you excel (Abeel, 1994).

Albuquerque's Twice Exceptional Children project provides middle schoolers an educational program with teachers who combine gifted education with special education. The product of collaboration between the Albuquerque Public School System and the University of New Mexico, it is a highly individualized program that has achieved remarkable success (Nielsen et al., 1993).

Other states have also funded special programs for gifted learning disabled students, but most do not have special programs. For many children, their families and schools, it can be a constant struggle to address the special needs of the GLD student.

Some parents decide to take their GLD child's learning into their own hands and home school. For a parent who has the time and resources, or is willing to invest the necessary time, this can be extremely beneficial for the child. Home schooling allows children to proceed at their own pace and to be challenged to their limit. It is personalized, progressive, individualized, child-centered, and flexible (Winner, 1996). Because of their natural tendencies toward isolation, however, special provisions must be made to ensure that the child has opportunities to practice social skills in natural environments.

Conclusion

The gifted learning disabled child faces tremendous challenges. Educators are only beginning to see beyond their disabilities and appreciate their potential. With accurate and early identification, well-trained and caring teachers, supportive parents, and access to special technology, the gifted learning disabled will have the chance to reach the high goals they set for themselves and become successful lifelong learners.

References

Abeel, S. *Reach for the Moon.* Duluth, Minn.: Pfeifer-Hamilton, 1994.

Baum, S. "Gifted but Learning Disabled." Class handout, University of San Francisco, Rosselli, 1996.

Clark, B. *Growing Up Gifted.* Columbus, Ohio: Merrill, 1983.

Daniels, P. *Teaching the Gifted Learning Disabled Child.* Rockville, Md.: Aspen, 1983.

Davis, R. *The Gift of Dyslexia.* Burlingame, Calif.: R.D. Davis, 1994.

Harris, D. M. "Understanding and Meeting the Needs of Gifted Learning Disabled Students." Class handout, University of San Francisco, Rosselli, 1996.

Huston, A. *Understanding Dyslexia.* Lanham, Md.: Madison Books, 1992.

Levinson, H. *Smart but Feeling Dumb.* New York: Warner, 1994.

Nielsen, M.; Higgens, L.; Hammond, A.; and Williams, R. "Gifted Children with Disabilities." *Gifted Child Today,* September 1993.

Nosek, K. *The Dyslexic Scholar.* Dallas, Tex.: Taylor Publishing, 1995.

Schmitt, A. *Brilliant Idiot.* Intercourse, Pa.: Good Books, 1992.

Smith, S. *Succeeding Against the Odds.* Los Angeles, Calif.: J.P. Tarcher, 1991.

Swesson, K. "Helping the Gifted/Learning Disabled." *Gifted Child Today,* September 1994.

Udall, A. "Gifted Learning Disabled Students." *Update on Gifted Education,* Fall 1991.

Whitmore, J. *Giftedness, Conflict and Underachievement.* Boston: Allyn & Bacon.

Whitmore, J., and Maker, C. *Intellectual Giftedness in Disabled Persons.* Rockville, Md.: Aspen.

Winner, E. *Gifted Children, Myths and Realities.* New York: Harper Collins, 1996.

CHAPTER 13

Teaching Able Learners in the Regular Classroom

Peggy S. Mayer, Lake Stevens School District

Students in quality middle schools reflect a broad range of ability, emotional development, and special needs and interests. This diversity contributes to the dynamic nature of teaching at the middle level and provides options for cross grade grouping, self-directed learning, individualized learning, flexible schedules, exploratory mini-courses—a range of vital and exciting options for organization and instruction.

As middle level schools move to a more inclusive model, including greater use of heterogeneous classrooms, teachers struggle for ways to serve the varying needs of all students. The fundamental premise of inclusion is also a fundamental premise of democratic schooling: All children are capable of learning, just as all children have gifts that make them unique and valuable.

High among those needs is the need to be accepted. To avoid the stigma of segregation and elitism, schools have moved toward the inclusion of students with diverse learning needs into the regular classroom.

Inclusion Philosophy: Classroom as Microcosm

The inclusive classroom is a microcosm of the middle school. A full spectrum of ability and talents are represented, contributing to a richness in both the classroom and the school at large. The strengths of one group serve as a model for others. Such a classroom can help all students feel welcomed, a valuable part of the learning community. The challenges faced by some students help fellow students become more sensitive, appreciative, and responsible.

All students can learn. It is important that students be integrated in as many ways as possible in order to promote their and their classmates' academic and emotional growth. The inclusive classroom tries to do this. However, differences in academic and social needs and learning styles do exist and must be addressed. Integration comes with both rewards and frustrations. The challenge for the teacher in the inclusive classroom is to make accommodations that maintain the benefits of integration, yet offer to all students the opportunity to experience a challenging curriculum and engaging instruction.

Can We Meet Their Needs?

Clear understanding of the needs of highly capable students is the first and most important step in creating programs to serve them. Educating staff members about the concerns and needs of these students is essential. The next step is to commit the time and resources necessary to adapt and support instruction. In addition, teachers need practice, if not additional training, in a variety of instructional methods.

Approaches to instruction that may be unproductive or seem unrealistic with the average student can often be very successful with the highly capable. As with virtually all aspects of middle level education, "one size does not fit all."

Another barrier to serving high performing students in the conventional classroom is time and space. Because of noise levels and distractions, it is difficult to have multiple groups functioning at one time on different topics in the same classroom. It is also untenable to have students demonstrate their task commitment and elaboration skills if they will be interrupted by the bell. Finally, we must be certain not to neglect these students' socio-emotional needs. In addition to the same issues that plague all middle school adolescents, these students carry their own set of issues.

Five critical or core issues must be addressed when striving to meet the needs of the highly capable students in the middle school:

1. Knowledge of the nature of talent and giftedness

2. Curriculum adaptation (including support materials)

3. Instructional methods for able learners

4. Flexibility of instructional setting

6. Counseling and advocacy.

The term "able learner" can be misleading, for if students are achieving at a high level, then it appears, by definition, that they are doing fine. If, however, they are achieving good grades and high scores in a mundane curriculum that fails to challenge them, things are not fine at all. Serving highly motivated and highly capable students requires helping them achieve according to their capability and sustaining their high motivation to learn.

What characteristics distinguish this group of students from the general student population? First, they can tolerate and need a faster pace of learning. Second, they have the ability to focus for longer periods of time, allowing more in-depth instruction. Third, these students more readily move to higher levels of thinking and reasoning, often using deductive and inductive reasoning very efficiently. They may have advanced vocabularies. They also can be perfectionists who see minor setbacks as major failures.

In contrast, some have decided the burden of being bright is too great, or too socially detrimental, and therefore mask their achievement. Such behavior demonstrates the normalcy of able learners as well. They are experiencing the changes of puberty, they want to fit in and be accepted, they need to grow and learn, and they need to feel a sense of accomplishment. Fortunately, there are strategies for achieving these goals in the regular classroom.

Curriculum Adaptation and Materials

Teachers have options when serving highly capable students in the classroom. They may chose to accelerate the curriculum in a linear fashion; elect depth and elaboration—laterally expanding a student's learning; or develop a "connective" world view for the student, helping him or her see the interrelatedness of the different content areas, how one subject melts into another, helping students understand the "connective tissues" of the world of knowledge and learning.

Pretests help teachers diagnose and prescribe an appropriate curriculum for able learners, particularly in inclusive classrooms. Such tools often help both the teacher and the district focus on the essential learnings within their scope and sequence and identify where the curriculum might be "flexed" for students with special needs. A clear vision of those essential learnings, not just within a teacher's particular grade level, but for the upcoming grade levels, is necessary if a teacher is to work with highly capable students. Likewise, a teacher should be aware of what is taught in the other subject areas at his or her grade level, and beyond, if possible. This general awareness will enable teachers to provide the best programs for the student, whether using the acceleration, intensification/enrichment, or integration models.

Curriculum compacting is the current language used to describe acceleration of curriculum. Its foundation is the high quality diagnostic pretest, which allows the teacher to determine exactly what the student already knows and can apply. At this point, the teacher may group students within the classroom to deliver information at a pace appropriate for each of three or four subgroups. When this grouping is in place, the teacher can then meet with students of each group, in this case the able learners, and provide them with the results of their testing.

Grammar, mathematics, the periodic tables, the dates and places of history—these are facts that able learners can acquire far more readily than the average student. Able learners have often ridden high in their classroom simply because they can assimilate such knowledge quickly, without ever having really performed any sophisticated original thinking. Curriculum compacting allows them to move through this material without becoming bogged down, and it provides the teacher and student with something very valuable: time.

All school leaders have heard teachers say, "But if I teach them that now, what will they have to learn later?" It sounds almost ludicrous, but it is true: Many teachers are afraid of curriculum compacting. They believe they are either minimizing the importance of the material or that they will place the child so far ahead of his or her peers that somehow they will run out of curriculum to teach.

In fact, such fears are not entirely groundless. In the early days of gifted programs, it was common to find very advanced students who had gaps in their early instruction; while they had mastered advanced concepts, some of their basic skill areas had never been mastered. Remaining highly accountable to the essential learnings can help avoid this; good pretesting and good prescriptive instruction can help correct it.

The second concern is that the teacher will run out of curriculum to offer the student. Of course teachers know they can never run out of things to teach students, but they might run out of materials, and out of the time it takes to design new materials and align them with a district's scope and sequence. Likewise, advanced materials may not seem age appropriate, even though a student is ready for the factual information contained therein. This is where the appeal of lateral expansion of the curriculum comes in.

Lateral expansion of the curriculum:

- Keeps the student working within the realm with which the classroom teacher is familiar.

- Keeps the student more or less with his or her peers as far as the general content of the curriculum. Projects, discussion, and interaction with students doing lateral expansion serve as enrichment for students in the general group.

- Can enrich the teacher's instruction, since materials brought in for the students in the lateral expansion group can also be used by teachers as they design lessons and enhance their own knowledge.

While the key to linear acceleration of curriculum is pretesting and a knowledge of the district's curriculum continuum, high quality questioning strategies are key to lateral expansion, followed by good instruction in researching skills and availability of reference materials and sources.

Lateral curriculum expansion increases the depth of the content covered and the sophistication with which it is treated. It can provide a teacher with the most workable methods for dealing with diverse ability levels, yet include the entire spectrum of students in discussions, films, etc. It is, however, labor intensive at the front end. This labor pays off, since once lessons are in place, they can be used for subsequent years either as a duplicate of the first year, or as a work in progress that the teacher or team of teachers can build on.

Instructional Methods

Questioning Strategies

Asking the types of questions that promote advanced thinking, promote real-life problem solving, and encourage students to view subject matter in an integrated manner is one of the most valuable things a teacher can do. Not only does it challenge the student, it focuses the teachers on what they are teaching and models questioning behavior, which is a significant characteristic of intelligent behavior.

Facts may be the realm of the knowledgeable person, but motivations, implications, and significance are the realm of the intelligent person, and alternatives and solutions are the realm of the wise person. The teacher has the power to direct the student in the process of thinking through quality questions so the student is still an authentic and original intellect, not just a source of correct answers. The able learner has probably mastered the knowledge level performance and has perhaps had a "free ride." Once truly challenged by high quality questions, requiring divergent and convergent thinking and creative problem solving, the high achieving student may be forced to work for the first time in a great while. What is just as exciting, students who have been passive may finally feel a challenge to think and rise to the occasion. It is not uncommon for teachers to hear some grumbling, as well. While the fact-driven curriculum may have been dull, it was probably also easy!

Grouping

Grouping is a sensitive topic. Grouping students by ability has fallen from favor because of the effects of labeling on motivation and performance, research on best academic practices, and the effects on integration. Yet, educators know they can best serve students by working with those of like ability and interests at certain times and in certain settings.

With the increased popularity of inclusion in the classroom, cooperative learning has become more widespread. Cooperative grouping can be an answer to grouping like-ability students for discussion and specific tasks, but it is also a flashpoint for danger. If teachers consistently structure groups with students of widely disparate ability, they may foster feelings of resentment among both the high and average achiever. The high achiever may insist on dominating the task rather than risk turning in lower quality work. The low achiever may either be reinforced in a passive role or fall into the pattern of being a "user," letting someone else do the work for him or her. Both the low and average performing students feel their ideas are never good enough or that there is no point in even competing with a more dominant student, even though, in fact, their ideas may be superior or their thinking more creative.

A better option is to group the able learners together with a specific task, and do likewise for average and less skilled students. All the tasks should represent part of a complete outcome, so each group recognizes its work as important to the end product.

Projects

Projects, both independent and group, are a traditional tool for dealing with highly capable students who always seem to be done sooner than other students and need something to keep them productively occupied. Projects should not take the place of direct instruction and group interaction. Independent work should be a part of the instruction used with these students, but not the primary method. These students should have the opportunity to do long-term and independent projects in an area of their own interest. Another problem with project work is that often these opportunities are only afforded the able learners. The project expectations for this highly capable group must be clearly identified, and should include authentic research strategies and reporting techniques. Plagiarism and lame paraphrasing should not be tolerated.

Individualization

Many school districts have language in their mission statements that implies individualization—phrases like "take all students from where they are as far as they can go" and "provide an education that meets the individual needs of each student." But it is easier said than done. It takes long hours of preparation work, organization, consistency of staff and goals over a period of years while a program is developed, time for teamwork and communication, and flexibility.

Flexibility: Time and Space

What kind of flexibility will support individualization within an inclusive classroom? One method is flexible schedules that provide common planning for teachers who are willing to take on the task. For example, if you are functioning in a middle school with three teams of teachers for seventh grade, you may choose to group the highest achievers within one team's classes so the burden of individualizing a program can be taken on by a truly committed group. Another approach would be to have the teachers in a given content area develop an advanced strand for their particular curriculum, much as some textbooks provide multiple levels of challenge to a particular skill activity. Once again, the staff would need common planning time, or time during a summer to develop their lessons.

Another area where flexibility is important is in scheduling. Many in-depth activities require, or at least benefit from longer periods. If a daily 45-minute schedule is locked in place, students cannot always become intensely involved in in-depth projects such as Internet research. Teachers must be open to some students having a more free-flowing schedule. This does not mean total randomness of student attendance or lack of accountability, but flexibility based on student maturity and performance, recognizing that it is the student's job to meet obligations in all his or her classes.

Flexibility goes beyond the classroom, beyond the school, and extends to the district as a whole. There will always be times when the most appropriate course to take with a student is to allow the student to challenge a class at a higher level on the curriculum continuum. This challenge must be based on good assessment tools and evaluation of the student's maturity and commitment. To be inflexible to this option means unnecessarily blocking student advancement.

Counseling and Advocacy

A final concern that must be addressed is counseling and advocacy. Many middle schools are understaffed in the counseling area and to compensate use a homeroom model or the teaching team. Students who have been identified for government monitored programs such as Title 1, LAP, and special education are served by their case managers and the LAP or specialist in the field. But this is not the situation for able students, although their need, while different in nature, is often just as great.

The administrator must ensure that a staff person is responsible for being an advocate for able students. They need someone whom they can respect and trust, and who knows and understands their particular challenges. This advocate may be a regular classroom teacher who works with these students, or it may be a district-designated specialist or a teacher who is well-suited because of his or her background, experience, and training to work with these students.

Whatever the case, this person can be a clearinghouse of information for students, parents, and fellow teachers; an understanding ear, and even a go-between, for the students and teachers; and an advocate for the students (and their teachers) in meetings, program decisions, funding allocations, and conferences.

It is unfair to assume that these students can and will always have the self-confidence, courage, or wherewithal to speak up for themselves. Often they just tolerate or become cynical.

When others think they are excelling, they feel inadequate, or like failures. They need a guide who can help them keep their perspective.

They have difficulty fitting in and finding intellectual peers. They are sometimes resented even by their teachers. They need special training in how to cope with these issues. They struggle to fit in with society, yet be true to themselves as well. They should believe the system is there for them, and that it is helping look out for their best interests. Many good books and quality workshops are available to principals wishing to prepare a staff member for this role of advocate for the highly capable.

Effective Strategies: Examples and Recommendations

Projects

An independent project is much like painting a house—the results are determined more by the preparation than by any other factor. Do a good job at the preparation stages and projects will be meaningful for students (not just busywork to get them out of your hair) and a meaningful means for teachers to evaluate student learning.

Projects whose general topics lend themselves to student choices, but which are carefully designed to address important objectives, can work well with highly capable students. The thoughtful planning of the projects makes them work well even though students are working independently. Select categories offer several options for projects, thus allowing students or groups to select different focus areas under the same general category. For example, consider decades; personalities; specific events (e.g., great disasters, revolutions); warriors and peacemakers; groups and organizations (e.g., AFL/CIO, NBA, Cherokee Nation, Amish, Black Panthers); specific inventions and discoveries; and places (e.g., most dangerous place on earth, best place to be a teenager, safest place on earth).

Specific steps to implement project learning include:

1. Teacher determines the general topic of the projects and helps students generate a list of options within that general topic area.

2. Students add to the list of topics with teacher approval.

3. Teacher determines the critical features of the topic option (including the critical categories of information that should be contained in the final product, critical areas of investigation, critical questions and issues to be explored).

4. Teacher may allow students to choose from a set of categories or features, a set number of which must be represented in the final project.

5. Teacher provides presentation model options such as oral/performance, research report , multi-media project, or other visual display. (Each category should have specific guidelines regarding what will be critical at the evaluation stage.)

6. Student determines presentation model from a list of options provided by the teacher.

7. Students complete a project plan before beginning any independent work. The proposal includes:

   a. Student-selected topic

   b. Student-selected presentation model

   c. Identification of resources and/or fieldwork required to complete project

   d. A timeline for completion

   e. Evaluation criteria to be used in self and teacher assessment.

Seminar Groups

An intelligent and well-educated individual should have the ability to listen and respond thoughtfully to the ideas of others. Clarity of self-expression, in any number of modes, is part of almost any school's essential learning requirements.

Writing is essentially thinking on paper. When a student writes well, he or she is usually thinking well. If students are to organize their thoughts on paper, they must first organize them in their minds.

Interacting with others, hearing and responding to their views, sharing our own, and reshaping and adjusting our thinking are the primary reasons we bring students together in an academic environment. Education is successful when students become better observers of their world, can assess it critically, consider possibilities, and propose solutions and new directions.

Seminar groups can be a tool for promoting all these things with students. Elements of a successful seminar program include:

1. Selecting meaningful, relevant, intriguing, controversial questions/topics for the seminars

2. Selecting high-quality related readings

3. Making available related readings

4. Giving students clear procedures for approaching the topic

5. Keeping groups to a workable size of four to eight students

6. Training group leaders to give meaningful commentary on student work

7. Guiding students on procedures for the seminar itself.

Determine how long students will need to read materials and write their papers, being sure to include some in-class time for independent work that can be monitored. A week, with some time provided in class for reading and composition, is usually adequate.

Present the seminar prompt. This may take the form of a question or questions, a famous quote or passage, or a quote taken from current events. Give students a "map" for how to approach the prompt:

1. Read the prompt carefully.

2. Look for critical vocabulary, or words that are ambiguous or unfamiliar.

3. Ask related questions: What is the person really saying? Do I have all the information I need? What biases are present? What do I need to find out in order to respond?

4. Take a position: Do you agree? Disagree? In whole or in part? With reservations?

5. Write an initial thesis statement.

Provide students with related reading. This may be an article, a section from the text, a news clip, or video. It may be printed for each student, or be on reserve in the library.

Now students need to continue the process:

6. Read the related readings.

7. Reassess, and perhaps recompose, their thesis statement.

8. Support their position with facts, evidence, arguments, examples.

9. Compose their final paper, 1–3 pages in length.

10. Conduct seminar (no one is allowed to participate without a paper, and students must read quote positions directly from their papers).

11. Students may be permitted to edit their papers, then resubmit them with new material or corrections.

One of the most important stages is the selection of the prompt. This is also the area that gives the teacher the most flexibility and provides one of the greatest strengths of seminars as a means of working with the highly capable in the regular classroom. Prompts can be directly tied to the curriculum, the tool to integrate two different subject areas or to form meaningful connections between content areas. They can incorporate current events and help students with values formation. Seminars can be vehicles through which the school reaches out into the community by inviting parents and other adults to volunteer ideas for seminar topics.

With creative program planning, an entire grade level team could be involved in seminars during a flex-time slot on a topic integrating all they have been studying in their various subjects. Principals, librarians, and support staff could be called in to lead groups. Participation of a wide range of adults as seminar leaders emphasize to students that the school is a learning community.

Individualization

It is an old standby, but it does work. First, the student is pretested. Then, students who have already mastered the information or skills planned for the class are guided to another topic or another aspect of the class topic and given a separate set of lessons.

The alternative track may be a more advanced level of the same content; it may be at a higher thinking level (perhaps they can work on application and synthesis while the rest of the class is still working for understanding); or it could be an entirely different subject. For example, in math, students who are beyond the rest of the class in computational skills could begin working on the algebra portion of their text. In art, students who have mastered basic technique could then work on artwork for the school's public areas or on designing art docentry displays for the library. Students can tutor those who are having trouble understanding concepts or skills. Students who have proven their mastery in study skills could go on to an individualized unit on vocabulary.

To make individualization a valid tool in the classroom, the process must keep the students at a task that is academically enriching and appropriate for their level of performance. It should not be used as a substitute for all types of instruction, because it might isolate the learner from classmates and their ideas. But it is beneficial in conjunction with the other methods for serving these students in the regular classroom.

A Word in Closing

It is not easy to meet the needs of each and every student. As educators, we try to do what is best for the whole student community and, at the same time, never sacrifice those students with high ability if that means lowering standards, minimizing expectations, or failing to provide necessary academic services. On the contrary, we should strive to improve the quality of education we are providing across the board—for all students under our care.

We can teach students to appreciate differences in style, ability, and interests without holding them back. It is our job to encourage and empower, not limit. When we make the commitment to teach students in an inclusive environment, it needs to be a commitment based on a clear understanding of what is involved in terms of time, money, training, and personnel. Only then will such moves be academically successful for all students.

CHAPTER 14

Quality Staff Development: A Plan for Meeting the Needs of Able Learners

Cassandra Countryman, Principal, Muirlands Middle School

The principal's vision and commitment to quality staff development are central to addressing the needs of high achieving students. The principal must possess the skills necessary to promote the vision, motivate the staff, and provide leadership in implementing the staff development program.

This is the story of my experience as a new principal of a middle level school. It captures both the frustration and the exhilaration embedded in my experience—converting a middle level school and at the same time detracking its program.

By utilizing site-based management and shared decision making, I worked with my teachers to determine the focus for our training program. Together, we agreed that staff development should focus on improving teaching skills, thereby improving learning outcomes for students. This collaborative effort identified several essential elements of a sound professional development initiative:

1. The principal as a leader and practitioner
2. The importance of collaboration with staff
3. Commitment to quality staff development activities
4. Empowering teachers and building commitment
5. Providing professional development for school leaders
6. Ensuring a content focus
7. Securing sufficient resources.

Principal as Leader/Practitioner

Upon assuming the principalship it became clear that my role would be quite different than my experience as a junior high and senior high school assistant principal. Through the auspices of the Edna McConnell Clark Foundation my district secured a grant for leadership training. This program helped me develop the skills to successfully lead and mentor my staff during our reform efforts.

One element of this training allowed me to conduct a personal assessment, defining my role as principal, clarifying my vision for the school, identifying my leadership style, and learning skills of collaboration and shared decision making. The result was a professional development program specifically tailored to enhance my professional growth.

A principal must provide leadership in developing and implementing quality staff development programs. He or she must have a strong commitment to this endeavor as well as a clear purpose and vision. To be successful, the vision must be shared by teachers.

Successful staff development efforts provide a broader, far-reaching approach to staff development. They respond to questions such as: What are the targeted outcomes? Who is benefiting?

How are they benefiting? How will you know when you have reached your goal? Where do you go from there? How does each component of staff development contribute to the vision and school goals? How can we measure the impact of the learnings from the staff development program on student achievement?

An example from my own school, Muirlands Middle School, illustrates this approach. Our vision states:

> **To prepare students to meet the challenges of a global, multi-cultural, and technological society, the Muirlands staff will create a setting that meets the needs of all ability levels, maintains high standards, enhances self-esteem, and provides a broad range of educational experiences.**

Each school year this statement guides the selection of school goals. One year, it led to the following goals:

- Improving student achievement through reading
- Schoolwide portfolio culture integrating content standards
- Developing new standards
- Parent outreach.

These goals were then used as I worked with the staff members to establish and refine our professional development priorities.

Collaboration with Staff

Effective principals work closely with staff members to design and implement staff development programs. Teachers are empowered to take an active role in deciding staff development priorities. A collaborative school culture, exemplified by site-based management and shared decision making, provides one mechanism for this involvement. Together the principal and teachers can design a staff development program than strengthens teaching skills and focuses on improved achievement for all students.

Commitment to Quality Staff Development

Commitment to quality staff development programs often requires seeking funds and resources to support such initiatives. Muirlands Middle School sought and received a grant from the Edna McConnell Clark Foundation to support our work. The grant allowed the staff to attend several conferences directly related to our school goals.

The primary goal in creating our staff development program was to enhance teaching and learning. We focused first on assessing staff needs. Then teachers worked with the principal to designate our priorities. Together we determined the objectives, standards, and assessments for the program. This collaborative effort build shared ownership and commitment to the project.

In spring 1991, we began considering detracking the school. One important consideration was the impact of detracking on gifted and high-achieving students. Our response was to commit to a high content, high expectation, and rigorous curriculum for all students. Students experienced the benefits of group work as well as individual work. Self-choice became an option for some students when they chose to work at the advanced level offered to all students or the most challenging level.

Support from the principal was important. It facilitated change and encouraged teachers to positively deal with the initial resistance received from some parents. Teachers were provided time during the summer to develop and plan a curriculum that would meet the needs of a diverse student population. The principal also supported the teachers' request that all new teachers hired at Muirlands commit to teaching in a heterogeneous classroom, and possess a GATE (Gifted and Talented Education) credential.

We provided staff development on working with an educationally diverse population; Anne Wheelock, among others, worked with teachers to write clear curriculum and develop assessment strategies.

The initial focus was on the sixth grade. Two years after implementation in all sixth grade classes, the seventh grade adopted a similar model, followed by the eighth grade. Currently, all humanities classes are detracked and offer all students a challenging, high quality curriculum complemented with high support to ensure success.

Teacher Empowerment and Commitment

Active, interested, and vested teacher commitment is critical to successful staff development initiatives. Teachers know the needs of their students and are best suited to provide input regarding the most effective programs and appropriate delivery models. Principals should encourage teachers to research new programs as well as develop curriculum. Visits to other schools and attendance at workshops and conferences provide alternative perspectives. Often new ideas emerge from these activities and can be fine-tuned to meet the specific needs of local schools.

At Muirlands Middle School one staff development program had a dramatic effect on student achievement—the Writing to Learn program. It has proved to be one of our most successful staff development programs. The program provided teachers the skills necessary to write curriculum and design assessment tools aligned with the curriculum. The program began with a small group of teachers and through this initial success grew annually. A major contributor to its success was the use of teachers as facilitators. Participants from previous years were trainers for subsequent years. A second factor in its success was teachers working with their own team members to write curriculum.

A second example of focused staff development was the PACE (Performance Assessment Collaboratives for Education) Project from Harvard University. Muirland teachers worked with teachers from schools across the country on assessment and portfolio development. Summer institutes at Harvard as well as national and local meetings with other PACE participants were attended by the principal and a cadre of teachers. This resulted in our developing a student portfolio system.

Quality staff development led teachers to become more reflective about their teaching. Teachers at Muirlands write almost all their own curriculum. They can explicitly address the needs of all students, including able learners, by ensuring the inclusion of higher order thinking skills and other instructional strategies.

Professional Development for School Leaders

Professional development for administrative staff is a key element in successful staff development programs. A quality program that trains and prepares principals to be site-based, shared decision-making leaders is essential. Components of such programs include:

- Defining and understanding the role of the middle level principal
- Understanding one's own leadership style
- Defining the vision of the school
- Refining communication skills
- Evaluation and assessment strategies
- Building teams and promoting collaboration.

Funding for staff development must be available to principals for their own professional growth as well as that of their staff members. In San Diego Unified School District "job alikes" are used as one method for continued professional growth. Middle level principals get together monthly to discuss issues and concerns specific to that level. The chance to collaborate with peers serves as an opportunity to gain greater understanding of strategies to enhance and refine one's leadership skills.

Content Focus

Based on experiences at Muirlands the following topics and activities should be considered in a comprehensive staff development program focused on improving achievement among all students:

- Development of the team concept
- Thematic curriculum planning and design
- Gifted and talented education training
- Curriculum compacting
- Planning conferences and workshops
- Strategies for detracking the school.

A variety of approaches can be used to deliver these suggested programs, including attendance at workshops and institutes, use of in-district consultants and lecturers, scheduling staff development days during the school year so the total staff can participate, paid summer planning and writing time, and attendance at university courses.

Summary

Principals must have the training and preparation for the role as instructional leader and to develop and implement a quality staff development program for their faculty. And, principals must take an active role in their own professional growth. A strong commitment to relevant continuous staff development that supports clearly defined and shared school goals is critical.

The staff development program for a school is created through site-based management and shared decision making and is essential to motivate staff.

Teachers who feel empowered to try new ideas and cause positive change find themselves at the center of many reform efforts. Because of a strong staff development program, the teachers on this middle school staff have developed the confidence to lead positive change.

Finally, the program must be focused on meeting the needs and improving the outcomes of high achieving students with a high content, rigorous, and challenging curricular program that stretches these students' capabilities.

Systemic professional growth is essential because making such a commitment ensures enhanced learning opportunities for students. There can be no more worthy goal.

Resources

California State Department of Education. *Caught in the Middle.* Sacramento, Calif.: CSDOE, 1987.

Fipp; Barry; Hargrave; and Countryman. "With Equity and Excellence for All." *Middle School Journal* 15(1996).

Kulik, J. A., and Kulik, C.-L.C. "Effects of Accelerated Instruction on Students." *Review of Educational Research* 54(1984): 409-25.

Oakes, J. *Keeping Track.* New Haven, Conn.: Yale University Press, 1985.

Slavin, R. E. "Are Cooperative Learning and 'Untracking' Harmful to the Gifted?" *Educational Leadership* 6(1991): 68-71.

————. "Point-Counterpoint: Ability Grouping, Cooperative Learning and the Gifted." *Journal for the Education of the Gifted* 1(1990a) 3-8.

————. "Response to Robinson: Cooperative Learning and the Gifted: Who Benefits?" *Journal for the Education of the Gifted* 1(1990b): 28-30.

Wheelock, A. *Crossing the Tracks.* New York: The New Press, 1992.